GOD:
ACTION AND REVE

STUDIES IN PHILOSOPHICAL THEOLOGY

Edited by: H.J Adriaanse & Vincent Brümmer
Advisory Board: John Clayton (Lancaster), Ingolf Dalferth (Tübingen), Jean Greisch (Paris), Anders Jeffner (Uppsala), Christoph Schwöbel (London)

Editorial Formula:
'Philosophical theology is the study of conceptual issues which arise in views of life, in religious thinking and in theology. Such conceptual issues relate to the logical coherence between and the presuppositions and implications of fundamental concepts in human thought, as well as the effects which historical and cultural changes have on these aspects of human thinking.'

1. Hent de Vries, *Theologie im Pianissimo & zwischen Rationalität und Dekonstruktion,* Kampen, 1989
2. Stanislas Breton, *La pensée du rien,* Kampen, 1992
3. Christoph Schwöbel, *God: Action and Revelation,* Kampen, 1992
4. Vincent Brümmer (ed.), *Interpreting the Universe as Creation,* Kampen, 1991

Christoph Schwöbel

GOD:
ACTION AND REVELATION

Kok Pharos Publishing House – Kampen – The Netherlands

Meinem Lehrer Carl Heinz Ratschow
mit herzlichem Dank für hilfreiche Begleitung
in theologicis et in vita

CIP-GEGEVENS KONINKLIJKE BIBLIOTHEEK, DEN HAAG

Schwöbel, Christoph

God: action and revelation / Christoph Schwöbel. – Kampen : Kok Pharos. – (Studies in philosophical theology ; no. 3)

ISBN 90-242-3097-7
NUGI 631/619
Trefw.: godsdienstfilosofie

© 1992, Kok Pharos Publishing House, Kampen, The Netherlands
Cover by Rob Lucas
ISBN 90 242 3097 7
NUGI 631/619 W-boek

Table of Contents

Part II
DIVINE REVELATION

Preface

The studies in this volume were originally written between 1986 and 1990 as contributions to conferences and seminars in England, Germany and the Netherlands. In spite of their different origins they present some basic elements of a systematic-theological proposal centred on the concept of divine action. The studies concentrate on one of the criteria of theological reflection set out in the 'Introduction', the criterion of the internal coherence of the rational reconstruction of the forms and contents of Christian faith. This does not indicate that the other criteria are of lesser importance for theological exploration. It seems to me, however, that the investigation of the internal plausibility of the truth claims asserted, presupposed and implied in Christian faith is a necessary condition for testing their external coherence with other beliefs and convictions we hold to be true. This also applies to an area of theological reflection which is, in my view, of paramount importance in contemporary multi-religious societies, the attempt to develop a theology of religions in the context of interreligious dialogue. For this task it is, however, an important prerequisite that Christian theology is clear about the perspective from which it engages in conversation with other religious convictions. Reflection on the internal plausibility of Christian truth claims is therefore a necessary element for conducting a dialogue between religious traditions.

The suggestions presented in this volume cannot claim to be in any sense systematically complete, nor can they claim to offer any final results of theological reflection. The theses which are defended have grown out of constructive and critical exchange with others and are intended as proposals for a continuing theological conversation. They are therefore, at best, an interim report from an on-going process of dialogue. This provisional character is both a reminder of the inexhaustibility of God's revelation and of the fallibility of human knowledge. The implications of this view are to my mind very clearly expressed by the authors of *Foundations* in 1912: 'We fully recognize the obligation of loyalty to the tradition of the Church to which we belong, we make no claims to irresponsibility, but...our responsibility is of a different kind. It is the responsibility of making experiments.'

The 'Introduction' was originally published in *King's Theological Review* X (1987), 51-57. Chapter 1 is a revised version of a paper originally published in German in *Vom Handeln Gottes. Marburger Jahrbuch Theologie* I, N.G.Elwert Verlag Marburg 1987, 56-81. Chapter 3 was first published in *Nederlands Theologisch Tijdschrift* 43 (1989), 122-138. The original German version of chapters 4 and 5 appeared in *Lebenserfahrung. Marburger Jahrbuch Theologie* III, N.G.Elwert Verlag Marburg 1990, 68-122. I am grateful for the permission to reuse these materials.

The 'Introduction' and chapters 1,3,4 and 5 were part of the published work submitted and accepted for the *Habilitation* in systematic theology at the Fachbereich Evangelische Theologie, Philipps-Universität Marburg in November 1991. I am grateful to the referees, Professors Wilfried Härle, Theodor Mahlmann and Michael Pye for their constructive criticism and encouraging assessment of my work.

The studies in this volume are very much the result of the on-going dialogue with friends and colleagues in England, Germany and the Netherlands. I thank my colleagues in the Research Institute in Systematic Theology where most of the papers were discussed, Colin Gunton, Brian Horne and Francis Watson, for the stimulating encouragement to clarify my thinking. Colin Gunton has not only shared my passion for theological debate over the last six years, he has also, with his wife Jenny, provided an environment of friendship for our family in which we feel at home in theological and other important respects. As a *donum superadditum* he has undertaken the arduous task of correcting my style, especially in the translations of chapters originally written in German.

The members of the *Pfullinger Arbeitskreis Theologie* where chapters 1,4 and 5 were first discussed have enabled me to keep in touch with theological conversation across the Channel. I am grateful to Ingolf Dalferth, Wilfried Härle and Eilert Herms for their incisive comments and helpful suggestions for the development of many of the thoughts presented in these pages. I would like to thank Wilfried Härle for his support and friendship, both in the form of theological critique and personal support. I am grateful to John Clayton for the insight and sympathy with which he has accompanied my attempts to find a personal mediation between the intellectual traditions of German-speaking theology and Anglo-Saxon philosophical and religious thought.

For many years friends and colleagues from the Netherlands have provided a lively and inspiring forum of theological and philosophical conversation. Chapter 3 and the 'Postscript' were first delivered at research seminars organized in connection with the academic link between the Faculty of Theology at Utrecht and the Department of Theology and Religious Studies at King's College London. It is due to Vincent Brümmer and Luco van den Brom that Utrecht has (literally and metaphorically) become a kind of half-way house between Marburg and London in my theological geography.

I owe an immense debt of gratitude to my wife Marlene and our children Martin, Christine, Johannes and Stephan for making the synthesis between theological interests, pastoral commitments and all other dimensions of life possible that is our family.

Ever since I did the first tentative steps towards theological thought my teacher Carl Heinz Ratschow has been a most perceptive critic and resourceful adviser - in theological matters and in many other questions. This book is dedicated to him as a small token of my gratitude.

King's College, London
January 1992   *Christoph Schwöbel*

Introduction
Doing Systematic Theology

1 WHAT IS THAT - SYSTEMATIC THEOLOGY?

Sometimes, when I am asked what I do for a job, I answer that I teach systematic theology. In most cases, I have to admit, this brings the conversation to a rather sudden end. But in some cases the people I talk to try to get beyond this cryptic answer. Knowing that academics, and especially those from my background, have an inclination to use abstract though somewhat incomprehensible concepts, they ask whether I could give an example of this strange activity from my work in recent years. I could answer that I have done some work on liberal theology at the turn of the century. 'So you are really a church historian', my conversation partner could say. Well aware that church historians are not so favourably disposed towards systematic theologians trying their hand at historical research, I could answer: 'No, not exactly. Apart from trying to understand a specific theological conception in its historical context, I have to relate it to the biblical message and have to bind out how the biblical sources are used in presenting an adequate account of Christian faith today.' 'So your work is rather like that of a biblical scholar', might be the reply. This makes me feel slightly uneasy, since I know that biblical exegetes are sometimes tempted - and not without reason - to summarize the excursions of systematic theologians into their field under the heading 'amateur's night'. And I try to explain that I am not so much concerned with the biblical texts in their original historical situation, but with the present validity of the truth-claims they imply. This, however, would seem to be trespassing on the land of the philosophers. I do not want to spell out all the possible exchanges with my - by now wholly imaginary - conversation partner. The difficulty in giving a straightforward answer to the question what 'doing systematic theology' means should already be sufficiently clear, namely, that systematic theology seems to be a strange mixture of all theological and some non-theological disciplines, borrowing bits and pieces here and there but never achieving a methodologically unambiguous coherent strategy. My main problem is therefore whether and how it is possible to give an account of doing systematic theology which presents it as an activity that is at least so coherent and intelligible that it would seem justified calling someone a lecturer in systematic theology. My first suggestion is very simple and it accounts for my rather inelegant title 'Doing Systematic Theology'. Systematic theology should not primarily be understood as a system of theological doctrines or theories, but as an activity. And since this activity is dependent on working with certain materials and using certain tools systematic theology has the character of a craft which in some rare cases achieves the quality of an art.[1] On this view, teaching systematic theology would not consist in presenting certain fixed doctrines, but in demonstrating and practising certain skills with the aim of en-

---

[1] Cf. John Clayton, 'Tillich and the Art of Theology', in: J.L.Adams, W.Pauck, R.L.Shinn (eds.), *The Thought of Paul Tillich*, San Francisco 1985, 278-289.

abling students to learn to practise this craft by themselves. The objective of studying systematic theology should be to acquire competence in doing systematic theology. And this would imply the ability to work with the materials of systematic theology in a way which is informed by certain criteria and methods. This view of systematic theology does not rule out that the activity of doing systematic theology results in a set of systematically ordered arguments and propositions which could be called a systematic theology. But this result is always dependent on the craftsmanship and expertise applied in the activity of doing systematic theology. I shall therefore try to show how the activity of doing systematic theology is related to the nature of Christian faith and which criteria would define competence in doing systematic theology. Nevertheless my account of this craft has more the character of leafing through the rule-book and sorting out the toolbag of systematic theologians. A more concrete description of doing systematic theology would mean analyzing or presenting a concrete example of this activity, and this would have to be much more specific than my general topic, 'doing systematic theology'.

2 THE SELF-EXPLICATION OF CHRISTIAN FAITH

One could define systematic theology as the self-explication of Christian faith with respect to the truth-claims and norms of action that are asserted, presupposed or implied by it. As Christian *dogmatics* systematic theology is the rational reconstruction of the forms and contents of Christian faith. As Christian *ethics* it is the reflection on the possibilities, aims and norms of action connected to the truth- claims of Christian faith. These truth-claims describe the situation of the agent in the world within the framework of the central Christian beliefs about the nature of reality and human destiny and thereby prescribe the basic orientation of human action in the world. The fact that our fundamental beliefs and convictions about the nature of reality determine our possibilities of action as well as the aims we try to achieve provides the essential connection between dogmatics and ethics which makes it possible to summarize both under the heading 'systematic theology'. In the rest of the paper I shall concentrate exclusively on systematic theology as dogmatics although this makes my account of doing systematic theology necessarily incomplete.

This view of systematic theology as the self-explication of Christian faith makes it dependent on Christian faith in its various expressions. Therefore, the work of the systematic theologian is never purely constructive. It is the rational reconstruction of what is given in the manifold expressions of Christian faith as they are presented in prayer, confessions of faith and Christian proclamation.[2] The reconstructive character of systematic theology implies that the propositions of systematic theology are always dependent on the assertions of Christian faith, and that the truth-claims of systematic theology are derived from the truth-claims of Christian faith.

---

[2] Cf. I.U.Dalferth, *Existenz Gottes und christlicher Glaube. Skizzen zu einer eschatologischen Theologie*, München 1984, 16-30.

The definition of systematic theology as the self-explication of Christian faith immediately raises the question what it is about the nature of Christian faith that makes the rational reconstruction of its contents possible and necessary. The possibility of systematic theology as the self-explication of Christian faith is given in the role of linguistic communication in the constitution of faith and in the linguistic character of its expressions.[3] In the Christian tradition faith is interpreted as a gift of the Spirit. The divine Spirit authenticates the Gospel of Jesus Christ as the revelation of the true relationship of the creator to the whole of creation and thereby makes possible the unconditional trust in God which determines the whole of the life of the Christian believer. On this trinitarian view of the constitution of Christian faith, which reflects the trinitarian structure of God's being and action, faith is constituted by divine action and passively received by the believer.[4] Its character is the active acknowledgement of its divine constitution in all spheres of life.

It is one of the fundamental elements of this understanding of the constitution of faith that the divine action in creating faith is the authentification of the human proclamation of the *external word* of the gospel of Jesus Christ by the *internal word* of the witness of the Holy Spirit. Faith presupposes the proclamation of the Gospel, the linguistic communication of the content of the revelation of God in Jesus Christ. And in this sense Christian faith is *fides ex auditu*. The rhetorical puzzlement of Paul's question: 'How could they have faith in one they have never heard of?' (Rom.10,14) is an apt illustration of the strength of his conclusion: 'We conclude that faith is awakened by the message, and the message that awakens it comes through the word of Christ.' (v.17)

It is the linguistic character of Christian faith-expression that makes its self-explication possible. Everything that can be expressed in a semiotic system (a system of signs, like a musical score or a blueprint) can be explicated. But only what is expressed in a linguistic system is capable of self-explication. The reflexive character of language distinguishes it from most of the other semiotic systems, and this is the reason why we normally have to use language in order to explicate non-linguistic semiotic systems. The fact that faith presupposes and implies the linguistic communication of the gospel makes the self-explication of faith in systematic theology possible.

The necessity of the self-explication of Christian faith is given in the fact that the act of faith presupposes certain truth-claims about the object of faith and its relation to reality which determine the character of faith as unconditional trust. The *fides qua creditur* implies *fides quae creditur*: 'belief in' implies 'belief that'.[5] The truth-claims implied in Christian faith are ontological in character, they concern the constitution and structure of reality. This makes it necessary for the Christian community to justify that the assertions of faith imply genuine truth-claims and that these truth-claims concern *what there is*, the nature of real-

---

[3] Cf. W.Härle, 'Widerspruchsfreiheit. Überlegungen zum Verhältnis von Glauben und Denken', *NZSTh* 28 (1986), 223-237, especially 229ff.

[4] For the view of divine action presupposed here cf. my article 'Divine Agency and Providence', *Modern Theology* 3 (1987), 225-244.

[5] For a more detailed description of this relationship cf. chapter 1 below.

ity. And this necessitates the self-explication of Christian faith in systematic theology. Furthermore, faith is claimed to be the basic orientation for the totality of human existence. This claim would be immediately falsified, if human rationality as an essential dimension of human existence would somehow be excluded from this existential orientation. And in order to show that faith does not exclude but includes rationality, the self-explication of faith as the rational reconstruction of the forms and content of Christian faith is required.[6]

Both the possibility as well as the necessity of the self-explication of Christian faith are implied in its character as a communal and a missionary faith. The existence of a Christian community of faith presupposes that the linguistic communication of the contents of faith is possible. The missionary character of Christian faith presupposes the claim to universal validity which is implied in the ontological character of the truth-claims of Christian faith. And it necessitates the self-explication of Christian faith for those belonging to the Christian community in order to justify its self-transcending character and for those who are outside the Christian community and who are invited to accept the Christian Gospel as the truth for their lives.

Apart from these structural characteristics of Christian faith one can also point to the experiential situation in which the necessity of the self-explication of Christian faith arises. The Christian Gospel claims that Jesus Christ is the revelation of God's reconciling love which overcomes the contradiction of human sin and enables justified humanity to live in community with God. This claim alone raises a host of philosophical problems about the relations of the eternal and the temporal, the necessary and the contingent and the universal and the particular. Existentially more important is that the world as we experience it seems to contradict this view of reality harshly. The existence of evil and suffering seem to call either the nature of God as love or God's power into question. It is at this point that Christian faith has to become reflective faith, if it wants to remain faith.[7] And this is the existential anchorage for the rational reconstruction of the contents of Christian faith in order to explore ways how the apparent contradiction between the claims of Christian faith and our experience of the way things go in the world can be resolved.

3 THE TASK OF SYSTEMATIC THEOLOGY

After we have seen how the relationship between systematic theology and Christian faith can be characterized in such a way that systematic theology can be understood as the self-explication of Christian faith, we can now attempt to characterize the task of systematic theology. Although systematic theology is a

---

[6] Cf. Härle, op. cit. (note 3), 230.

[7] Cf. C.H.Ratschow, 'Das Christentum als denkende Religion', in: *Von den Wandlungen Gottes. Beiträge zur systematischen Theologie*, Berlin 1986, 3-23.

theoretical activity, it is provoked by very practical problems and its final aim is a practical one.[8]

The need for the self-explication of Christian faith arises out of the concrete experience of dissensus in the Christian community concerning the interpretation of the forms and contents of Christian faith. There has never been a time in the history of the church when there was no conflict and disagreement about Christian faith. Usually these conflicts concern the foundations of the community of faith and its relationship to those outside the community. When both kinds of problems are taken together they raise the question of the identity of the Christian community.[9] The reasons for dissensus can take a variety of forms. They may be located in internal difficulties with the practice of Christian faith, they can result from the way Christian faith is presented to those outside the Christian community, and they can be the result of external pressures on the Christian community. Whatever its causes, the dissensus becomes the starting-point of systematic theology when it concerns the interpretation of the fundamental truth-claims of Christian faith. The task of systematic theology in this situation of dissensus is to propose a new consensus in the community of believers which reaffirms the foundations of that community in such a way that the difficulties which called the old consensus into question can be resolved. In trying to propose this new consensus systematic theology has to suggest an adequate interpretation of Christian faith which can be acceptable within the Christian community, which defines its relationship to those outside the Christian community, and thereby affirms the identity of the Christian community.

If systematic theology is called to its task by the existence of dissensus in the Christian community and if its task consists in helping to propose consensus, the task itself would seem to have a two-fold character. On the one hand, it can be seen to consist in the attempt at justifying the present validity and relevance of Christian faith in our situation today. This could be dubbed the *historical-hermeneutical* task of systematic theology. On the other hand the task of systematic theology can be seen to consist in giving reasons for validating the intelligibility and coherence of the truth-claims implied in Christian faith. This could be called the *systematic-analytical* task of systematic theology. This two-fold character of the task of systematic theology reflects two central characteristics of Christian faith: firstly, that it is grounded in a particular historical event and exists in a historical community which describes its identity by referring to this event; and secondly, that it implies a comprehensive view of reality which is claimed to be both coherent and universally valid.

Both aspects of the task of systematic theology are clearly interrelated and overlap constantly in the actual practice of doing systematic theology.

---

[8] This is especially emphasized in E.Herms' exposition of the character and task of theology, cf. *Theologie - eine Erfahrungswissenschaft*, München 1978, and *Theorie für die Praxis - Beiträge zur Theologie*, München 1982.

[9] Cf. S.W.Sykes, *The Identity of Christianity. Theologians and the Essence of Christianity from Schleiermacher to Barth*, London 1984; see especially 11-34 about the relationship of conflict and identity.

Nevertheless, they must be clearly distinguished, because the present relevance and acceptability of a given statement is not identical with its truth. If the distinction between these two tasks is blurred, this usually results in two common types of mistakes in systematic theology. The first type is very often found in programmatically revisionary conceptions of systematic theology. It usually amounts to asserting that the recent history of human self-interpretation in the West renders certain ways of expressing the Christian faith impossible. 'After Feuerbach (Kant, Marx, Freud...) we cannot have a realistic (metaphysical, personal...) understanding of God anymore...' would be an example of this type of reasoning. It is based on the category mistake of conflating an alleged historical necessity with logical necessity. And taken seriously, the task of validating the alleged historical necessity would be more difficult than demonstrating the logical possibility or coherence of the statement which is said to have been rendered impossible.

The opposite mistake which can sometimes be found in the work of those who see their task in defending traditional Christian doctrines is to prove the logical possibility of a given statement without paying any attention to the question whether this statement is still an authentic and relevant expression of faith in the Christian community today.

4 SOME CHARACTERISTICS OF CHRISTIAN FAITH

After we have tried to characterize the task of systematic theology we can now take a closer look at the *criteria*[10] which determine the actual practice of doing systematic theology and which make it possible to assess whether and to what extent systematic reflection has solved its task. I want to suggest that the criteria of doing systematic theology are grounded in the characteristics of Christian faith.

First of all, Christian faith refers to Jesus Christ as its historical ground and as its focus of belief. This inherent Christocentricity, which should not be confused with christocentrism as an organizing principle in presenting a systematic theology, is grounded in the confession of faith that Jesus is the Christ. This implies seeing Jesus Christ as the ultimate revelation of God in whom the relationship between God the creator and sinful humanity is restored by God's reconciling love, so that human beings can live in accordance with their created destiny as far as they participate in the reality of salvation in Christ. Christian faith has always insisted on the particularity of God's revelation in the historical individual Jesus of Nazareth who is confessed as the Christ, as the one who is seen by Christians as the realization of God's righteousness which was expected in Israel and as the salvation for all humankind. This means, on the one hand, that God's revelation in Jesus Christ cannot be transformed into a transhistorical metaphysical or moral principle. On the other hand, this implies that all Christian beliefs

---

[10] In German-speaking theology the discussion about the criteria of Christian dogmatics was inaugurated by A.Jeffner, *Kriterien christlicher Glaubenslehre. Eine prinzipielle Untersuchung heutiger protestantischer Dogmatik im deutschen Sprachbereich*, Uppsala 1977.

are shaped by the fundamental role ascribed to Jesus Christ as the ultimate revelation of God.

This essential feature of Christian faith accounts for the crucial importance of Scripture for Christian faith. It is understood in the Christian community as the authentic record of God's revelation in Jesus as the Christ, as the witness of the response of faith to Jesus which is summarized in the title-term 'the Christ' and as the fundamental interpretative framework of narrative, law, prophecy and wisdom of the Hebrew scriptures which provided the basic categories for the interpretation of God's action in Jesus Christ. The essentially christo-morphic structure of Christian faith justifies the role of the bible as the book of the church, because it is the book of Christ.

Secondly, Christian faith is characterized by its historical and communal character. The historical character of Christian faith comprises two elements: on the one hand, Christian faith is constantly referred to its origin; on the other hand, it is historical in the sense that it perceives its historical ground and focus through the tradition which mediates its significance. The communal character of Christian faith is not only an implication of the linguistic character of its central expressions. It can be traced back to the social content of Jesus' message of the Kingdom as the community of God and reconciled humanity, which entails the restoration of the created sociality which is threatened by the disruptive effects of sin.

The historical and communal character of Christian faith are closely interrelated, since the Christian community understands itself as constituted by God's revelation in Jesus Christ and since it determines its identity by referring to its historical origin. Nevertheless, Christian faith as a communal and historical faith exists in different Christian churches and these churches differ from each other precisely in the way how they construe the reference to Jesus Christ as the origin of the Christian community and how they understand the structure of the Christian community. Whatever the reasons for their separate existence, Christian communities usually state these reasons (which are implied in their construal of Christian identity) not in dogmatic treatises but in confessions of faith which function as the authoritative traditions for the practice of Christian faith. In the historical existence of Christianity the Christian community has its identity only in the form of a confessional and denominational identity. And through this specific confessional community and its authoritative traditions the community of faith is perceived and interpreted.

Thirdly, Christian faith is not only characterised by its reference to Jesus Christ and by its historical and communal character, but also claims to be relevant for the present situation. This claim finds its expression in various forms, ranging from relevance for the individual life-style to the issues discussed in society at large. Implied in this claim to relevance is the conviction that the beliefs implied in Christian faith provide the fundamental orientation for the questions and needs of our present situation. Again, this characteristic is not unconnected to the other two features mentioned above. The relevance of Christian faith is understood as the relevance of Jesus Christ, his message, deeds and suffering, as the revelation of the relationship of God the creator to humanity for our present situation. And it is one of the motives for the adaptation of the Christian community to the changing conditions of relevance in human history. On the strength of its claim to relevance the historical community of faith participates in historical change and becomes itself a major force of historical change.

The fourth characteristic of Christian faith is that it implies a view of reality which claims to be intelligible, meaningful and coherent. We have already mentioned that this is shown by the character of Christian faith as a missionary faith. The claim to intelligibility and coherence is a corollary of the role of linguistic communication in constituting and expressing Christian faith. Intelligibility and coherence is furthermore a necessary condition for the character of Christian faith as asserting genuine truth-claims. A given statement can only function as a truth-claim if it is logically and semantically correctly construed and if it has a propositional content which has not been falsified. The assertions of Christian faith are not exempt from this requirement.

The basic condition for intelligibility or coherence is that the law of non-contradiction - paradoxically known as *principium contradictionis* -is observed.[11] This principle is much more than a theorem in the propositional calculus. It states the fundamental condition for all linguistic and indeed, semiotic, communication. In its most basic form it refers to the semiotic act of signifying something as something. The law of non-contradiction states that this is only possible if the same sign is not ascribed to the thing signified and denied at the same time and in the same respect. If this law is violated, communication becomes meaningless and, in fact, impossible. That Alice and Humpty Dumpty can continue their conversation after Humpty has announced 'When I use a word...it means just what I choose it to mean - neither more nor less' is only possible, because he remains fairly conventional in his choice of meanings and does not consistently violate the law of non-contradiction. (Long words, like 'impenetrability' which he chooses to mean 'that we've had enough of that subject, and it would do just as well if you'd mention what you mean to do next, as I suppose you don't mean to stop here all the rest of your life' are, of course, an exception.) The character of Christian faith as *fides ex auditu*, as being constituted by communication and as resulting in communication, implies the claim that the Christian faith is internally coherent and intelligible at least in the minimal sense of not violating the law of non-contradiction.

The fifth characteristic of Christian faith is that its ontological truth-claims are not restricted to one aspect or sphere of reality but refer to reality as a whole. Their ontological character is the reason for their claim to universal validity. As ontological truth-claims the assertions of Christian faith must be compatible with all other true propositions. And this formal requirement is strongly emphasized by the comprehensiveness of Christian faith. Without this compatibility Christian faith could not be a form of life which determines the whole of the believer's existence, it would have to inhabit a special sphere without any connection to the other spheres of life. But precisely that is excluded by the ontological character of Christian truth-claims.

---

[11] For the following argument cf. W.Härle, op. cit. (note 3) 227f.

My main contention is that these five characteristics of Christian faith determine the criteria of systematic theology as the self-explication of Christian faith. They enable us to assess whether systematic theology is done in a competent or in an incompetent way. One could divide the whole set of criteria into two groups. The first group - the criteria of adequacy - belong to the historical-hermeneutical aspect of the task of systematic theology. The second group - the criteria of coherence - concern the systematic-analytical task of systematic theology.

Let us first turn to the *criteria of adequacy*. The first criterion of this group is that the assertions of systematic theology should be in accordance with *Scripture*.[12] It is the function of this criterion to make sure that systematic theology conforms to the fundamental structure of Christian faith as referring to Jesus Christ as its historical ground and thematic focus. Reference to Jesus as the Christ is only possible through the medium of Scripture. This implies that the conformity of systematic theology to Scripture cannot be understood as reference to a canon of infallible texts.This strategy and attitude would be more appropriate within an Islamic framework where the Qur'an is indeed identified with the revelation. For Christian faith the authority of Scripture is 'eccentric' (J.McIntyre) insofar as it refers back to the authority of the revelation of God in Jesus Christ. Conformity with Scripture is a criterion for the adequacy of systematic theology, because God's action in Christ is not accessible in any other way than through the medium of Scripture. And this determines the way in which this criterion should be used in systematic theology. Scripture should be used in such a manner that the texts are explored with respect to the way in which they report, express and interpret the expectation and experience of the revelation of God in Jesus Christ. And this perspective determines the way in which systematic theology solves the problem of the unity and diversity of the witness of Scripture.

In using adequacy to the biblical scriptures as a criterion for doing systematic theology, Scripture is viewed in a two-fold perspective. On the one hand, the Bible is the book of the church and systematic theology has to refer to its use in the church today. On the other hand, it is a collection of texts which all have their own origins and which are shaped by the historical, cultural and sociological circumstances of their respective *milieu*. In combining both aspects in its use of Scripture systematic theologians are heavily dependent on the work of their exegetical colleagues. Only if the original intention of the texts and their present use in the church can be combined in a unified perspective, can conformity with Scripture function as a genuine criterion of doing systematic theology. It should, however, always be kept in mind that conformity with Scripture is only the manner in which the conformity of systematic theology with God's

---

[12] Cf. W. Härle, 'Lehre und Lehrbeanstandung', in: *Zeitschrift für evangelisches Kirchenrecht* 30 (1985), 283-317. See also Jeffner, op. cit., 34ff. and David H. Kelsey, *Uses of Scripture in Recent Theology*, New Haven 1976.

revelation in Jesus Christ can be established. In this way this criterion functions as the criterion of *authenticity* for a Christian systematic theology.

The second criterion of this group is the conformity of systematic theology with the authoritative traditions of a given historical community of faith. The authoritative traditions to which the systematic theologian appeals safeguard the continuity of systematic theology with the history of the church and its connection to the community of faith. The authority of these traditions is usually implied in their own self-ascribed status. As confessions of faith they intend and claim to be in accordance with the fundamental witness of faith in Scripture. Their authority is therefore derivative. If the authority of Scripture is secondary to the primary authority of God's revelation in Christ, the authority of authoritative traditions is tertiary.[13]

The authoritative traditions of the Christian churches summarize and interpret the Christian Gospel in order to present the consensus of a specific Christian community concerning the understanding of God's revelation in Christ. On the path from dissensus to consensus they present the old consensus, and it has to be examined how far the interpretation of the old consensus can help in achieving a new consensus. If it is precisely the validity of the old consensus which is called into question it has to be asked how far the old consensus is really in accord with Scripture or whether it has to be expanded and corrected. If this examination comes to a negative result a new consensus will have to be proposed in a new authoritative tradition. But this is a task for the church in which systematic theology can only lend a helping hand. As a summary of the fundamental truths of Scripture the authoritative traditions of the Christian churches provide a framework for interpreting Scripture and can be used as the fundamental set of rules for the use of Scripture in a given Christian community. It would, however, be disastrous if this grammatical use of the authoritative traditions would be played off against the ontological character of Christian truth-claims, because their regulative function is precisely that of determining what should be regarded as a genuine Christian truth-claim and how it should be interpreted.

Since the authoritative traditions guaranteeing the historical continuity of the Christian community are themselves historical documents, the systematic theologian has to depend on the help of the church historians for their interpretation. Only if the historical character of these traditions and their claim to authority for the present can be combined in a unified perspective, can the appeal to authoritative traditions function as a criterion for doing systematic theology. And since the historical continuity of the community of faith is only given in different churches and denominations, this criterion establishes the *confessional identity* of a systematic theology.

The third criterion of adequacy is that the self-explication of Christian faith must be adequate to the present situation. This criterion, which states the relevance of Christian faith for today, has frequently played a major role in modern theology - especially since modernity defined its self-understanding by its discontinuity with the preceding history of Christianity. Nevertheless, this criterion is highly problematical. Demanding an independent criterion to secure the

---

[13] Cf. W.Härle, op. cit., 303.

adequacy to the present situation for the self-explication of Christian faith would imply that Christian faith does not in itself entail its validity and relevance for today. And this would be an implicit challenge to the claim to universal validity of Christian faith which is grounded in the ontological character of the Christian assertions about God's revelation in Jesus Christ. This would deprive the whole enterprise of systematic theology of its basis. Therefore it is necessary to interpret the present validity and relevance of Christian faith as an *implication* of the universality of the fundamental truth-claims of Christian faith.[14] If Christian faith claims to be valid for the whole of humanity at all times, it must also be valid for us today. This, in turn, implies that relevance cannot be treated as a criterion for the *content* of the self-explication of Christian faith, but rather as a criterion for the *presentation* and *exposition* of the self-explication of Christian faith which spells out its relevance for today.

The application of these criteria constitutes the historical-hermeneutical aspect of systematic theology. As criteria of adequacy they function as norms for doing systematic theology. Apart from that, they can also be used as descriptive tools for distinguishing certain types of systematic theology. The priority ascribed to one criterion and the virtual neglect of one or both of the others characterizes biblicism, traditionalism and modernism. While it is probably unavoidable that any given way of doing systematic theology displays tendencies towards one or the other of these types, this nevertheless implies the danger of neglecting the internal relatedness of these criteria and consequently misconstruing their respective status.

Furthermore, the status attached to these criteria differs from one Christian denomination to another. Therefore these criteria also function as instruments for characterizing the distinctive denominational character of a given way of doing systematic theology.

We must now turn to the *criteria of coherence* which describe the systematic-analytical aspect of the task of systematic theology. The first criterion of this group is the *internal coherence* of the concepts, propositions and arguments of the self-explication of Christian faith. I have already tried to show that this criterion is presupposed in Christian faith insofar as the linguistic communication of the Christian Gospel is a presupposition for the possibility of Christian faith, and insofar as intelligibility is a necessary condition for the truth-claims of Christian faith.

The necessity of operating with this criterion is given in the fact that Christian faith is presented in a wide variety of modes of expression which comprise almost all linguistic forms: narratives, parables, metaphors, analogies etc. The task of the self-explication of Christian faith with regard to its internal coherence is to explore the relations between these sometimes *prima facie* contradictory or at least paradoxical modes of expression by determining their respective meaning. This implies the task of offering a *conceptual* reconstruction of the basic forms of linguistic expression in the church. The translation into conceptual language is inevitable, because only concepts can be sufficiently

---

[14] This has been demonstrated with exemplary precision in Härle, op. cit., 304f.

clarified with respect to their intension, their content of meaning, and their extension, their reference to what they signify. And this clarification has to go all the way from concepts to propositions and to the connections of propositions in arguments. Interpreting the use of this criterion as conceptual reconstruction implies that the self-explication of Christian faith does not aim at asserting anything different from the primary expression of Christian faith in prayer, confessions of faith and Christian proclamation, but it intends to say the same thing differently, namely in a conceptual way. The material identity should be preserved in the formal difference.[15] It can be that the difficulties of the conceptual reconstruction of the primary expressions of faith show that these primary expressions seem to be inadequate in a certain respect. However, the criterion by which it could be decided that they have to be changed is not the fact that they do not fit the theoretical model employed in their conceptual reconstruction, but that they misrepresent the revelation of God in Jesus Christ which can be disclosed in the process of reconstruction.

It is this criterion of internal coherence which accounts for the systematic character of systematic theology and which justifies the rather pretentious name 'systematic theology'. Much of the heated debate about the 'system' in systematic theology falls flat if the system is seen as the natural consequence of the claim to internal coherence implied in Christian faith.

The last criterion, the *external coherence* of systematic theology, which tries to validate the compatibility of the assertions of Christian faith with all other true propositions is the most problematical of all criteria of systematic theology. We have already seen that this criterion is logically necessary, because it is implied in the character of Christian claims as presenting genuine truth-claims which must be compatible with all other true propositions. The theological necessity of this criterion could be developed by pointing to the fact that the revelation of God in Jesus Christ is the revelation of the creator and that it is the inherent rationality of his creative action which makes the rational structure of the world and of the human mind possible. External coherence is also an existential requirement, if Christians do not want to live with a divided mind which keeps their religious belief in intellectual quarantine isolated from the knowledge on which they rely in all other matters - a kind of holy, or rather unholy - schizophrenia which is totally incompatible with the character of Christian faith.

Although the necessity of this criterion is as evident as the fact that it does not subject the self-explication of Christian faith under an alien law but is required by the nature of Christian faith itself, it is nevertheless exceedingly difficult to operate with this criterion. The main difficulty is that we can never be entirely certain that what we believe and claim to be true is actually true. The fallibility of human beings forbids the rigid use of this criterion. The difficulty is not peculiar to systematic theology. Think how many scientific discoveries of recent times would have had to be rejected at the time when they were first

---

[15] Cf. I.U.Dalferth, op. cit. (note 2), 25.

introduced, because they openly contradicted what was believed to be true at that time.[16]

There is no easy way of resolving this dilemma. There are, however, a number of considerations which help to resolve at least some of its difficulties. First of all, if we do not look at the problem as the abstract relationship of different propositions but try to understand it as the kind of coherence that is required for our basic orientation in the world, we can see that this coherence can incorporate change (the acquisition of new knowledge and correction of former convictions) without the collapse of the whole belief-system. Secondly, we have to pay attention to the specific logical status of the propositions of systematic theology as the reconstruction of the propositional content of Christian faith. Because basic propositions of systematic theology assert, presuppose or imply ontological truth-claims, they do not have the same status as empirical or theoretical statements about particular entities, classes of entities or universal properties of classes of entities. Their respective logical status determines the rules for ascertaining the compatibility of the propositions of systematic theology with other truth-claims. The abortive controversy about 'science vs. religion' in the second half of the 19th century is a striking example of the category mistakes that can occur if one does not pay attention to this distinction and to the self-misunderstanding of religion and science which it produces. Thirdly, it has to be kept in mind that even as a criterion of truth coherence is only a necessary and not a sufficient criterion.[17] This should make us careful to recognize the limitations of this criterion and not to collapse all the other criteria into this single criterion. And fourthly, our difficulty is a forceful reminder of the general fallibility of all human knowledge from which the self-explication of Christian faith cannot claim to be exempt. To keep this in mind would not have to be a disadvantage, if it makes us aware that even the most skilful use of these criteria must be accompanied by that humility which is appropriate to the subject-matter of theology and a necessary requirement for doing theology at all.[18]

6 CRITERIA AND METHODS

The use of these five criteria constitutes the activity of doing systematic theology. In my view, each of these criteria represents a necessary element of doing systematic theology and jointly they provide a sufficient basis for characterizing the activity of doing systematic theology. These criteria can be used for different purposes in the actual process of doing systematic theology. They can function descriptively as a guide-line for the conceptual description of the content of Christian faith. They can be used analytically in examining and evaluating historical and contemporary examples of systematic theology and for testing their relevance for the present task of systematic theology. The descriptive as well as the analytical use of these criteria serves as the basis for their normative

---

[16] Cf. W. Härle, *Systematische Philosophie*, München-Mainz 1982, 180ff.

[17] Cf. W. Härle, op.cit., 183 and my article 'Wahrheit', *Taschenlexikon Religion und Theologie*, 4th ed. Göttingen 1983, vol.V, 283-289.

[18] Cf. John Calvin, *Institutes of the Christian Religion* Book I, chap. I, 2.

use in proposing a rational reconstruction of the forms and contents of Christian faith which helps the Christian community to overcome its dissensus and achieve a new consensus. It may well be possible that these criteria are incomplete or that they have to be interpreted in a different way. But this discussion is itself a task of systematic theology which thereby reflects its relationship to Christian faith which makes systematic theology possible as well as necessary, and whose characteristics determine the criteria of doing systematic theology. Any suggestion to introduce different criteria or to modify the proposed criteria necessarily involves construing the characteristics of Christian faith in another way and therefore belongs also to the self-explication of Christian faith.

These criteria also help to determine the methods used in systematic theology. Systematic theology does not have a special method of its own, Rather, the use of specific methods depends on whether they are adequate for applying the criteria of systematic theology. And since these criteria suggest certain methods, exegetical and historical methods for the criteria of scripture and tradition, sociological and psychological methods for the criterion of relevance and philosophical methods for the criteria of coherence, systematic theology cannot do better than to apply these methods as they are developed in their respective disciplines. Nevertheless, these methods will be used for achieving a different aim, that of the self-explication of Christian faith as the rational reconstruction of its forms and contents with respect to the truth-claims it implies. If one talks about *the* method of systematic theology, one usually refers to the specific combination of methods borrowed from other theological disciplines for the task of systematic theology.

One question still remains to be answered. If the criteria and the methods of doing systematic theology can be described in this way, what are the criteria for assessing the result of doing systematic theology, namely, a conception of systematic theology? It follows from the account I have tried to develop that a conception of systematic theology must satisfy the same criteria as those of doing systematic theology and the additional criterion of giving reasons for the way it uses these criteria. The only additional criterion is a strictly methodological one.

This way of presenting the activity of doing systematic theology might provoke the question whether it is not unnecessarily complicated compared to the striking simplicity which characterizes the greatest examples of systematic theology. I could only answer by pointing out that even the simplest activities like tying one's shoe-laces seem to be extraordinarily complicated once we try to describe them. I am, however, wondering whether the next time I am asked what I do for a job I should not answer that I teach Christian Doctrine.

Part I
DIVINE ACTION

1 Divine Action and Christian Faith

1 FUNDAMENTAL YET OPAQUE: DISCOURSE ABOUT DIVINE ACTION

Discourse about divine action is as fundamental in Christian faith as it is fundamentally unclear in Christian theology.[1] The fundamental role of discourse about divine action can be shown in all activities expressing Christian faith. In *prayer* reference to divine action indicates the basis for addressing God and determines the way in which somebody relates to God in prayer.[2] In prayers of *praise* specific attributes of God are referred to which are seen as characteristic for God's action in relation to humanity and the world. *Thanksgiving* refers explicitly to what God has done and does in such a way that it benefits the person who offers prayers of thanksgiving. *Petitionary prayer* would not make sense if it were not understood as asking God to act. *Lamentations* also refer not just to the circumstances of the believer's life in the world, but to these circumstances insofar as they are the result of divine and human action. It would therefore seem correct to say that prayer in all its forms presupposes and expresses a relationship between God, the believer and the world which is established and shaped by God's action and which is the context for the agency of the believer.

This relationship which is established and shaped by divine action is professed in *confessions of faith* in the community of believers and before the world as the foundation and content of faith. God's action is the common focus of what is confessed as determining the life of the community of believers in the world. In this way God's creative action is professed as the condition for the existence of created being. The narrative exposition of the history and fate of Jesus Christ is expressed as the story of the history and fate of the Son of God which, as the self-disclosure of God, has its unity in its reference to God's action in Christ. In confessing faith in the Holy Spirit the Christian community states that God's

---

[1] There have been significant attempts in recent years to clarify the concept of divine agency cf. W.Härle, 'Werk Gottes - Werk des Menschen', *NThT* 34 (1980), 213-224. Cf. also V. White, *The Fall of a Sparrow. A Concept of Special Divine Action*, Exeter 1985; M. Wiles, God's Action in the World, London 1986; K. Ward, *Divine Action*, London 1990; Mats J. Hansson, *Understanding an Act of God. An Essay in Philosophical Theology*, Studia Doctrinae Christianae Upsaliensia 33, Acta Universitatis Upsaliensis, Uppsala 1991. The conception developed in this chapter I first outlined in the paper 'Divine Agency and Providence', *Modern Theology* 3 (1987), 225-244.

[2] Cf. Vincent Brümmer, *What Are We Doing When We Pray? A Philosophical Inquiry*, London 1984, especially chapter 5 'Prayer and the Agency of God', 60-73.

grace is the condition for its life as the church and gives expression to its hope that God's action will grant eternal life through the resurrection of the dead. The trinitarian structure of the confession of faith asserts God as the unitary agent in the personal particularity of his agency as Father, Son and Spirit. With regard to the content of the confession of faith this makes it clear that God's action is the common framework of reference for all confessional statements in the sense that only that which can be seen as divine action can become the content of confessions of faith.

Christian *proclamation* as the process of communication which provokes and expresses faith refers through the *verbum externum* of Scripture to God's action in Israel and in Jesus Christ as the paradigm for all divine action. It has the aim of expressing the memory God's action in Israel and in Jesus Christ as the basis for a true presentation of human understanding of reality. Proclamation is furthermore motivated by the hope that the truth of its discourse about God's action in Israel and in Jesus Christ is made evident in such a way that it becomes certain for the believer as the true destiny of human life. This implies that the memory of God's acts in Israel and in Jesus Christ and the expectation of God's action which is grounded in this memory is ascertained in the experience of the life of the believer and can thus be acknowledged as true. Christian proclamation not only refers to God's action by asserting the memory and expectation of God's action as it is expressed in the biblical traditions as universal truth. It is furthermore motivated by the hope that this truth is made certain through God's action in the *testimonium internum* of the Holy Spirit and can in this way become the ground and content of Christian faith.

This brief sketch of a number of basic aspects of Christian worship shows that divine action which is presupposed and proclaimed in the practice of worship and expressed in the discourse of faith not only plays a central role for Christian faith, but is constitutive for it. Without divine action there could be no Christian faith and therefore the discourse of Christian faith is grounded in all its forms on discourse of divine action. The way in which God's action is referred to also shows that Christian discourse is not based on a purely formal concept of divine action, but that it expresses specific relations in which God, humanity and the world are related in a way determined by God. This means that all talk about divine agency presupposes a specific understanding of humankind and of its possibilities of action, and of the world as its field of action which, in turn, shapes the ways in which we can speak about divine action. One cannot talk about divine action without (at least implicitly) saying something about human agency and the world as the field of human action. And it is claimed in Christian faith that one cannot speak about human agency and the world as a field of human action without (at least implicitly) saying something about divine action. Only by paying attention to these interconnections can the understanding of reality in Christian faith be structurally complete and only in this connection can the ontological truth claims of Christian faith be correctly determined.[3]

---

3 Schleiermacher has expressed this in classical form: 'Alle Sätze, welche die christliche Glaubenslehre aufzustellen hat, können gefaßt werden entweder als Beschreibungen menschlicher Lebenszustände, oder als Begriffe von göttlichen

Against this background of the fundamental role of discourse about divine action in Christian faith, which reflects the constitutive role of divine action for faith, the fundamental opacity of the concept of divine action in Christian theology appears highly problematical. This opaqueness finds its expression in the fact that Christian dogmatics constantly employs concepts like 'creation', 'reconciliation' and 'redemption' which imply notions of divine action, but seldom explicates them sufficiently. Where attempts at explicating these implicit concepts of divine agency are undertaken, they often rely on traditional models, like the distinction between primary and secondary causality. This, however, can lead to contradictory impressions, since these models are not without further clarification compatible with the notion of God as a personal agent. If the concept of divine action which is presupposed in dogmatic concepts like creation and redemption is not clarified this leads not only to a loss of clarity with regard to individual *loci* of Christian dogmatics, but also with regard to their relationship in the overall structure of Christian dogmatics. It follows from the central place of the concept of divine action in Christian faith that difficulties in giving clear conceptual expression to it are mirrored in almost every doctrine of Christian dogmatics.

The symptoms which indicate the opacity of theological concepts of divine action do not sufficiently reveal the reasons for this situation. They can only be understood against the background of the fundamental criticism of the meaningfulness of discourse about God in modern intellectual history. The decisive elements of this criticism for the understanding of discourse about divine action are represented in three types of criticism which appeared in historical succession.[4]

The *epistemological* criticism in the tradition of Kantian philosophy denies that metaphysical states of affairs and therefore also a transcendent God can be a possible object of human knowledge. If this applies to the agent presupposed in the expression 'divine action' then it applies necessarily also to the actions ascribed to such an agent. Therefore the expression 'divine action' cannot have cognitive meaning and cannot be employed in constative speech acts: it must have non-cognitive meaning.

Materialist criticism denies the factual existence of an agent referred to in the expression 'divine action' and the factual existence of any actions ascribed to this putative agent.[5] Since according to a materialistic view of reality, reality as a

---

Handlungsweisen, oder als Aussagen von Beschaffenheiten der Welt; und alle diese drei Formen haben immer nebeneinander bestanden.' *Der christliche Glaube*, 2nd edition, §30 (quoted from the edition of M.Redeker, vol. 1, Berlin 1960), 163.

[4] These three types of criticism and there relevance for the doctrine of God is discussed in detail in an unpublished manuscript by Eilert Herms 'Grundprobleme der Gotteslehre'. He offers an extensive counter-critique of all three types of criticism.

[5] The representatives of this strand of criticism in 19th century Germany are Ludwig Büchner, Jakob Moleschott and Karl Vogt. They are connected to the earlier epistemological criticism of theological discourse through d'Holbach and Helvetius. Still informative is the exposition of P.Volkmann, *Die materialistische Epoche des 19. Jahrhunderts*, 1909. In recent years similar considerations, based on different

whole should be understood as a conglomerate of interacting particles of matter, there is no place in such a view for God as agent nor for any actions ascribed to God.

The criticism of *logical empiricism* denies that sentences in which the expression 'divine action' is used in a referential sense succeed in making meaningful statements. On the basis of the criterion of meaning provided by the test of empirical verifiability or falsifiability the alleged agent cannot be identified, and action cannot be meaningfully ascribed to this agent.[6] Discourse about divine agency represents on this view neither a cognitively inaccessible state of affairs, nor a non-existent fiction; it is quite simply 'meaningless'.

The far-reaching character of these three forms of criticism can be seen from its implications for the understanding of human agency. According to the epistemological critique of discourse about divine action the ground of freedom which is presupposed in human intentional action would also be part of the metaphysical realm which is not a possible object of human knowledge. According to the materialistic type of criticism, which is also represented in modern behaviourism, not only talk about God, but also talk about intentional human action is to be given up because it can be reduced to statements about the probability of the occurrence of certain events.[7] In the context of the logical empiricist critique discourse about persons which intends to express more than their spatio-temporal identifiability as sources of action is as meaningless as talk about God.[8]

This seems to suggest that the criticism of discourse about divine action implies a view of human agency which renders its foundations and intentional structure as being beyond the realms of knowledge or as non-existent and discourse about it as meaningless. One could raise the question whether the converse is true as well, so that the reconstruction of the concept of divine agency implies a view of human agency which can account for the ground of human freedom, for the intentional structure of human action and for the personal character of human agents.

The criticism of discourse about divine action which we can find in the intellectual history of the 19th and 20th century has led to two different theological reactions. On the one hand, discourse about divine action is completely reinterpreted or replaced by a) conceiving of the doctrine of God in a conceptuality which refrains from referring to an acting God in order to escape the epistemological, materialist and logical empiricist criticism; or it is attempted b) to translate discourse about divine action into descriptions of

---

scientific theories, but characterized by a similar philosophical tendency, have been voiced by representatives of the school of sociobiology.

[6] The most influential and most succinct exposition of this view was A.J.Ayer, *Language, Logic and Truth* (1946), Pelican edition Harmondsworth 1971, 151-158.

[7] Cf. Thomas F. Tracy, *God, Action and Embodiment*, Grand Rapids 1984, especially 6-20.

[8] This is explicitly indicated by Ayer, op.cit., 154.

particular forms of human self-understanding.[9] On the other hand, the criticism of discourse of divine action is rejected as an alien imposition upon theo-logy and a return to biblical forms of language as an adequate exposition of the 'God who acts' is called for, as in the North American school of 'biblical theology'.[10]

Both forms of the former type are, at least *prima facie*, discontinuous with dis-course about divine action in Christian faith. This provokes the question whether they provide an adequate basis for the theological exposition of Christian faith. The second form of this type of reaction which translates discourse about divine action into descriptions of human self-understanding raises the question whether these descriptions of human self-understanding must, from a theological point of view, remain underdetermined since they can no longer refer to the conditions of adequate self-understanding in terms of divine action. The latter type of reaction can preserve a *formal* continuity with discourse about divine action in Christian faith, but this is achieved at the expense of neglecting the task of Christian theology to give a coherent exposition of the view of reality of Christian faith. This creates a discontinuity with the *content* of discourse on divine action in Christian faith which provides the foundation for such a view of reality.[11] The example of the school of 'biblical theo-logy' illustrates moreover that an attempt at reconstituting discourse of divine action which simply ignores its modern critique runs the risk of also ignoring the common presupposition of both the traditional doctrine of God and of its modern critique, i.e. that God may not be understood as a worldly agent and that divine action must therefore be thought of as categoreally distinct from human action. Because most forms of Christian theology are situated between these extreme forms of reacting to the criticism of divine action and are influenced from both sides there is often a loss of clarity in the theological exposition of discourse of divine action.

This situation which we have characterized with regard to its symptoms and causes, and with regard to some attempts at resolving its difficulties, has one major problematical consequence. If Christian theology does not succeed in finding a coherent conceptual exposition of discourse about divine action, the status of theology as rational self-explication of Christian faith is called into question. The theological task consists, therefore, in trying to offer a conceptual reconstruction of discourse about divine action which can preserve a continuity of content with discourse of divine agency in Christian faith and, at the same time, can establish possibilities for critically confronting the criticism of discourse on divine action.

In view of the challenges of this task we can only attempt to offer a contribution to the resolution of some of the problems. Our approach starts from

---

[9] An example of tendency a) would be the theology of Paul Tillich; for tendency b) one could refer to Herbert Braun's theology or, more recently, to Don Cupitt's thought since the publication of *Taking Leave of God*, London 1980.

[10] Cf. G.E.Wright, *God Who Acts: Biblical Theology as Recital*, London 1972.

[11] For a critical assessment of the conceptions of 'biblical theology' cf. L.B.Gilkey,'Cosmology, Ontology and the Travail of Biblical Language, in: *JR* 41 (1961), 194-205, now in: O.C.Thomas (ed.), *God's Activity in the World. The Contemporary Problem* , AAR Studies in Religion 31, Chico Calif. 1983, 23-43.

the exposition of Christian faith as an *act* which rests on certain conditions for its possibility which are identified in the language of divine action as the *content* of Christian belief as it is expressed in confessions of faith (2). This requires us to reconstruct the various dimensions of divine action which make the act of faith possible and which are confessed as the content of belief as internally related types of action (3). Subsequently it has to be shown how this description of types of action can be coherently expressed in a model of divine agency (4). This, however, raises the question of how this view of divine action can be understood in relation to God's being (5). Only then will it become possible to indicate possible strategies for responding to the criticisms of discourse on divine action (6).

2 THE ACT OF FAITH AND THE CONTENT OF BELIEF

The theological tradition distinguishes between faith as *act* (*fides qua creditur*) and the *content* of belief (*fides quae creditur*). The act of faith is commonly understood as the unconditional existential trust which forms the fundamental orientation of human agency.[12] Understood in this sense faith designates not only a specific relationship to God, but includes also specific relationships of believers to themselves, to their shared social world and to their cultural and natural environment which are determined by their relationship to God. Insofar as faith is understood as the fundamental framework of orientation for believers it shapes their view of the possibilities of human action and informs their understanding of the norms and aims of their agency. It can therefore be said that for believers faith is constitutive for their role as agents in the world.

Faith can be characterized as *unconditional* trust, because as the fundamental act of human agency faith cannot be seen as being rooted in another form of human action. If this were the case, the action making faith possible would be the fundamental act of human action and would as such represent the fundamental orientation of all human agency. The unconditional character of faith indicates that Christian faith is passively constituted. Faith as the fundamental act of human existence is not actively constituted *by* human beings, but is constituted *for* human beings. The condition for the possibility of faith is already presupposed in the act of faith and can therefore only be passively received.

In Christian faith this condition of its possibility is understood as the certainty-creating disclosure of the truth of the Gospel of Christ as the truth about the constitution and character of reality.[13] Faith as the act of

---

[12] Cf. the exposition of the relationship between the act of faith and the content of belief based on Luther's commentary on the first commandment in W.Härle, 'Widerspruchs-freiheit. Überlegungen zum Verhältnis von Glauben und Denken', *NZSTh* 28 (1986), 223-237.

[13] Cf. the exposition of the constitutive role of certainty for the possibility of free agency which consists in the fact that certainty is constituted by the disclosure of truth in E.Herms, 'Die eschatologische Existenz des neuen Menschen', *ZThK* 83 (1986), 463-483, especially 470ff. The following argument concerning the function of faith as the basic orientation for all action which faith possesses in virtue of the certainty of the truth of the Gospel of Christ applies only to *right* faith which is to

unconditional trust is the active acknowledgement of the certainty of the truth of the Gospel as the fundamental orientation for all human actions. This certainty is constitutive for the basic orientation of personal agency insofar as the selection of certain aims of action in intentional action presupposes certainty concerning the possibilities of action, the aims of action and the conditions for its realisation. Certainty as the basis for intentional action always rests on a specific view of the possibilities and norms of action which is claimed to be true. The condition for the possibility of certainty is therefore the truth of a specific view of the situation of the agent.

The disclosure of truth which makes certainty possible is seen in Christian faith as the truth of God's revelation in Christ. This implies that this truth is not actively produced by the believer, but is passively disclosed to the believer and actively acknowledged by the believer. Disclosure is always the disclosure of something. If the content of God's revelation in Christ is to be the fundamental orientation for all actions in the fundamental act of faith, then it cannot have an arbitrary content, but must reveal the constitution and character of reality in such a way that it can be seen as the field of action for personal agents. Since the truth that is disclosed in revelation includes the conditions of agency which are not themselves constituted by the agent, and since these conditions comprise not only certainty concerning the truth of a view of reality, but also the character and structure of reality itself, reality itself must also be seen as passively constituted. Certainty is only possible with regard to truth, and there can only be truth with regard to what is the case, that is, in traditional language, as correspondence between a proposition and the reality expressed in that proposition.

If this whole structure is understood as the constitution of faith and if the overall manner of the constitution of faith is to be characterized as passive constitution, then it is also claimed that every link in this chain of conditions for the possibility of faith has the same structure which is characterized as passive constitution. This means that certainty as well as the disclosure of truth and reality itself are understood as passively constituted.

Reflection on the conditions of the possibility of faith as the act of unconditional trust illustrates the connection between faith as act and belief as assent to specific propositions expressing the content of belief. In our exposition the conditions for the possibility of the *act* of faith are precisely what is asserted as the *content* of belief. Only that can be asserted as the content of faith which constitutes the act of faith, and only that act can be seen as the act of faith which is constituted by the conditions for the constitution of faith which are asserted as the content of belief.

In confessions of faith the conditions for the constitution of faith are stated as the content of belief by being expressed in the language of divine agency. What

---

be distinguished from superstition. This qualification is necessary since it is in the context of modern epistemology not possible to infer truth from the existence of certainty because of the fundamental fallibility of human beings. Certainty is not a sufficient condition of truth, but truth is a necessary condition for 'real' certainty and 'right' faith. This distinction corresponds to the later medieval use of the concept of *certitas* where *certitas* concerning p implies that p is true.

is constituted *for* faith, is expressed as being constituted *by* God. What is seen as the foundation of all human agency in faith is interpreted as being rooted in divine agency. Divine agency is referred to in such a way that it expresses the condition of the possibility of all human agency.

In this context discourse of divine action must be strictly related to what enables faith as the fundamental act of human agency. God's action is therefore expressed as that which makes certainty possible and thus provides the basis for the selection of aims of action. Since the certainty that is granted in this way rests on truth, God's action is depicted as the constitution of reality which is disclosed in revelation and made certain in inspiration.

This way of talking about God as agent identifies God as the only being humans should relate to in the act of unconditional trust because God is depicted as the ground of all certainty, truth and reality. At the same time unconditional trust is identified as the only appropriate relation of humans to the God who is characterised in this way.

In the discourse of Christian faith God's action in creating certainty, truth and reality is expressed in language about God's action in the Spirit, about God's revelation in Christ and by talking about God the creator. If this form of discourse is analysed in its epistemic structure according to the *ratio cognoscendi* one has to start from the action of God the Spirit in creating the certainty of faith concerning the truth of God's revelation in Christ as the truth about the relationship of the creator to creation. If we inquire about the ontological relationship of these dimensions of agency according to the *ratio essendi* we have to start from the agency of God the creator which is revealed in Christ and made certain in the Spirit.

The ontological exposition of these types of divine action does not have to present an objectifying account which abstracts from the experience of divine action in faith. By viewing the passive constitution of faith for the believer as active constitution through divine action we also determine the ontological status of faith. Faith is recognized as having the status of created being which through the disclosure of the truth of the constitution of reality has become transparent for itself in such a way that its created status can be acknowledged in the act of unconditional trust in its creator.[14] Faith participates in the ontological status of all created reality, but it is the specific distinction of human creatures that they can become certain of the truth of their ontological status as created beings and respond to God their creator in the unconditional trust of faith. Discourse about divine action is from the perspective of faith therefore not abstractive and as such objectifying, but it has a *self-involving* character.[15] This can be brought out by explicating the view of human agency and the world as a field of action which is implied in discourse about divine agency. However, it is primary for faith as an exemplar of created being that it participates in the

---

[14] Cf. E.Herms, 'Die Wirklichkeit des Glaubens. Beobachtungen und Erwägungen zur Lehre vom ordo salutis', *EvTh* 42 (1982), 541-566.

[15] Cf. for this concept D.D.Evans, *The Logic of Self-Involvement. A Philosophical Study of Everyday Language with Special Reference to the Christian Use of Language about God as Creator*, London 1963.

general structure of passively constituted being, i.e. in its createdness. Therefore it seems appropriate for a conceptual account of divine action to start from discourse about God the creator.

3 DIVINE AGENCY: A RECONSTRUCTION

Theological tradition has summarized God's creative agency, the first type of divine action, in the concept of *creatio ex nihilo*.[16] This notion points to the unconditional character of God's creative action which rests on no other condition than God's creativity. God's action is described as essentially creative and universal so that everything that exists presupposes God's creative activity as the condition for its being. The character of God's activity is conceived as establishing the conditions for existence of everything that is not God. This posits a radical distinction between God as the one who in his creative agency is the creative ground of all being and the world whose being is grounded in God's creative agency. Seeing God's agency in this way as the ground of created being gives to created being the status of *contingent* being. This, in turn, requires us to see God's creative activity as the unity of creation and conservation, summarized in the concept of *creatio continuata*. If God's creative action were located only at a specific point at the beginning of time which is no longer necessary for the continuing existence of created being, then we would have to assume for created being a change in ontological status from contingent being to necessary being. This is excluded by interpreting God's creative agency both as *creatio ex nihilo* and as *creatio continuata*.

This correlation of creation and conservation, however, contains one conceptual difficulty. If God's action is interpreted as *creatio ex nihilo* 'in the beginning', then God's action is the sufficient condition for the existence of the world. If God's action as *creatio continuata* is understood in this sense, then everything that happens in the world would be completely determined in the divine decree.[17] Neither the relative autonomy of natural processes in the world which we express in the probabilistic statements of natural laws nor human freedom would be possible. Is it conceivable to understand God's creative action as sufficient condition for the existence of the world and as necessary condition for every occurrence in the world? This would be plausible if the creation of the world could be understood as the establishment of a network of relationships which God maintains in his action as conservation in such a way that he acts as the necessary, but not as the sufficient condition for all occurrences in the world. This interpretation of God's creative action as sufficient condition for the existence of the world in the initial act of creation and as necessary condition for all occurrences in the world in the conservation of creation implies the notion of a divine self-limitation. On this view, God maintains the world in its created structures and freely limits the exercise of divine omnipotence in respecting the

---

[16] Cf. the precise interpretation of the *creatio ex nihilo* formula in E.Wölfel, *Welt als Schöpfung. Zu den Fundamentalsätzen der christlichen Schöpfungslehre*, München 1981.

[17] Cf. for the discussion of this problem Brümmer, op. cit. (n.2), p.59ff.

existence and structure of creation. This is reflected in the fact that the relational structure of the world which includes the relative autonomy of natural processes as well as the finite freedom of human agents is understood in Christian faith as a good order in which righteousness and salvation can be actualized.

The distinction of the human creature in the world as creation is expressed in the theological tradition in the metaphor of the image of God.[18] This distinction of the human creation, summarized in the concept of the human person, can be characterized as the ability to relate actively to the relatedness which constitutes human existence and which is grounded in God's creative action. This ascribes to human beings the ability to relate to God, to themselves in their social context, and to their cultural and natural environment. This ability includes as finite freedom the possibility to relate actively to the passive relatedness which is given for human life. This can either happen in such a way that the ability for active relationships and the passively constituted structure of relatedness which is given to human beings are acknowledged as grounded in God's creative action; or it can happen in such a way that God's creative action as the ground of finite human freedom and as the ground of being of the given structure of relatedness in God's creative action is denied, so that human beings act as if their freedom were sovereign and creative, radically self-produced freedom.

Christian discourse about the Fall and about sin states that this denial, the contradiction of human freedom against its ground in God's creative freedom, is the factual situation of human beings in the world. It is characterized by the fact that human beings retain the capacity for intentional action, but do not possess knowledge of the ground of human freedom and of the world in God's creative action so that human beings have to act in the absence of the fundamental orientation of certainty with regard to the truth of the constitution of reality. The fact that God maintains and sustains the world in its created structures in spite of the rebellion of sin is understood in Christian faith as an expression of God's faithfulness. This implies that sin has no independent ontological status. The world and the human creatures remain God's creation in spite of the human contradiction of sin.

This fundamental asymmetry between God's creative agency and the agency of created beings implies that the relationship between God and humanity which had been broken by sin cannot be restored from the side of humanity. The restoration of this relationship lies outside the scope of human possibilities of action, precisely because human agency is not sovereign, absolutely creative action. Christian faith is rooted in the conviction that God has restored the broken relationship with humanity in the revelation in Christ and has in this way cancelled the consequences of the rebellion of sin. Summarizing the renewal of the relationship between God and creation in the concept of *revelation* as the second type of divine action does not mean that other metaphors of Christian

---

18 Cf. W.Härle, 'Die Rechtfertigungslehre als Grundlegung der Anthropologie, in: W.Härle and E.Herms (eds.), *Rechtfertigung. Das Wirklichkeitsverständnis des christlichen Glaubens*, Göttingen 1979, 79-100; and I.U.Dalferth/E.Jüngel, 'Person und Gottebenbildlichkeit', *Christlicher Glaube in moderner Gesellschaft* 24, Freiburg-Basel-Wien 1981, 57-99.

teaching for the restoration or recreation of this relationship such as reconciliation, atonement etc., are thereby made redundant. What is meant here is that God's action in restoring the broken relationship to creation can best be expressed in the concept of revelation so that this concept becomes the framework for the interpretation of other soteriological metaphors.[19]

Theological discourse about God's revelation in Jesus Christ asserts that in Jesus Christ God discloses for human experience the truth about his relationship to humanity and to the world. In this view of revelation it is presupposed that what is disclosed by God in Christ could not be known by human persons in any other way because of the contradiction of sin. God's revelation in Christ enables human beings to relate in faith to God and the world in such a way that God is acknowledged as the ground of all created being and as the source of salvation. The content of this revelation is interpreted as God's faithfulness to a world which is lost if left to its own resources. The faithfulness in which God upholds his relationship to the world is disclosed to sinful humanity, it is claimed, as the revelation of grace and truth in Jesus Christ. From the perspective of sin this revelation is radically discontinuous with sinful existence and its view of reality. However, where this revelation is acknowledged in faith as the truth about God's relationship to the world and to humanity it is made manifest that this revelation has no other content than God's faithfulness to the purpose of his creative action to bring about righteousness and salvation for his creation.

If God's faithfulness is seen in such a strong sense as the content of God's revelation in Christ, this would seem to imply that the *mode* of God's revelation does not contradict its content. Traditional Christology has attempted to do justice to this insight by insisting that Jesus Christ as God's revelation is not a *tertium quid* between God and humanity, neither angel nor superman, but true God and true man. This implies for Christology that God's revelation occurs in the human action and passion of Christ in such a way that it becomes the ultimate disclosure of God's relationship to creation.

In Jesus' deeds and suffering which are consistently characterized by unconditional obedience to the will of God the Father his relationship to God is depicted as a relationship free of contradiction and rebellion so that in all his actions God is acknowledged as the sole condition for their possibility. In this radical obedience to the will of God the Father Jesus' history and destiny becomes transparent for God's creative action as that which enables the witness of Jesus' life.

This can be expressed in a two-fold thesis: Jesus Christ is the revelation of true humanity insofar as in his relationship to God the true destiny of humanity as it is made possible by God is realized. Jesus Christ is the revelation of God insofar as *in this relationship* God's relationship to humanity is disclosed as the condition of the possibility of the true relationship of humanity to God.

The revelation of God in Jesus Christ reveals nothing other than the relationship of God to the world and to humanity which is established in God's creative action as the condition for the possibility of the appropriate relationship

---

[19] For a more detailed account of the theological status of the concept of revelation see chapter 4 below.

33

of human beings to God. However, since this relationship is disclosed in the reality of experience as God's action which overcomes the contradiction of sin, God's action can now be experienced in Jesus' deeds and suffering as its creative ground, so that God can be identified as agent in this experience.

This view of God's revelatory action has profound implications not only for our understanding of God as agent, but also for our view of the world and our understanding of human agency.The truth about God's creative agency as the ground of being of all created reality becomes accessible to human experience in God's revelatory action in the medium of created reality. This makes possible a view of reality where reality is not only understood as constituted by God, but also as the medium of God's self-disclosure. Discourse about God's creative action expresses the character of the world as God's creation and discourse about God's revelatory action characterizes the world as the context in which God's relationship to creation can be experienced. God's creative action determines the character of the world as the context of the exercise of the created and finite freedom of human agents. God's revelatory action in Jesus Christ makes Jesus' action and passion evident as the foundation of true insight into the character of human freedom and as the paradigm for the exercise of this freedom. In this way God's revelation in Christ discloses the character of the world as the context for the exercise of created freedom and gives insight into the norms and rules of human action by which human action can correspond to the created destiny of humanity in all relationships of human existence.

In Christian faith not only the constitution of reality (creation) and the disclosure of the truth about the constitution of reality (revelation) is ascribed to God's agency, but also the creation of certainty with regard to the disclosed truth about the constitution of reality. This specific aspect of divine agency is expressed in discourse about the *inspiration* of the believer by God the Spirit, the third type of divine action. The point of this discourse about God the Spirit is that it does not express a new content over and above God's agency in creation and revelation. Rather, God's inspiring action constitutes certainty about God's revelation in Jesus Christ as the truth about God's relationship to the reconciled creation. This certainty is not the result of an actively conducted strategy of verification concerning the truth of revelation, but is the passively constituted insight into this truth. God's agency in the Spirit re-presents the truth of God's revelation in Christ in such a way that it becomes evident for me as truth about my personal life. Therefore, God's action in the Spirit is, as the re-presentation of the truth of revelation, also the personalization of this truth as the foundation of the life of the individual believer. In this way the life of the believer becomes transparent for itself as it is grounded in God's creative action and enlightened by God's revelatory action.

Certainty which is constituted in this way makes possible faith as the active acknowledgement of God's creative, revelatory and inspiring action. Faith can become the fundamental orientation for human life, because certainty with regard to the structure of reality is a constitutive condition for successful intentional action. Intentional action is only possible on the basis of certainty with regard to the truth of an agent's knowledge of his possibilities of action and with regard to those policies of action which enable the agent successfully to relate an intention and its actualisation. By creating certainty concerning the character of reality

God's inspiration reconstitutes human being as agents. Just as sin includes the disorientation and ultimately the destruction of the capacity to act, because as a state of deception about the character of reality sin can only produce self-deception about the possibilities of action in the agent, so faith includes the reconstitution of the capacity to act by granting certainty about the constitution of reality and the agent's possibilities and potentialities of action. In this process the world is reconstituted for human agents as the space for the exercise of finite freedom. According to the view of reality of Christian faith, God's creative agency establishes the existence of the world, God's revelatory action establishes the accessibility of the world as God's creation for human experience and God's inspiring action is the foundation for the shaping and organising of the world by human agents in the framework of created finite freedom.

Our reconstruction of discourse about divine action in Christian faith distinguishes three types of divine agency: God's creative action as the constitution of created being, God's revelatory action as the disclosure of truth about the relationship of God the creator to his reconciled creation and God's inspiring action as the enabling of certainty concerning the truth about the constitution of reality. These three types of divine agency are internally related so that God's inspiring action creates certainty precisely with regard to the truth of the relationship of the creator to creation established in God's creative agency as it is disclosed in God's revelatory action in Christ. This reconstruction of the three types of divine agency implies a view of human agency according to which human beings are reconstituted as agents in God's inspiring action by being granted certainty about the truth of the created destiny of human personal agents, as it it is disclosed in the paradigm of Jesus Christ's action and passion. The world appears in this conception as the space for the exercise of finite human freedom which, because it's constitution is disclosed in revelation, can be shaped in acts of organisation and interpretation.

According to the conviction of Christian faith, God's revelation in Jesus Christ is eschatologically ultimate in that it will not be surpassed by further revelations. The certainty of faith created by the Spirit is therefore not a new revelation in the sense of disclosing a new content, but the personal appropriation of the truth of the revelation in Christ. If God's revelation in Christ which is the disclosure of the truth about the relationship of the God the creator to his reconciled creation is eschatologically ultimate, it follows that God's perfecting agency is not an independent type of action in addition to God's creative, revelatory and inspiring action. God's eschatological action has to be described as the perfecting of his creative, revelatory and inspiring action.

The *eschaton* in which the ultimate purpose of God's agency is perfected can in this way be described as the state in which the three types of divine action are coextensive so that God's creative action is universally revelatory and inspiring action. In the eschaton God's universal creative action is universally disclosed and made certain, and it can therefore bring about the inclusion of all believers in the eschatological reality of God and his perfected creation. The state in which God's creative, revelatory and inspiring action have become coextensive has traditionally been described as the *beatific vision* in which the certainty of faith has become universally evident. Before the *eschaton* the truth about God's relationship to the world is mediated through the communicative acts of

35

proclaiming and hearing the witness to God's revelation which is re-presented and authenticated in the Spirit as the personal certainty about my being and as a universal truth claim about all being. In the *eschaton* it will be present, that is the hope of Christian faith, as immediate vision and universally verified truth.

This attempt to present the eschatological dimension of God's action in the interrelationship of the three types of divine action enables us to relate precisely the *now already* of present experience and the *not yet* of the immediate vision of the eschatological reality of God's community with his creation. In faith the believer *already* participates in the eschatological reality, because God's creative, revelatory and inspiring action achieves its purpose by becoming the foundation of the life of the believer in the certainty of faith. This certainty implies the universal truth claim of God's revelation in Christ for all reality, although its universal and public verification can *not yet* be experienced, but remains the content of Christian hope.

4 PERSONAL AGENCY VERSUS TRANSCENDENTAL RELATION: CAN THE CONFLICT BE RESOLVED?

Our reconstruction of discourse about divine action in Christian faith rests on the presupposition that God's activity can plausibly be presented as personal agency. This implicit presupposition must now be explicated. In this context the conception of the three internally related types of action functions both as the basis of the model of divine action and as a qualification for this model.

If an event is described as the result of intentional action it is implied that this event would not have occurred if it had not been brought about by an agent whose action can be named as the necessary condition for the occurrence of the event. Furthermore, it is presupposed that the agent pursues a particular purpose with the action and that his or her action can be regulated to bring about the purpose. It is moreover assumed that the action-directing intention is the result of a conscious choice of aims of action and that the regulation of action is the result of a conscious choice of means of action. With these presuppositions we ascribe to the agent freedom of choice and freedom of action.[20] Only if these conditions are met does it become possible to describe an event as the result of intentional action and ascribe it to an agent who possesses knowledge of the aims and means of action and competence for the employment of these means of action. If an event can be described as the result of intentional action then the ascription of the event to the intentional agency of a free agent provides a sufficient explanation for the occurrence of the event.

The description of God's activity in creation, revelation and inspiration in terms of the model of personal agency is *possible* because discourse about divine action in Christian faith presupposes that the conditions for intentional

---

[20] Cf. the definition of the concept of intentional action in A.Kenny, *Will, Freedom and Power*, Oxford 1975, 56. A classic treatment of the concept of intentionality is still G.E.M.Anscombe, *Intention*, 2nd ed., Ithaca 1963.

agency we have outlined apply eminently in the case of God.[21] The reconstruction of discourse about God's activity in terms of personal agency is *necessary* since only this model can account for the unconditional character of God's action which is implied in discourse about creation, revelation and inspiration. These types of discourse presuppose that referring to God's agency offers sufficient reasons for the existence of the world, the disclosure of truth about its fundamental constitution in the world and for the creation of certainty concerning this truth. This can only be assumed on the basis of the interpretation of God's activity as intentional action.

A brief comparison with the model of causality can clarify this assumption underlying the discourse of Christian faith about divine action. A given event cannot be completely explained by referring its occurrence to a cause, because the concept of a cause cannot explain the occurrence of an event so completely that further explanations would be redundant. Why a cause C_1 produces an event as its effect can only be explained by referring to further causes C_{2-n}, so that C_1 appears itself as an event which can be explained by reference to C_{2-n}. C_1 appears as the medium of the effect of C_{2-n}, C_2 as the medium of C_{3-n}, and so on. An infinite regress seems inevitable. The attempt of halting this regress by employing the concept of *causa sui* destroys the conceptuality of causality and is therefore more an indication of the problem than its solution. It is different with the model of intentional action where the description of an event as the result of intentional action offers a sufficient explanation which does not lead into an infinite regress of further explanations.[22] This shows that the model of causality is at best a secondary explanatory model for the regulation of actions of personal agents, but not suitable as the primary model for the reconstruction of personal agency.

The interpretation of God's activity in terms of the model of personal agency is furthermore necessary since the internal relation of creation, revelation and inspiration discloses the purpose of God's action in revelation and inspires believers to find the orientation of their actions in doing the will of the creator so that their purposes are defined by God's purpose for his creation. This soteriological and eschatological direction of divine agency which defines the direction of the life of faith requires explication in terms of personal agency.

Discourse about God's action in creation, revelation and inspiration moreover includes, as we have attempted to show, the notion of a self-limitation of the

---

[21] For the theological employment of the model of personal action cf. R.H.King, *The Meaning of God*, London 1974, and C.M.Wood, 'The Events in Which God Acts', *Heythrop Journal* 22 (1981), 278-284.

[22] 'The conception of cause both includes and excludes the idea of the the "production" of an effect. In consequence, whatever we assign as the cause of an event is something which is not itself capable of producing an effect, but only, as it were, of transmitting it. It is a means through which something else produces an occurrence. In other words, the "cause" turns out to be merely another event which must be itself referred to another cause. An infinite regress of causes faces us in every case.' J.Macmurray, *The Self as Agent*, London 1956, 153. Cf. also Tracy, op.cit. (n.7), 21-44.

exercise of God's power. This notion which gives language about God's faithfulness its specific content presupposes the model of personal agency, since self-limitation is an implication of the selection of intentions and means of action in intentional action.

Another important reason for the interpretation of divine activity in terms of personal agency is that Christian discourse about divine action ascribes to God attributes like faithfulness, mercy and loving kindness which can only be predicated of personal agents on the basis of their intentional actions.[23] The ascription of such attributes is based on the experience of actions which document a consistent pattern of action and which can be interpreted as expressing the agent's intentions because the pattern of action is the result of a conscious choice of a policy of action. Predicating personal attributes of God requires that God be seen as a personal agent.

We have attempted to argue that it is possible and necessary to interpret God's activity in creation, revelation and inspiration in terms of the model of personal agency. The next step is to show why discourse about God's action requires the theological qualification of the model of personal agency. In creation, revelation and inspiration God's action is interpreted as bringing about and sustaining a finite world, as disclosure of truth about the world as creation and as granting certainty concerning this truth. In all three types of action God's agency is absolutely constitutive for finite being and finite agents. This constitutive relation indicates that there is a fundamental difference between God's agency and the agency of finite agents. This difference consists in the fact that God's action is the ground of the possibility of the agency of finite agents.

This categorical difference between divine and human agency is expressed in the traditional divine attributes of omnipotence, omnipresence, eternity and omniscience.[24] These attributes have to be strictly related to God's action in creation, revelation and inspiration and to the model of personal agency in which these three types of action are described in order to avoid the dilemma that the personal attributes ascribed to God are immediately denied by ascribing metaphysical attributes to God.[25] This dilemma can only be avoided if omnipotence, omnipresence, eternity and omniscience are interpreted as qualifiers of the model of personal agency for God's action.

God's omnipotence is accordingly not to be interpreted as God's ability to do anything that is logically possible, but as God's power by which he creates a world *ex nihilo*, through which he discloses the truth about his relationship to the world and to humanity in the world and through which he authenticates this truth as the certainty of faith. God's power consists centrally in that his action is the sufficient condition for the existence of the world and a necessary condition for everything that happens in the world. This interpretation of divine

---

[23] Cf. Tracy op. cit., part I.

[24] The following considerations are, as can easily be detected, inspired by Schleiermacher's exploration of the divine attributes. Cf. Schleiermacher, op.cit. (n.3), §50-55. For a more detailed account cf. chapter 2 below.

[25] Cf. the discussion of this dilemma in F.G.Kirkpatrick, 'Understanding an Act of God', in O.C.Thomas op.cit. (n.11), 124-125.

omnipotence includes the notion of divine self-limitation in the exercise of God's power by the existence and structure of creation. In contrast to the limited power of finite agents whose agency is externally limited by their bodily existence (and with that by a limited time and space of action) and by the existence of other agents, God is only limited by himself, that is by his creative will. For human action this external limitation of the possibilities of action implies that the scope for the self-regulation of action is restricted. This, in turn, implies that that there is a gap between an intention and its actualisation so that we cannot do everything we might intend. Furthermore, not everything we do is also intended by us, since intentional action is only part of our behaviour. All these external limitations of finite agency cannot be ascribed to God. God's agency is completely self-regulated agency.

If omnipotence is defined in this way it implies God's omnipresence insofar as God is seen as universally present to creation as its creative power of being. If omnipresence is interpreted within the framework of the three types of action of creation, revelation and inspiration, this means that God reveals himself in the spatio-temporal world of experience as its creative ground and that he is able to make the truth of his revelation everywhere present in order to grant certainty of faith. The spatial limitations which apply to created being cannot be applied to God, since God's agency as completely self-regulated agency includes God's omnipresent power and his omnipotent presence.

Since God's creative action is interpreted as the constitution of a temporal world, then God cannot be seen as being subject to the temporal limitations of a created world. However, if God's agency is seen as the necessary condition of all worldly occurrences then divine eternity cannot be interpreted as atemporality, strictly beyond time. God's eternity as the creative ground of a temporal world must include the ability to disclose the truth about the constitution and conservation of the temporal world in time and to authenticate it for temporally existing persons.

In the context of the model of personal agency, divine omniscience is to be interpreted strictly as that form of knowledge which enables and accompanies God's action in creation, revelation and inspiration. The knowledge of God therefore participates in the self-regulating character of divine action which includes the free limitation of God's power by the creation and conservation of a world of relatively independent natural processes and created agents with finite freedom. This implies that God's knowledge is self-limited through the free actions of his creatures in such a way that God knows the future not as eternal presence, but as the future, as the sum of all possibilities which are given in the world at a particular moment in time.[26]

It becomes clear when we introduce the metaphysical attributes of God into the interpretation of the model of personal divine agency that the model of intentional agency can only be applied to God if certain important qualifications are made. These qualifications, however, neither destroy the model of personal agency nor is God's action made to appear as an inferior type of personal agency.

---

[26] Cf. P.T.Geach, 'The Future', in: *New Blackfriars* 54(1973), 208-218. This view is further developed in a theological context by Brümmer op.cit (n.2), 40ff.

Rather, it becomes evident that God's action represents the *perfection* of intentional action as completely self-regulated action and that the metaphysical attributes of God indicate the respects in which God's action as perfect action is distinguished from human action.[27]

With this exposition of the model of personal agency one decisive element of discourse about divine action as the sum of the conditions of the possibility of faith has not yet been sufficiently explained. When we understand God's creative agency as the constitution of created being, God's revelatory agency as the constitution of truth and God's action in inspiration as the creation of certainty concerning the truth of God's revelation, then the relationship between God and creation has to be conceived as a *transcendental* relation in the sense that discourse about divine action states the universal condition of the possibility that something exists and that it can become the object of true and certain knowledge.[28] If the relationship between God and the creation is described *exclusively* as a transcendental relation, this has the theologically unproblematical consequence that we cannot conceive of created being apart from its relation to its ground of being in God. However, it also has the theologically very problematical consequence that the notion of the ground of being always includes the concept of the being constituted by it. Theologically this relationship between being and the ground of being leads to the postulate of the eternity of the world. If we were to rely exclusively on the interpretation of the God-world relationship as a transcendental relation it would also follow that we could not predicate personal attributes of God since these attributes presuppose the notion of a personal agent which is not included in the view of the relationship between God as the ground of being and created being as a transcendental relation. The most problematical implication of using the model of a transcendental relation for depicting the relationship between God and the world is perhaps that it does not permit us to talk in any meaningful sense about God's freedom, including the divine freedom of self-limitation. Talk about God's freedom also presupposes that God is a personal agent capable of intentional action.[29]

These difficulties illustrate a basic problem of the model of a transcendental relation and it can be seen in the fact that although this model enables us to offer a conceptual reconstruction of one decisive element of the structure of the *relationship* between God and the world, at the same time it restricts the

---

[27] Cf. here the instructive discussion in the last chapter 'God and the Perfection of Agency' in Thomas F.Tracy's book (n.7), 124-154.

[28] For the interpretation of the God-world relationship as a transcendental relation cf. E.Herms, 'Gottes Wirklichkeit', in: W.Härle/R. Preul (eds.), *Marburger Jahrbuch Theo-logie I*, Marburg 1987, 82-101.

[29] A strong conception of divine freedom as it can be developed on the basis of the model of personal agency is necessary if we are to preserve the distinction between divine and human agency and has proved to be absolutely essential for the theological understanding of grace or for the doctrine of the church. This is very well brought out in the context of ecclesiology by Eilert Herms, 'Evangelische Katholiken?' now in his collection of essays: *Von der Glaubensfreiheit zur Kirchengemeinschaft: Plädoyer für eine realistische Ökumene*, Marburg 1989, 51-62

description of the *terms of this relation* to the description of the relationship itself. The problems which this conception presents become clear when we raise the question whether the same concepts can be employed for speaking about God as the ground of being and for speaking about the world and humanity as the form of being which has its ground in God. Can we talk about God's 'existence', or about divine 'action', or are we employing concepts for talking about God which can only be used with reference to finite being and finite agents? At this point all the traditional problems of a theological conception of language about God reappear.

At this point we notice an important difference between a philosophical and a Christian theological doctrine of God. A philosophical conception of God could possibly be content with suggesting a theoretical model for the relationship of God and the world and with restricting the exposition of the terms of this relationship to what can be said within the framework of the suggested model. A Christian theological doctrine of God which is conceived as the rational reconstruction of the forms and contents of the discourse of Christian faith cannot be satisfied with such an attitude, but has to look for possibilities of finding appropriate conceptual reconstructions for the view of reality expressed in Christian faith.[30] It cannot therefore test the adequacy of Christian discourse of faith by asking whether it meets the requirements of the proposed theoretical model, but has to assess the adequacy of its models of reconstruction by testing them against Christian discourse. In this process of rational reconstruction it is very likely that forms of Christian discourse of faith will also be criticized. The criterion of such criticism, however, is not incompatibility with a theoretical model of interpretation, but incompatibility with the fundamental content of the revelation in Christ.

In the context of these considerations, the problems of understanding the God-world-relationship in terms of the model of a transcendental relation become clear. On the one hand, the model can provide an exposition of the relationship which seems appropriate to the view of reality expressed in Christian discourse; on the other hand, the model appears to imply far-reaching restrictions for all talk about God as a personal agent so that it seems to be incompatible not only with the forms, but also with the content of the discourse of Christian faith.

Can this choice between the model of a transcendental relation and the model of personal agency be avoided? It appears that both models can be constructively integrated when the concept of agency is consistently interpreted in an ontological sense, so that all being can be conceived as the result of action. God's action would have to be interpreted as making possible created being in its processes and events so that the contingent status of finite being could be understood precisely as its dependence on God's action in making it possible and letting it be actual. The transcendental character of this relationship would have to be conceived as *the* structural characteristic of divine action constituting the fundamental categorical distinction between God the creator and the created being of the world. When the concept of agency is interpreted in this sense as the

---

[30] For this interpretation of the task of Christian theology cf. I.U.Dalferth, *Existenz Gottes und christlicher Glaube*, München 1984, 16-30.

fundamental category of ontology, the concept of divine agency designates the ground of all created being. On this view, ontology becomes a modal theory of divine action. Everything that is would have to be interpreted as being made either possible or necessary 'by God' so that 'by God' would have to be unterstood as 'constituted by God's action'. God would have to be conceived as the by itself possible and necessary ground of all worldly being and occurrences in such a way that 'by itself' designates the self-constitutive character of divine agency.[31]

This has further implications for the interpretation of God's metaphysical attributes. They would appear not only as the conceptual expression of the perfections of divine action, but would have to be seen as the exposition of the modal status of divine action by which God makes possible the relationship between divine being and the being of the world in creation, revelation and inspiration. God's omnipotence would have to be conceived as the specific mode in which God makes the being and processes of the world possible and necessary. God's omnipresence would express the way in which God is present to all worldly occurrences as the ground of their possibility. God's eternity would consequently have to be conceived as the ground of the possibility of time in which God is present for time in its modes of past, present and future as the condition for its possibility. The concept of God's omniscience presents in this view the fundamental accessibility of worldly events and processes for finite knowers as being rooted in their disclosedness for God.

This modal ontology of divine action would have the status of a theory which would have to demonstrate the compatibility of the model of personal agency and of a transcendental relation, which both seem to be required for a reconstruction of the discourse of Christian faith about divine action, by explicating their ontological implications. We can here only indicate the task of developing such a theory. However, our consideration seems to show that the apparent antinomy between both models can be overcome if the concept of action is conceived as an ontological concept which expresses the distinction and relation between divine action as it makes possible the processes of the world and human action on the one hand, and on the other hand, the processes of the world and human action as they are made possible by divine action.

5 TOWARDS A TRINITARIAN THEORY OF DIVINE AGENCY

In the theological tradition the doctrine of the Trinity offers possibilities for determining the relationship between the three types of divine action we have distinguished and for understanding their particularity and unity as rooted in God's triune being. It has to be observed that the doctrine of the Trinity has a different logical status from, for instance, the doctrine of creation or the doctrine of the church. It provides as the summary description of God's being and action a fundamental matrix which structures all material statements in Christian dogmatics. Its place in the *prolegomena* or *epilegomena* of dogmatics is a

---

[31] Cf. the philosophical theology in W.Härle, *Systematische Philosophie*, München-Mainz 1982, 228-250.

strong indication for its status as a the structural matrix for all doctrinal statements.

Our proposal for the reconstruction of discourse about divine action gives expression to the trinitarian structure of Christian faith by distinguishing and relating the three types of divine action in creation, revelation and inspiration as the action of Father, Son and Spirit. This enables us to individuate three different types of action and, at the same time, to identify God as the one agent in these three types of action. We have tried to show that the action of God the Spirit creates certainty precisely with regard to the truth of the revelation of the Son which is the disclosure of the true relationship of the Father to creation. This interconnection between the three types of action points to the common intention underlying all three types of action which enables us to identify God as agent in these actions. This interrelatedness of the three types of action implies that creation is already established in a relationship between the creator and creation which is directed towards its disclosure in such a way that this disclosure enables certainty concerning the truth about God's relationship to the world and its purpose. By acknowledging the truth about God's relationship to the world in faith as the fundamental orientation for their actions believers are thus included in the actualisation of God's intentions. The unitary intention which is contained in the internal relatedness of the three types of action is expressed in the insight of traditional trinitarian theology: *opera trinitatis ad extra sunt indivisa.* By demonstrating the internal relationship of the three types of action our proposal can account for the critical and constructive intention of the conception of the economic Trinity to assert the action of Father, Son and Spirit in creation, reconciliation and salvation as the action of the same God.

The theological conception of the immanent Trinity presents the relations of God to the world as they are developed in the doctrine of the economic Trinity as being rooted in the trinitarian relationality of God's being. The immanent relationality of God's being is the source and basis of God's relations to the world. God's action in creation, revelation and inspiration in the divine economy is therefore to be regarded as constituted in God's relational being in its immanent personal interaction. God's relational being in the mutual communion of the persons of Father, Son and Spirit, whose relationship towards one another is constituted in forms of action particular to each person *(opera trinitatis ad intra sunt divisa)* is the condition for the possibility of the unitary intention which regulates God's action in the divine economy. When it is interpreted in this way the doctrine of the immanent Trinity has a function analogous to that of the thesis of the ontological primacy of the concept of action. Being is interpreted as constituted in God's action in the divine economy which, in turn, is the expression of God's immanent relationality in God's relationship to the world. God's action in the divine economy can therefore be regarded as completely self-regulated agency, because it is rooted in God's immanent action as completely self-productive agency. The doctrine of the immanent Trinity as the expression of the eternal personal communion of Father, Son and Spirit explains why God's relationship to humanity in the divine economy is a personal relationship although the personal being of God is not constituted in the personal relationship of the creator to the personal creatures.

43

For discourse about divine action the doctrine of the economic Trinity functions as a fundamental rule for all statements about divine action in Christian dogmatics. The doctrine of the immanent Trinity offers a theological justification for this rule by interpreting the trinitarian structure of God's relationship to the world as rooted in the relationality of God's triune being. Employing the doctrine of the Trinity as the regulative matrix of all statements about divine action takes the apophatic character of all statements about the Trinity into account in a way which repeats an inherent element of trinitarian reflection in the Christian tradition both in the East and in the West. This apophatic character of all statements about the Trinity is the ultimate horizon of all attempts at reconstructing the trinitarian logic of the discourse of faith.

6 RESPONDING TO THE CRITICS

Can this reconstruction of discourse on divine action offer a basis for responding to the critical objections against the plausibility of language about God and divine action as they have been offered from the perspective of Kantian epistemology, ideological materialism or logical empiricism? We cannot offer anything like a full justification at this point, but we can at least sketch very briefly possible strategies of response.

With regard to the epistemological critique we can point out that the fundamental conditions of knowledge are not given apart from a specific view of reality. They can only be defined in the context of a view of reality which defines the field of possible knowledge. There is no ontology-neutral theory of knowledge. It is, however, a fundamental characteristic of discourse about divine action that it is not implied in a given view of reality, but that it constitutes such a view of reality. The epistemological justification of discourse about divine action is therefore only possible as the critical assessment of the epistemic possibilities of a view of reality constituted by this form of discourse. A response to the epistemological criticism can therefore not be offered on an 'ontology-free' ground. It can only be attempted as the dialogical assessment of the epistemic possibilities of the understanding of reality for which discourse about divine action has a foundational status in conversation and comparison with other views of reality which reject such discourse as epistemologically unjustifiable.

Discussion about the objections of materialism that God and divine action are not only unknowable, but non-existent, can be conducted on the ground which is acknowledged by materialists as being existent. Such a ground is the field of human behaviour and of the processes and events of the world. The central question of such a debate would be whether the view of reality for which reference to divine action is constitutive is able to make more sense or less sense of human action in the world and of the processes of the world than a materialistic view which is restricted to the analysis of regularities in the constitution and interaction of particles of matter and to the description of behaviour in terms of elaborate stimulus and response mechanisms.

A response to the objections of logical empiricism can be attempted by offering criteria for the identification of God as an agent which clarify how actions can be ascribed to this agent. The description of the types of action of 'creation' and 'revelation' open up different ways for the individuation of God's actions and for the identification of God as agent. By talking about God as creator a unique relationship is asserted of this agent to the world of our experience which can be employed as a criterion for the identification of this agent and for the individuation of divine actions. Since God is understood as the author of the revelation in Jesus Christ, God's actions would have to be identifiable as that which enables Jesus' action and passion. And insofar as the story of Jesus is made co-present to our story and to the reality of our experience through God's action in the Spirit there is one narrative which locates both us and God's revelation and could thus provide the basis for the identity-description of God in this narrative.[32]

These remarks can only indicate possible strategies of response, but they cannot anticipate success or failure of the attempt at responding to the critics. Even in these brief reflections it becomes clear that the chances for a satisfactory response increase in the extent in which it is possible to provide a systematic reconstruction of discourse about divine action in Christian faith. For this task different models will have to be investigated than the models of personal agency and of a transcendental relation which we have discussed here.[33] All such attempts have to be motivated by the intention to show that the clarity of systematic reconstructions of the concept of divine action can - at least in tendency - correspond to the central role of discourse about divine action in Christian faith.

---

[32] Cf. Tracy (n.7), 73-84.

[33] Cf. Grace M. Jantzen, *God's World, God's Body*, London 1984.

2 Exploring the Logic of Perfection: Divine Attributes and Divine Agency

1 A STRUCTURAL PROBLEM IN CHRISTIAN THOUGHT

Anyone who says that the Christian understanding of God presents in its historical development and systematic exposition many philosophical antinomies, paradoxes and confusions, can hardly claim much originality for such a statement. In view of the difficulties accompanying the history of Christian thought one could be tempted to explain the on-going attractiveness of the Christian view of God in the manner of Karl Barth by quoting the phrase *Dei providentia - hominum confusione*.[1] However, that this tag which seems only too plausible in many situations offers more consolation than explanation can be seen from the fact that it is relatively unlikely that anyone would attempt to add to the classical five ways of proving God's existence a sixth, negative and indirect proof *e confusione hominum*.

The fact that certain configurations of problems and the philosophical antinomies, paradoxes and confusions they contain regularly return in the history of the rational exposition of the Christian understanding of God points to more than the limitations of human reason and the inexhaustibility of the subject-matter of theological and philosophical reflection. The reappearance of the antinomies and paradoxes after every attempt at resolving them seems to indicate that we have to deal here with structural problems of the Christian understanding of God. Structural problems can be seen as such problems which do not arise from a specific conceptual exposition of the Christian view of God (there remain enough of those), but which appear in every such exposition, because they belong to the basic constitution of the Christian conception of God. Without the element constituting these problems the Christian view of God could not be authentically and plausibly expounded. Structural problems are distinguished from other kinds of problems by the fact that every attempt at offering a solution for them can only be seen as adequate if it also justifies why the problem could appear in the first place. The justification of the problem in its attempted solution indicates that the initial problem was not simply a mistake, but arises out of genuine aspects of the situation which is seen as problematical, calling for a resolution. I hope that these abstract remarks will become more concrete when we consider the structural problem which I want to investigate in this chapter: the antinomy between the conception of the divine attributes in philosophical theology and discourse about divine action in Christian faith.

---

[1] For an interesting early example of Barth's use of the phrase cf. Barth's letter to Martin Rade, dated 31.8.1914(!), in: *Karl Barth - Martin Rade. Ein Briefwechsel.* Mit einer Einleitung herausgegeben von Christoph Schwöbel, Gütersloh 1981, 97.

2 DIVINE PERFECTIONS AND THEISTIC PROOFS

The traditional conception of the so-called metaphysical attributes of God in philosophical theology which has shaped the exposition of the Christian view of God since the cultural compromise of Christianity with Greek metaphysics is closely related to the overall project of philosophical theology: to give reasons for the rational intelligibility of the world and of human being in the world in the framework of a *conception of God*. This project presupposes as a fundamental postulate of human rationality that there is an explanation of why there is something and not nothing, and why what there is, is as it is. Philosophical theology rests in all its histo-rical variations on the presupposition that there is an intelligible order of the universe which is accessible to rational explanation.

This basic orientation towards making reality intelligible by explanation, which underlies as the fundamental postulate of rationality all concrete attempts at offering explanations, always takes the form of a *theology* if it assumes the possibility of a *complete explanation* of reality. Com-pleteness of explanation in this sense does not only comprise all aspects of reality, but also includes an answer to the question of the ground of existence: why is there something and not nothing? The thesis put forward by all forms of *theistic* philosophical theology is that there is a being which as the complete explanation of itself is also the ultimate ground for the explanation of everything else.[2] This thesis always has a cosmological and an anthropological as well as a theological content. Human rationality, the rational intelligibility of the world and the existence of God as the universal principle of explanation and the ground of existence are seen as mutually dependent.

The mutual dependence of theology, cosmology and anthropology can be seen in exemplary fashion in the theistic proofs, the classical repertory pieces of the philosophical theology of theism. They demonstrate in different ways what it would mean if the world were completely accessible to rational explanation. And they do this by offering rational arguments for the existence of a being, which because it is completely self-explanatory, is the ground of the existence and intelligibility of the world. In doing this they offer basic descriptions of the constitution of the world and of human being in the world. This can be illustrated briefly from the classical five ways of demonstrating the existence of God.[3] I do not claim that these ways are cogent as demonstrations of the existence of God, certainly not in the simplified form in which we present them. They serve here simply as an illustration for the way in which the postulate of complete expla-

---

[2] An excellent contemporary version of this argument is developed by Keith Ward, *Rational Theology and the Creativity of God*, Oxford 1982, 1-23.

[3] A good exposition of Thomas Aqunias' classical account of the five ways can be found in F.C.Coplestone, *Aquinas*, Harmondsworth 1955, 107-126. The most incisive critical discussion is still A.Kenny, *The Five Ways*, London 1969. For an illuminating survey of interpretations of the theistic proofs and a comprehensive bibliography see John Clayton, art. 'Gottesbeweise II.III', in: *Theologische Realenzyklopädie* vol. XIII, Berlin-New York 1984, 724-784.

nation which is crucial to the project of philosophical theology shapes a specific understanding of God and the divine attributes.

If, *first of all*, all change in the world is caused by something, and if all change can be explained by referring to its antecedent conditions, and if, furthermore, the principle of complete explanation which excludes an infinite regress of antecedent conditions is valid, then it seems plausible to postulate a first cause of all change which is neither from without nor through itself subject to change, and which is therefore immutable and imperishable.

If, *secondly*, because of the non-reflexivity of efficient causality nothing is brought about by itself, then it seems plausible to postulate a first cause of everything which itself is not the effect of a cause. This first cause cannot, given the principle of complete explanation be an element of a series of causes, but must be the eternal cause of all causes in the temporal sequence.

If, *thirdly*, against the backdrop of our experience that some things exist contingently and are what they are contingently, we conduct the thought experiment that all things were contingent, we would arrive at the notion that everything could cease to be and cease to be what it is at a certain point. At this point nothing would exist, and nothing, evidently, comes from nothing. If, however, there is something, not everything can be contingent. There must be at least one necessary being. This argument also presupposes the principle of complete explanation, because only if this is valid, is it possible to proceed from reflection about something which is necessary, because it is necessitated by something else *(ab alio)*, to what is in itself *(a se)* necessary and necessarily as it is.

If, *fourthly*, we investigate the comparative structure of the world, the gradations we observe in everything there is, we are led to postulate the existence of a superlative, which is instantiated in a being perfect in every respect so that this being, as the ground of the relative perfections of the world, must itself be absolutely perfect.[4] If there are limited degrees of goodness, there must be a supreme good as the cause of all goodness. And since goodness and being are convertible so that the degree of goodness indicates he degree of being, the highest good is also the highest being as the ground of being and the cause of every perfection in the world which is in itself the most perfect being. The principle of complete explanation offers again the decisive hint to the logic of the argument. If the complete explanation for the existence and intelligibility of the world can only be provided through an immutable, uncaused and necessary being, then there can be no perfection in the world which does not have its ground and supreme instantiation in this being. This argument establishes that the logic of divine attributes must be seen as a logic of perfection.

If we proceed, *fifthly*, from the observation that we experience the world not only in quantitative gradations of perfection, but also as exhibiting an order in which purposes are actualized, we can postulate from the uniformity of this ordered structure a unitary cause through which everything is ordered towards a purpose. If applied in this way, the principle of complete explanation not only relates to the present state of reality, but also to its end, the state which will be achieved through the complete actualization of all purposes in the world. This

---

[4] For a critical discussion of this notion of perfection cf. K.Ward, op. cit., 49-66.

end is defined by the nature of the final cause of everything there is which determines all purposive processes in the world. The principle of complete explanation in the philosophical theology of theism comprises the question of the ground of existence, as well as the question of its structure and its final end. The answer is in all cases the same: God.

The notion of plausibility which is presupposed in these five ways which we have sketched out in their basic outlines can be most successfully described if it is seen neither as straightforward deduction nor as induction. The different arguments seem most persuasive if they are seen a conceptual analysis of concepts we employ in the explanation of the world, under the presupposition of the regulative principle of the complete intelligibility of the world. The result which is suggested by this analysis is that our way of using explanatory concepts presupposes the existence of God as a necessary condition for our interpretation of reality. The five ways conduct such an analysis for concepts like 'change', 'cause', 'existence', 'contingence', 'necessity', 'perfection', 'order' and 'purpose', and they come to the conclusion that the coherence of our interpretation of reality is only secured by the coherence of our understanding of God.

Viewed from this perspective the much disputed relationship of the five ways to the ontological proof can be seen as one of complementarity.[5] While the five ways argue from the intelligibility of the world to the coherence of the notion of God, the ontological proof demonstrates that the concept of God, if coherently developed, implies existence, and this, in turn offers proof for the intelligibility of the world. The move from coherence to existence presupposes precisely the concept of God which the five ways develop as the necessary condition for the intelligibility of the world, i.e. the concept of a perfect being which as the complete explanation of itself is the explanation of everything there is, and which is as such immutable, eternal and perfect in every respect. The additional point offered by the ontological proof is that God either exists or is impossible. This defines indirectly the semantics of the concept of a necessary being. A necessary being must exist in every possible world. If anything is possible, then this being is necessary. If this necessary being is not, then nothing is possible. The assertion of the non-existence of God states the possibility that this necessary being does not exist. This, however, is precisely the state in which nothing is possible. Since the assertion of God's non-existence affirms one possibility while at the same time denying every possibility, it is self-contradictory.[6] This argument extends to the realm of possibilities the notion of God, who as the only self-explanatory being, is the ground of the explanation of everything else and in this way enables us to see God as *ens realissimum*, as the necessary ground of all possibilities.

I have chosen this approach *via* the theistic proofs in order to show how closely the conception of the metaphysical attributes of God is connected to the overall project of philosophical theology. The interpretation of reality which is

---

[5] This is lucidly argued by Keith Ward, op. cit., 24-48, especially 33.

[6] A clear exposition of the ontological proofs in its classical and modern versions is Hubertus G. Hubbeling, *Einführung in die Religionsphilosophie*, Göttingen 1981, 78-87.

provided by the theistic proofs is only coherent if God can be seen as a being with specific attributes. As the universal ground of existence and explanation God must be understood as necessary, immutable, uncaused, omnipotent, eternal, omnipresent, omniscient and in every respect perfect. The first way points to the immutability of God; the second describes God as uncaused and entails his omnipotence and eternity; the third way explains God's status as that of necessary being which implies that God possess all divine attributes necessarily; the fourth way interprets the attributes of God as divine perfections and so clarifies the logic of predicating attributes of God; the fifth way, finally, presents the divine attributes as the ground of purposeful order in the world. The ontological proof demonstrates that there is no difference between the divine attributes and the divine essence and offers the strongest arguments for the singularity and uniqueness of God. All other metaphysical attributes can by different routes be derived from these arguments: divine simplicity as non-compositeness, for instance, from the second way and from the concept of perfection presupposed in the fourth way. It has to be kept in mind that this view of God is correlated with an understanding of the world according to which the world is seen as a rationally structured and purposefully ordered whole. Humans are, in turn, interpreted as those beings which, while participating in the being of the world, can also know its relation to God as the ground and end of the world and of human beings in it.

3 THE ATTRIBUTES OF AN ACTING GOD

When this conception of God and the divine attributes is confronted with discourse about divine action which has shaped Christian faith from its earliest beginnings, we immediately become aware of a marked contrast. The Bible talks in many ways of God's action. Discourse about divine action is the central focus of different groups and literary genres of texts. The historical narratives of the Hebrew Scriptures present the memory of God's mighty acts as the foundation for the present experience of reality. The prophetic writings express in judgement and promise the expectation of God's action, and the order it brings about is the guide-line for their social and religious criticism. Wisdom literature describes the order of human actions and the world order in nature and history as being rooted in God's action which makes righteousness possible. Biblical discourse about divine agency and the fundamental aspects of the understanding of God as agent are perhaps most clearly documented in the psalms where God's action forms the horizon for human praise, intercession, thanksgiving and lamentation.

Discourse about God's action as the comprehensive horizon of biblical theology is just as central in the New Testament writings as in the Hebrew Scriptures, since all New Testament writers claim that God brings about his righteousness and salvation in the words, deeds and suffering of Jesus Christ. The differences between the various theological conceptions of the New Testament can be illustrated by investigating how different writers conceive of God's action and how they relate it to the action and passion of Christ.

The Christian church has retained the various forms of biblical discourse about divine agency, and it has given it a paradigmatic function as the criterion for its own talk of God's actions by practising proclamation as the exposition of Scripture. In its proclamation the church not only uses God's activity as it is witnessed in Scripture as the paradigm for the memory and experience of God's action in the present. The witness of the church is furthermore determined by the confidence that God will actively authenticate the truth of its witness to his action by his Spirit and in this way make faith possible. In consequence, the church can understand itself - as in the theology of the Reformers - as *creatura verbi divini*, as the product of God's communicative action.[7]

The conception of divine agency which is constitutive for Christian faith becomes clear in the basic forms of prayer in the biblical traditions and in the worship of the church. Thanksgiving, praise and petition all presuppose, as Vincent Brümmer has shown,[8] that God's action is intentional action, informed by God's purposes and directed towards the achievement of God's goals, and this implies freedom in the selection of the aims and means of action. Its is characteristic for the biblical traditions as well as for the Christian church that they never use discourse about God's action only as the exposition of some kind of formal capacity for action, but that it is conceived in specific fundamental acts like creation, reconciliation and redemption which determine the relationship between God, the world and humankind and which are presented in confessions of faith as the content of belief which is the foundation for the act of faith.

Discourse about divine action makes it possible for the biblical traditions to identify God as this specific God (e.g. Yahweh, or, the one who raised Jesus from the dead) and to individuate the actions ascribed to him. Through his actions God is identifiable as a specific agent; more than that, God identifies himself through his actions, a fact which is theologically expressed by the concept of revelation. God can thus be proclaimed as the one who has created heaven and earth, led the people of Israel out of the slave-house of Egypt, raised Jesus from the dead, etc. In the context of reflection on the divine attributes it is clear that the so-called moral, or better, personal attributes of God, his love, his mercy, righteousness, faithfulness, etc., presuppose this conception of divine action which is expressed in the biblical traditions and in the discourse of the church. They characterize actions which as intentional actions are distinguished from mere behaviour that follows a mechanism of stimulus and response. Insofar as they describe the fundamental patterns of the Intentional actions of a personal agent these personal attributes can also be predicated of the agent. The description of an action, of a pattern of activity and of an agent as merciful or faithful is only possible if the action in question is part of a comprehensive policy of action which expresses the character of the agent. To talk of God's personal at-

---

[7] For a discussion of this view in the ecclesiology of Luther and Calvin cf. my article, 'The Creature of the Word. Recovering the Ecclesiology of the Reformers', in: C.E.Gunton, D.W.Hardy (eds.), *On Being the Church. Essays on the Christian Community*, Edinburgh 1989, 110-155.

[8] Cf. V.Brümmer, *What Are We Doing When We Pray?*, London 1984, especially 60-73.

tributes seems therefore necessarily correlated with the model of intentional, and that is, personal action.[9]

4 A FUNDAMENTAL DILEMMA IN CHRISTIAN DISCOURSE ABOUT GOD

A fundamental dilemma of the Christian understanding of God seems to consist in the fact that it combines both forms of discourse in its conceptual exposition: reflection on the necessary, eternal, immutable, omnipotent and omnipresent ground of the existence of the world and discourse about God's action which as intentional action is the condition for ascribing mercy, faithfulness and forgiveness to God. Both groups of statements seem to be necessary for an authentically Christian and rationally plausible view of God, but they do not seem to be compatible. The attributes of the conception of God in philosophical theology cannot be predicated of God as agent in the sense in which God is depicted in the biblical traditions and in the discourse of Christian faith. Agency in the sense expressed in the biblical traditions and in the discourse of Christian faith cannot be ascribed to the God who is presented in the conception of the metaphysical attributes of God. We can illustrate this dilemma with reference to the attributes of divine eternity and immutability.

The theistic proofs seem to be correlated to a concept of God which implies eternity as a necessary attribute of God. In philosophical theology God's eternity has often been interpreted in terms of Boethius' classical definition as 'complete possession all at once of illimitable life',[10] as atemporal eternity. Eternity in this sense not only implies that God is not subject to the perishing characteristic of finite created being, but also that as an atemporal being God has no location in time and no temporal duration and that temporal indicators cannot be predicated of him. Precisely what is excluded in this way, however, constitutes the necessary conditions for individuating actions and for identifying agents. It follows that the concept of God in philosophical theology, if it implies God's eternity interpreted as atemporality does not permit us to conceive of divine action as the personal intentional action that the biblical writings do.

Conversely, it has to be said that biblical discourse about divine agency which does not shy away from individuation God's action by temporal descriptions and of identifying God as an agent in the framework of time excludes the philosophical concept of divine eternity as atemporality. If one wants to retain both the notion of divine eternity and discourse about divine agency, it becomes necessary

---

[9] Cf. my paper 'Divine Agency and Providence', *Modern Theology* 3 (1987), 225-244.

[10] *'Aeternitas igitur est interminabilis vitae tota simul et perfecta possesio'* CP 422, 9-11, in: H.F.Stewart, E.K.Rand, S.J.Trester (eds.), *Boethius: The Theological Tractates and The Consolation of Philosophy*, London-Cambridge Mass. 1973. For a precise restatement of Boethius' position see Eleonora Stump and Norman Kretzmann, 'Eternity', in: Thomas V.Morris (ed.), *The Concept of God*, Oxford 1987, 219-252. A critique of views based on Boethius' conception is provided by Nicholas Wolterstorff, 'God Everlasting', in: Steven H.Cahn, David Shatz (eds.), *Contemporary Philo-sophy of Religion*, New York-Oxford 1982, 77-98.

to modify both the understanding of eternity as atemporality and the concept of agency ascribed to God.

We encounter similar difficulties with the concept of divine immutability. The notion that God cannot undergo change is, as we have seen, explicitly developed in the first way, but is also presupposed in the other four classical ways. In philosophical theology divine immutability has traditionally been defined in one of two ways both of which demonstrate the close connection to the theistic proofs. If we start - following Platonic thought - from the concept of perfection, then change in a perfect being can only mean loss of perfection and can therefore not be attributed to God. If we start from the modal status of the concept of God, we can conclude - with the Aristotelian tradition - that there are no unactualized possibilities in God as *actus purus*, so that not only the *fact* of change in God but the very *possibility* of change in God must be denied.

In contrast to that we find that the biblical traditions talk of change in God precisely in the sense of the kind of mutability which is implied in the concept of agency if it refers to personal action, the freely chosen intentional action of personal agents. This is underlined by the fact that these traditions not only talk about divine action, but about God's *interaction* with creation, and this can hardly be conceived without some notion of mutability. Contrary to the concept of the immutability of God in philosophical theology, the biblical notion of the constancy of God, which underlies his faithfulness, presupposes God's free intentional agency which includes his capacity for change. It would be meaningless to ascribe faithfulness to a being which is not able to change, because it would thereby lose its perfection or because it possesses no unactualized potentialities. Faithfulness can only be meaningfully ascribed to a being which, because of its capacity for free intentional action, could act differently from the way in which its actions document faithfulness.

The dilemma seems to be clear: either we hold fast to the traditional interpretation of the metaphysical attributes of God in philosophical theo-logy, and then we cannot talk about divine action as personal intentional action; or we remain faithful to discourse about divine agency in the biblical traditions and in Christian faith, and take leave of the traditional interpretation of the metaphysical attributes of God in philosophical theology.

This dilemma not only appears in the exposition of the Christian view of God, it also reappears in the understanding of the world and of human existence in the world. If we characterize God's relationship to humanity and to the world in terms of the traditional interpretation of the metaphysical attributes, it seems difficult to avoid the conclusion that God's omnipotence, eternity and omniscience deny the reality of human freedom. The world could no longer be understood as providing the space for free human action. On the other hand, if we see God's personal action as central, we could be confronted with the problem that God and human beings appear as, in principle, similar agents, only distinguished by their different power, but whose actions are located on the same level. The world would consequently appear as the space for either cooperation or competition between the divine and the human agents. This illustrates the inherent risks of both, the conception of God's metaphysical attributes and discourse about God's agency. The doctrine of the metaphysical attributes of God seems to tend to stress God's transcendence at the expense of his relationship to the world, whereas discourse about God's personal action is in danger of emphasizing God's relationship with the world at the expense of divine transcendence. One tendency calls the categoreal distinction of God and world in question, the other their relatedness.

This may be the reason why the conceptual exposition of the Christian view of God has in its main strands preserved both forms of discourse, leading to the situation that the dilemma between the conception of God's metaphysical attributes and discourse about God's agency has been handed on in the tradition and confronts each generation anew. Nevertheless there have been many attempts in the history of theology and philosophy to solve the dilemma by cutting through the Gordian knot and cancelling the 'eternal covenant' between faith and knowledge. A classical example of such attempts is Pascal's radical separation of the God of Abraham, Isaac and Jacob from the God of the philosophers. If this separation is consistently pursued theological discourse about the God of faith is cut loose from philosophical reflection on God as the universal ground of all being and meaning. This could lead to the danger that the universal horizon of Christian belief in God the creator is abandoned for the tunnel vision of an exclusive concern for personal salvation. A similar danger occurs in contemporary demands for a narrative theology if it is propagated as a replacement for the arduous work of conceptual reconstruction of theology. It cannot be denied that there are clear affinities between the concept of divine action as the paradigm of Christian theology and the category of a narrative, since agents can be identified and actions individuated in the medium of narratives. However, without a conceptual explication of theological talk about divine action its ontological status remains unclear, and we could not confidently distinguish between stories about God and stories about Cinderella. A third possibility to do away with the dilemma also fails to stand up' to closer inspection. *Prima facie* it seems plausible to allocate discourse about divine action to the 'poetic' language of faith and worship and to reserve the doctrine of the divine attributes to the rational exploration of the concept of God. In view of the incompatibilities between both forms of discourse as they become apparent in our dilemma it does not, however, even seem possible to interpret one form of discourse as the 'poetic' expression of the other. It cannot be established that both forms of discourse, the 'poetic' and the conceptual, have the same referent.

Faced with these problems one can only admire the wisdom of the main strands of Christian thought in preserving both forms of discourse together, and thus enduring the dilemma, instead of simply abolishing it. The relative advantage of this situation, however, does not imply that we should simply choose to retain the dilemma and refrain from attempts at resolving it. It can, I think, be shown from both horns of the dilemma that its resolution is necessary.

5 REASONS FOR RESOLVING THE DILEMMA

We have seen that the project of a philosophical theology presupposes the postulate of complete explanation which extends the explanatory enterprise to all aspects of reality. The fourth of the five ways makes this explicitly clear in that it attempts to demonstrate divine perfection as the ground of all values we encounter in the world. Since we encounter attributes like love, mercy and faithfulness in interpersonal human relationships, it could be argued that these attributes must also be rooted in God's perfection. Seeing these personal attributes as grounded in the perfection of God would, however, imply that God has to be understood in some sense as a personal agent, because otherwise these predicates could not be ascribed to him. If this implication is denied, then the logic of perfection as a whole would be called into question. There would therefore seem to be good reasons for attempting to resolve the dilemma between the metaphysical divine attributes and the notion of God as agent.

The need for overcoming the dilemma is also illustrated by the fifth way which combines through the concept of purposive order the concept of the ground of existence and that of the end of existence, so that God appears as ground and goal of all being. The conceptuality of 'purpose' and 'end' has, however, its original context in the description of intentional action, or requires, as in the case of final causality, explication through categories of action. If the argument of the fifth way is to be applied to the same being which is described by the other ways as immutable, eternal, necessary and perfect in every respect, then some attempt must be made to reconcile these metaphysical attributes with the concept of agency.

There is yet another argument for the resolution of the dilemma which could be produced from the camp of philosophical theology. Philosophical theology has from the beginning insisted that the requirements for the concept of God based on the postulate of the rational intelligibility of the world and the requirements of religious worship have to coincide. Only a deity which can satisfy the conceptual criteria of the concept of God can be acknowledged as the one who is to be worshipped. This argument becomes meaningless if the one who is to be worshipped according to the criteria of the concept of God developed in philosophical reflection lacks all personal attributes. These attributes, however, presuppose the concept of personal action.

The necessity for resolving the dilemma can also be demonstrated from the perspective of the other horn of the dilemma, discourse about divine action. Where the biblical writings or the discourse of Christian faith talk about divine action, all the characteristic elements of the concept of agency are employed, but there always is a clear distinction between divine and human agency in order to show their proper relation. God and human beings do not act in equal cooperation or competition on the same level. God's action in creation, reconciliation and redemption is characterised in such a way that it is presented as the ground of the possibility and the guide-line for human being and action. This distinction and relation of divine and human action is an essential feature of the distinctive view of reality of the biblical writings and of Christian faith. This ontological intention of discourse about divine action demands that theological reflection on the concept of divine action resolve the dilemma between the metaphysical attributes of God and discourse about divine agency, because it identifies as the subject of action the one who is presented by philosophical theology as the ground of the existence and intelligibility of the world. In order to express the distinction between divine and human action which is the presupposition for its correct relation, theological reconstruction of the concept of divine action has to introduce descriptions of God as agent in contrast to finite agents and they point to attributes similar to those employed in philosophical theology as God's metaphysical attributes.

There is still another reason to be found in discourse about divine agency for resolving the dilemma between the concepts of God's metaphysical attributes and of divine agency. Faith as unconditional trust can be directed only to such an entity to which the personal attributes of faithfulness, righteousness and trustworthiness can be ascribed, i.e. to a personal agent. But if faith is to be distinguished from superstition, it cannot be directed towards a finite entity, but can only relate to the one who, as the ground and end of all being, is also the ground and destiny of human existence.[11] All these qualifications, however, point in the direction of a description of God which seems at least potentially quite similar to that offered by the metaphysical attributes in philosophical theology.

6 A POSSIBLE RESOLUTION?

All this raises the question: is there a plausible way of resolving the dilemma? Is there a possibility of relating statements about the metaphysical divine attributes to discourse about divine action so that they appear no longer incompatible, or does that amount to an attempt at squaring the circle? The following considerations are intended to establish the possibility of a resolution of our dilemma in two ways. First of all, I will try to show how a reconstruction of discourse on divine agency leads to a conception of divine attributes, and I will then attempt to argue that reflection on God as the ground of the existence and intelligibility of the world opens up an avenue for a conception of God's agency.

The confession of Christian faith presents that which makes the act of faith as an act of unconditional trust possible as the content of faith by talking about God's actions. The way in which it refers to God's agency is by no means a simple summary, but it offers, as we can see for instance in the Apostles' Creed, a carefully worked out theological structure which can be analysed as the exposition of three internally related types of action. These three types of action which are expressed by talking about the work of the Father, the story of the Son and the operation of the Spirit can be characterized as the foundation of existence *(Existenzbegründung)*, the disclosure of existence *(Existenzerschließung)* and the orientation of existence *(Existenzorientierung)*.

The internal relatedness of these three types of action becomes clear, if we follow the *ratio cognoscendi* and start from God's action as Spirit. A central element of discourse about the agency of God the Spirit is that God creates certainty about the truth of the revelation in Christ which makes faith possible. In the Spirit God authenticates the truth of the divine self-disclosure in Christ which is the truth about God's being in relation to his creation. Following the *ratio essendi* one has to say that God's creative action intends the disclosure of the truth about God's relation to creation in the created order so that human creatures are enabled by the Spirit's authentification of the truth of God's self-disclosure in Christ to relate to God in accordance with their created destiny. If we

---

[11] Cf. W.Härle, 'Widerspruchsfreiheit'. Überlegungen zum Verhältnis von Glauben und Denken', *NZSTh* 28 (1986), 223-237, esp. 232ff.

construe the internal relatedness of the action of God, Father, Son and Spirit in such a way, we can express the unity of divine agency in the differentiation of God' actions in the divine economy. This is the essential element of truth in the in other ways very problematical thesis of Western trinitarian thought *opera trinitatis ad extra sunt indivisa.*[12]

On the basis of this proposal for the reconstruction of discourse about divine agency we can predicate of God as attributes primarily the characteristics of his relation to his creation as its is established by God's action in creation, revelation and inspiration if these are interpreted as the ways in which God creates, reconciles and perfects the world. Furthermore, if God always achieves what he intends and if God's will and God's essence cannot be separated, then the attributes of his relation to the world apply also to God's being. According to our model the predication of attributes to God is possible on the basis of the insight of faith as the acknowledgment of God's self-disclosure which reveals the unity of his intention in the relationship of the different types of divine action. God's *love* has a special significance here, because it is claimed in Christian faith that love is the perfect expression of the unity of divine intention in the variety of divine actions and of the structure of his relationship to humanity and the world. Schleiermacher has combined love as the first of God's attributes relating to redemption with *wisdom* which is defined as the principle which orders and determines the world for the divine self-communication active in redemption.[13] In the framework of our proposal divine wisdom is the communication about God's intention as love which is an inherent part of the actualisation of this intention and which enables human beings to respond God in faith, love and hope.

We have characterized the condition for the possibility of faith as certainty with regard to the truth of God's self-disclosure in revelation which is the disclosure of human existence insofar as it presents it with the truth about its destiny as it is determined by the will of the creator. Since this truth is authenticated for human beings as sinners living in a state of estrangement from God, it is the realisation and actualisation of God's *right-eousness*. By disclosing the truth about his relationship to the world in the world, God overcomes the power of deception, enables sinners to acknowledge their alienation from God and promises righteousness to those who accept God's self-disclosure as the truth for their existence. This understanding of God's righteousness includes God's *holiness*, because human sin is not simply renamed as righteousness. The promise of righteousness is only given to those who recognize everything that contradicts the will of the creator as sin, as estrangement from God and rebellion against God. Insofar as God reveals his righteousness as the truth about his relationship to his creation in his creation, his self-disclosure is a powerful expression of his faithfulness by which he sustains his creation, despite and against the rebellion of sin, in the structures in which he created it.

---

[12] Cf. R.W.Jenson, 'The Triune God', in C.E.Braaten, R.W.Jenson (eds.), *Christian Dogmatics* vol.I, Philadelphia 1984, 79-191, especially 149ff.

[13] Cf. F.D.E. Schleiermacher, *Der christliche Glaube 1821/22*, §184, vol.II, Berlin 1984, 350.

All these attributes which we can only sketch here very briefly are, as Thomas Tracy has argued, *'character trait predicates'*,[14] personal attributes which can be predicated of the intentional actions of personal agents. If they express comprehensive and consistent policies of action they can also be ascribed to the agents themselves. For intentional actions it is required that agents have *power*, i.e. the ability to realize their intentions in their actions. In the case of actions which establish or presuppose real relations it is necessary that agents have *space* in which to execute their actions. Furthermore it is necessary that intention and action are connected in a *temporal sequence* which can be bridged by the agent. And it is finally required that agents possess *knowledge* of their intentions, possibilities of action, means of action and the aims which enable them to form an intention by selecting one from different goals of action and to execute it successfully. If these requirements cannot be met, it becomes impossible, or at least very difficult, to individuate actions.

Finite agents are externally limited in all these respects. Their capacity to act, their power, is limited by externally given restrictions of their possibilities of action: the existence of other agents, a limited space for action, a limited time to act and the restrictions of fallible, finite knowledge. Power, space, time and knowledge are constitutive conditions for intentional action, but the way in which they are given to us makes it clear that our agency is by no means a perfect and unconditional form of agency. Since it is only partly self-regulated, it is a restricted and conditioned form of agency.

The fact that God's action is seen from the perspective of Christian faith as creation, redemption and perfection of the world, requires that divine agency is categoreally distinguished from the agency of finite agents. In the context of the model of divine agency, this distinction can be introduced by qualifying the conditions for personal intentional action which are the basis for the ascription of personal attributes to God by reference to the metaphysical divine attributes which distinguish the perfection of divine agency as completely self-regulated agency from the limited mode of action of finite agents. Instead of the limited power of finite agents we can talk about God's *omnipotence* which is restricted by nothing apart from God's own creative agency. It is the power by which God establishes the existence and structure of created being, through which he reveals his relationship to creation in the created order and authenticates the truth of his revelation as the condition for the possibility of faith. Instead of talking about the limited space of finite agents we have to refer to God's *omni-presence* through which God is present to creation as its creative ground in such a way that he discloses this relationship in the spatio-temporal world of experience as the condition for the possibility of the certainty of faith. Instead of talking about the limited time of finite agents we can talk about God's *eternity* as the mode in which God is for all times present to a temporal world as its creative ground in such a way that he discloses in time for human beings as temporally existing creatures the truth about the relationship of creation to the creator. And, finally, instead of the limited knowledge of finite agents we have to talk about the exclusively self-regulated omniscience of God which comprehends the totality of

---

[14] Cf. Thomas F. Tracy, *God, Action and Embodiment*, Grand Rapids 1984, 3-20.

his acts in such a way that it is only restricted by the structure of creation which God intended and brought about.

This qualification of God's personal attributes through the metaphysical divine attributes is necessary so that in discourse about God's love, wisdom, righteousness, holiness and faithfulness we are really talking about *God's* attributes, the attributes of the creator, reconciler and redeemer of the world. Therefore we are not introducing with these attributes a foreign philosophical element into discourse about divine action. What we do is to make essential implications of Christian discourse about God and God's action explicit.

7 RELATIONAL ATTRIBUTES

Can the possible resolution of the dilemma between discourse about divine action and the conception of God's metaphysical attributes also be demonstrated from the dilemma's other horn, the traditional metaphysical attributes of God? We tried to show at the beginning how closely the understanding of the metaphysical attributes of God is related to the overall project of philosophical theology to offer an explanation for the existence and intelligibility of the world in the framework of a view of God. The doctrine of the divine attributes is in this way part of the exposition of the relationship between God as the ground of being and the being of the world. I will argue that this relationship cannot be adequately conceived on the basis of the traditional interpretation of God's metaphysical attributes, since they tend to stress divine transcendence to such an extent that God can no longer be understood as the creative ground of the being of the world.

The traditional interpretation of divine omnipotence developed by the dominant Thomist tradition of philosophical theology indicates these difficulties. Since the concept of power refers to possibilities of action, divine omnipotence is commonly defined as the power to do everything possible. From this we have to exclude the self-contradictory, because what cannot be conceived without contradiction cannot be conceived as possible. God's omnipotence is therefore the power to do everything that is logically possible. We arrive in this way at a concept of omnipotence which excludes logical impossibility, but does not exclude arbitrariness in its exercise.

A further difficulty stems from the fact that every concept of power is relative to the other essential attributes a being possesses. If we see, as in the traditional interpretation of God's attributes, eternity as timelessness and immutability as changelessness as belonging to God's essential attributes, we arrive at a concept of omnipotence which excludes God's being able to relate to a temporally structured world of change. The traditional interpretation of divine omnipotence seems to confront us with the choice between an omnipotent God whose omnipotence excludes only the logically impossible, but not arbitrariness, and an omnipotent God who cannot relate to a temporal world subject to contingent change.

An alternative to these difficulties is offered by the approach of interpreting the metaphysical attributes of God as qualified by God's personal attributes of love, righteousness, faithfulness etc. God's power can then be seen as different from sheer arbitrariness in that it is consistently determined by God's will to do everything to bring about his purpose of establishing a community of love and righteousness with human creatures. If one defining characteristic of a community of love is that it involves a self-restriction of power in order to allow the other the free response of love, then divine omnipotence can be seen as consistently self-restricted in its exercise through the intention of God's agency. If God's omnipotence is determined along these lines, it is no longer seen exclusively in terms of abstract possibilities of action, but as the power of God of actualizing his creative, reconciling and redeeming will.

A similar argument can be presented for the metaphysical attributes of eternity, omnipresence and omniscience. If eternity is interpreted as sheer timelessness, then this raises the problem whether the relationship between God and the world can still be conceived as the relationship between the ground of being and the being of the world which forms the framework for reflection on the metaphysical attributes. The definition of God's omnipresence as non-spatiality creates similar problems of how to conceive God as the ground of being of a world of spatial extension. These difficulties appear in their most striking form in the traditional interpretation of divine omniscience. There are two main ways of conceiving of divine omniscience. Either God's knowledge is seen as completely limitless so that 'for every proposition p, if p, then God knows p'. In this interpretation divine omniscience is an implicit denial of the freedom of finite agents, since future contingent events which are the result of the actions of finite agents would be known by God even before they were brought about. On the other hand God's knowledge can be interpreted as the knowledge of an atemporal and absolutely non-spatial being. This, of course, leads to the conclusion that God does not and cannot know a temporally and spatially ordered world, since for the knowledge of an atemporal, non-spatial immutable being there would be no difference between propositions which are true at the time t_1 but not at the time t_2, at the place l_1 but not at l_2. If, however, the context for the ascription of omniscience to God is God's agency in creation, redemption and perfection as it is presupposed in God's personal attributes, omniscience must be understood as a *relational* predicate, determined by the relations which God establishes in his creative, redemptive and perfecting agency. This relational form of God's knowledge implies that he knows the structure of time not as eternal presence, but that he knows the past as the past, the present as the present and the future as the future.

This illustrates a general point of the strategy of interpreting the relationship between God's personal attributes and God's metaphysical attributes as one of mutual qualification in the context of a conception of divine agency. On this view, not only the personal attributes of God, but also the metaphysical attributes have to be interpreted as relational predicates.[15] This can avoid the pitfall of many traditional interpretations of God's metaphysical attributes which emphasise the *distinction* between God and the world to such an extent that the conceptual description of God's attributes denies God's *relation* to the world. This strategy of mutual qualification between metaphysical and personal at-

---

15 Cf. the lucid discussion of the ontological presuppositions of 'relational' and 'non-relational' predicates in V.Brümmer, op. cit., 36ff.

tributes is therefore not in contradiction to the project of philosophical theology. Rather, it restores its original intention to explain the existence and intelligibility of the world through the exposition of its relation to God as the ground of its being and intelligibility.

8 THE COMPLEMENTARITY OF DIVINE ATTRIBUTES

Our exploration of the logic of divine perfection has led to a result which seems to indicate that a satisfactory resolution of our dilemma between traditional interpretations of the metaphysical divine attributes in philosophical theology and discourse about divine action in Christian faith cannot be based on one of the forms of discourse which make up the dilemma alone. Our considerations seem to suggest that both the conception of divine action and the theory of God's metaphysical attributes are, in spite of the tensions between them, necessary elements of a comprehensive conception of the attributes of God the creator, reconciler and redeemer of the world, the ground of all being, truth and meaning. Although they seem *prima facie* in direct contradiction, their relationship can be conceived as *complementary*, if it is understood as one of mutual qualification. If metaphysical attributes, based on the enterprise of philosophical theology of making the existence and intelligibility of the world plausible in the framework of a conception of God, and personal attributes, based on the model of divine action understood in terms of personal agency, are seen as related through mutual qualification, some of the crucial pitfalls of each respective approach can be avoided.

By qualifying discourse about God's action and about God's personal attributes through the metaphysical divine attributes, the categoreal distinction which provides the basis for conceiving the proper relationship between divine and human agency can be safeguarded. By qualifying discourse about God's metaphysical attributes through God's personal attributes in the framework of a model of personal agency which leads to their reinterpretation as relational predicates, the fundamental relation between God as the ground of all being, meaning and truth to the world as God's creation can be safeguarded which is the basis of philosophical theology's project to explain the existence and intelligibility of the world by reference to God.

This complementarity by mutual qualification points to one central element of complementarity in the respective approaches of philosophy and theology to reflection about God. In Christian theology discourse about divine action in Christian theology which identifies God as a particular agent of particular actions which are individuated in narrative categories is, if it is to make sense of the claims it makes for this God, called to show that this God who is identified in his actions meets the requirements of the *concept* of God. It is challenged to demonstrate that God who is confessed as creator, reconciler and redeemer of the world is 'something than which nothing greater can be thought', in short: the most perfect being. Philosophical reflection on God which attempts to offer a conceptual description of God and his attributes is called to show that the concept of God it elaborates describes the one in whom believers have unconditional trust in the act of *faith*. It is challenged to demonstrate that the philosophical concept of God is not just a theoretical construct, but can relate to the fundamental orientation believers express in a view of reality which sees God as the ground of all being, meaning and truth. Our argument would suggest that of the two modes of thinking about God neither can meet its respective challenges without being aided by the other.

It is, however, not only in the relationship between theological and philosophical reflection on God that the structural problem from which we started appears. It also reappears in the very centre of the Christian understanding of God, the doctrine of the *Trinity*. Trinitarian discourse combines a forceful emphasis on the persons of the Father, the Son and the Spirit in their distinctive personal particularity and communal relatedness on the one hand with an equally stringent emphasis on the unity of the divine essence on the other. It is in the insistence of orthodox trinitarian thought that neither may be collapsed into the other, nor both sublated in the alleged synthesis of a God above the Father, the Son and the Spirit, that the question of the relationship of personal and essential attributes of God is kept alive at the heart of Christian theology. It would therefore seem that the ultimate testing-ground for the resolution of our dilemma in Christian theology lies here, in the relationship of person and essence in the Trinity.

Anyone who grapples with a problem like the relationship of divine action and divine attributes in an attempt at exploring the logic of divine perfection cannot hope to bring reflection on such a wide-ranging theme to a satisfactory conclusion, but has to be content to break off even if the result of such reflections leads to little more than *prolegomena* for a future treatment of the problem. What I hope to have achieved in this chapter, be it only by the fragmentary character of my considerations, is a justification of the problem.

3 God's Goodness and Human Morality

1 CONTEMPORARY MORAL PHILOSOPHY AND ITS THEOLOGICAL PAST

Contemporary moral philosophy has in recent years been characterized by a scrupulous self-examination provoked by an acute sense of crisis which is shared by a number of eminent practitioners in the field. One of the decisive symptoms of this crisis is the awareness that in a time where there is a growing demand for moral orientation in various areas of public and private life which is documented by the establishment of centres of ethical reflection on the moral issues encountered in medical research and practice, business, law and politics, the practitioners of moral philosophy often experience their inability to supply the goods. The problem is not the lack of moral justifications and theories concerning the rules regulating the moral life. Rather, it seems to consist in our apparent inability to integrate the different rules and justifications in one coherent framework which could lend unity and order to our moral concerns.[1] This situation has provoked the reemergence of a kind of ethical reflection that attempts to relate the ambiguities of present-day moral philosophy to its historical genesis and to see it in connection with processes of social and ideological change.[2]

In the context of these reflections Alasdair MacIntyre has pointed out that one of the crucial features of modern European morality is that it is 'post-theistic'.[3] The significance of this can be seen in the fact that 'much of the "ordinary language" of contemporary morality' is a survival from theism'.[4] Strong evidence supporting this interpretation is for MacIntyre that words expressing moral demands and duties like 'ought' and 'should' acquire 'a peculiar force'[5] when they are used against the background of an 'obligation' or 'requirement' to act in a particular way. This 'peculiar force' becomes apparent when these normative concepts are seen in the context of a law conception of ethics which, when applied universally, presupposes - as G.E.M. Anscombe has argued - some notion of a divine law-giver.[6] Where this theistic background is missing, as in modern moral philosophy, the strategies of supplying a different account of interpreting the nature of moral obligation or of reinterpreting the concepts presupposed in key-terms of

---

[1] Cf. Alasdair MacIntyre, 'Moral Philosophy: What Next?', in: Stanley Hauerwas and Alasdair MacIntyre (eds.), *Revisions: Changing Perspectives in Moral Philosophy*, Notre Dame-London 1983, 1-15, 5ff.

[2] An outstanding study of this kind is Alasdair MacIntyre, *After Virtue. A Study in Moral Theory*, London 1981.

[3] MacIntyre (note 1), 7.

[4] Op. cit. 8.

[5] Op. cit. 7.

[6] Cf. G.E.M. Anscombe, 'Modern Moral Philosophy', *Philosophy* 1958, 1-19.

moral discourse are - as MacIntyre argues - not simply different accounts of a single subject matter, but an attempt at constructing or inventing different kinds of moral projects.[7]

The absence of an integrating view of the nature of reality and a corresponding view of the nature of moral obligation which was supplied by belief in a *summum bonum* that shaped the theistic past of European morality is in this context interpreted as the reason for two interrelated developments in modern moral philosophy. The first is the interpretation of morality as a matter of choices concerning which the individual is absolutely sovereign and autonomous. This autonomy results from the fact that the notion of choice does not only apply to particular courses of action, but more radically to the reasons that could count as good reasons for choosing one course of action rather than another. The absolutizing of the notion of choice leads according to MacIntyre's analysis to a shortcircuiting of moral discourse which can in this way refrain from reflecting on the virtues, their relationship to the passions and their respective relationship to reason. Where the notion of choice becomes the key-concept of moral philosophy, philosophical psychology can be expelled from the realm of moral reflection. The concentration on the notion of choice which was occassioned by the abandonment of the theistic framework led, according to MacIntyre, secondly to a view of morality in terms of principles and rules which are conceived as the primary objects of choice. It is precisely in this area that MacIntyre locates one of the principal weaknesses of contemporary moral philosophy in its inability to evaluate rival claims that can both be supported by a variety of rules and principles.[8]

MacIntyre's analysis suggests that an understanding of the function of the conception of God for the definition of the nature of moral goodness and moral obligation, including its relationship to the goods as objects of human striving and aspiration, is required for the critical interpretation and assessment of the problems of contemporary moral philosophy. Unless moral philosophy understands the transformations that occurred in its emancipation from its theological roots, there is for MacIntyre little hope that moral philosophy can come to an understanding of its present problems which would help to contain the crisis in which it finds itself. This kind of analysis provokes the question whether these critical views can be turned into constructive insights, whether there are possibilities of employing the conception of God constructively in an attempt to overcome the dilemma of modern European morality and of contemporary moral reflection. Such an attempt would have to address the question of the unity and order of our moral universe systematically and would have to deal with the problem of relating human choices and the principles that are chosen for moral orientation to the way in which human beings are related to the reality in which they

---

[7] MacIntyre (note 1), 8.
[8] Op. cit. 10f.

live. Such an exploration of the possibilities of the conception of God for developing a more adequate understanding of human morality and a less restricted strategy of moral philosophy is presented in Iris Murdoch's essay 'On "God" and "Good"'.[9]

2 'GOD' AND 'GOOD'

Iris Murdoch's analysis of the deficiencies of contemporary moral philosophy overlaps with that of MacIntyre in several respects, perhaps most significantly in the demand of a philosophical psychology that can connect the insights of modern psychology (and here she thinks primarily of Freud) with the language and practise of morality. Her critique of the inadequacies of modern analytic moral philosophy is strongly connected to her criticism of what many people would see as its philosophical antidote, namely existentialism, which she attacks as an 'unrealistic and over-optimistic doctrine and the purveyor of certain false values' (68). She summarizes her critical points in the following diagnosis of the ills of contemporary moral philosophy: 'Briefly put, our picture of ourselves has become too grand, we have isolated, and identified ourselves with, an unrealistic conception of will, we have lost the vision of a reality separate from ourselves, and we have no adequate conception of original sin.' (69)

What looks like a list of somewhat disconnected symptoms is, however, soon shown to form a consistent pattern in which moral philosophy participates and prolongs the crisis of morality. This is shown by pointing to the dominance of the notion of the self viewed as an isolated will as the vantage point of moral philosophy. This contrasts sharply with the doctrine of original sin which Miss Murdoch finds in the works of Freud where the self is presented as an 'egocentric system of quasi-mechanical energy' (72). She claims that it is this view of the self which enables moral philosophy to acquire a realistic conception of the problems of morality and which points to the present tasks of morality and moral philosophy. In this sense she says: 'In the moral life the enemy is the fat relentless ego. Moral philosophy is properly...the discussion of this ego and of the techniques (if any) for its defeat.' (72f.)

Viewed from this perspective one of the central problems of moral philosophy is raised by the question: 'Are there any techniques for the purification and reorientation of an energy which is naturally selfish, in such a way that when moments of choice arrive we shall be sure of acting rightly?' (74) In the context of the consideration of these techniques of purification, religious concepts and practices are introduced into the discussion, especially a concept of the focus of moral orientation without which techniques of purification and reorientation such as prayer would loose their motivation and effectiveness for the moral life. The programme of enquiry is mapped out in the following way: 'I shall suggest that

---

[9] In: Hauerwas/MacIntyre (note 1), 69-91. Page references in the rext refer to this essay.

God was (or is) *a single perfect non-representable and necessarily real object of attention*; and I shall go on to suggest that moral philosophy should attempt to retain a central concept which has all these characteristics.' (75) Yet, in spite of the theological form of the inquiry the theologian should resist the temptation to turn it from the outset into a properly theological enterprise, since the basic pre-supposition of the enquiry is the question: 'What becomes of such a technique in a world without God, and can it be transformed to supply at least part of the answer to our central question?' (74)

In her attempt to redefine the concept of goodness along the lines of the concept of God Iris Murdoch starts, *first of all*, with the notion of an 'object of attention'. It is described as 'something which is a source of energy' (75) and which provides basic orientation for our being in the world, although it is at times quite impervious to the conscious activity of the will. This notion of an object of attention already points to the *second* characteristic, that of a unitary focus of our orientation. The evidence produced for this thesis comes from reflection on the virtues, where it can be shown that the attempt of defining one virtue leads to a description of its relations to other virtues. This is taken as the reason for the fact that 'reflection rightly tends to unify the moral world' (77). The *third* characteristic, transcendence, is connected to Miss Murdoch's insistence on a strong connection between morality and realism which is expressed in the phrase that 'morality, goodness, is a form of realism' (ibid.). It is at this point that the notion of realism is connected to the view of the selfish ego that defines original sin in Miss Murdoch's Freudian perspective. 'The chief enemy of excellence in morality (and also in art) is personal fantasy: the tissue of self-aggrandizing and consoling wishes and dreams which prevents one from seeing what is there outside one.' (78) The analogy with beauty suggests that the transcendence of goodness might be compared to the 'indestructibility' and 'incorruptibility' of beauty. This analogy breaks down at the point where one can claim that the transcendence of the beautiful can be experienced, whereas the transcendence of the Good is clearly something that is not empirically accessible. This notion of transcendence becomes a little clearer when it is linked to the *fourth* characteristic taken from the understanding of God and applied to the characterization of the good. This is the idea of perfection. It is interpreted as dependent on a specific context, a 'field of study' in which the idea of perfection produces by its very unattainability a 'sense of direction' and a specific authority (80).

The description of the Good as the focus for the moral life revolves around two related issues which come to the fore time and again when Iris Murdoch tries to approach this ideal through various descriptions and analogies whose very perceptiveness stands in the way of a more precise but possibly barren conceptual clarity. The first issue is that of *realism* which is developed in two directions, that of trying to ascertain the reality of the Good, and that of attempting to show how this unitary focus of attention enables us to perceive what is really there without the distortions of the self. The good life '*is* the checking of selfishness in the interest of seeing the real'. In this sense the necessity of the Good is '*an aspect of the kind of necessity involved in any technique for exhibiting fact"* (82). Therefore one can make a connection between the three classical trancendentalia of traditional metaphysics through which it is possible to understand realism, 'the ability to perceive what is true', *via* the analogy of beauty as a 'moral achievement'. And this leads to the further assumption 'that true vision occasions right conduct' (83).

A second characteristic feature of Iris Murdoch's prospect for a reorientation of morality is its dependence on religious concepts, acts and symbols. This applies not only to the development of the notion of 'Good' from the analogy with 'God', but also to the postulate of a mysticism which is conceived as 'a nondogmatic essentially unformulated faith in the reality of the Good' (89). Furthermore, she considers the possibility of a common 'machinery of salvation' for all mortals and reflects on the possibility and (perhaps necessity) of a notion of sacrament which 'provides an external visible place for an internal invisible act of the spirit'. This is characteristically located in the 'temporally located spiritual experience' of the apprehension of beauty, 'which is a source of good energy' (85). And, of course, prayer remains her primary example for the 'purification' and 'reorientation' of the energy of the self (75). Yet, it is the underlying assumption of this conception - which, however, 'may be challenged', 'that "there is no God" and that the influence of religion is waning rapidly' (90).

What this conception is intended to show - and in this sense the analogy between 'God' and 'Good' is developed - is that there is an intrinsic relationship between facts and values and that this relationship has to be explored by means of a realistic philosophical psychology. Nevertheless, there are a number of serious difficulties in the account given of goodness as the 'single perfect transcendent non-representable and necessarily real object of attention' which can raise doubts concerning the validity of the analogy between 'God' and 'Good'. The primary difficulty seems to consist in the fact that on these presuppositions goodness has to be interpreted as an absolute value and not as a relational concept. This necessitates conceiving our relation to goodness as an intentional relation (therefore the talk about the object of attention) and not as a real relation which, in turn, creates a number of problems for the realist objective of the whole enterprise. This difficulty becomes very clear in the interpretation of the central moral category of love as an impersonal attitude that necessarily implies detachment. This has the curious implication that it is for Miss Murdoch easier to develop her conception of love as an attitude relating to absolute values like goodness and beauty than as an interpersonal relationship (cf.80, 83f, 90). Because of this conception of love, that is always presented in categories of 'visual' perception (cf.83), the whole reorientation of the project of morality is presented in terms of *theoria* and not in terms of *praxis*. Last but not least, this conception of the reorientation of morality has a very strong conception of the self determined by 'possessive' energy under the conditions of 'Freudian' original sin, but a severely restricted view of the self that overcomes this state of sin in its orientation towards goodness. It is interesting that this orientation towards goodness enables us to see the 'separateness and differentness' (83) of other people which should prevent us from treating persons as things, but does not generate a notion of the sociality of human beings. This, in turn, provokes the question: who is to be the subject of this process of moral reorientation? Is the one who achieves the required purification and reorientation of the self in the contemplation of goodness as the proper object of attention in any sense less solitary than the grand individual moral will that dominates so much of modern ethical theory?

These difficulties should make anyone who wants to attempt to offer a theological response to these considerations careful not to follow the easy route of suggesting that Iris Murdoch's strategy of ascribing the status of 'God' to 'the Good' is unnecessary since God exists as the object of attention for the reorientation of morality that is so eloquently demanded. In contrast to such a strategy I want to show that the notion of goodness has to be conceived along different lines when it is understood not as a surrogate for the concept of God but as a divine attribute. In trying to develop this approach I want to suggest that such an approach can avoid the pitfalls of a view of goodness as an absolute value while at the same time offering similar possibilities for the reconciliation of fact and value in morality and for the development of a realistic moral philosophy. First of all, I want to discuss how an understanding of goodness as a divine attribute can be developed from the conception of divine agency that is asserted, presupposed and implied in the various expressions of faith in the context of the church. Secondly, I will attempt to show that such a view of God's goodness has a number of crucial consequences for the conception of goodness in the context of human morality. Thirdly, I will indicate briefly the implications of such a conception for the task of a theological response to the crises of moral reflection.

3 GOD'S GOODNESS AND THE LOGIC OF DIVINE ACTION

It would betray considerable self-deception on the part of the theologian or the philosopher of religion, if one would approach the problem of determining the character of goodness as a divine attribute and of relating it to human morality simply by way of abstract reflection and would attempt to construe its relationship to human morality from this perspective. MacIntyre and Murdoch are correct in assuming that ours is a post-theistic age, insofar as a shared belief in God cannot be presupposed as the unifying cultural framework for the interpretation of reality. Therefore it seems reasonable to approach the question of the relationship of God's goodness and human morality from a context which is distinguished from the post-theistic spirit of the times precisely by the fact that it is characterized by belief in God which is no longer universally accepted in Western culture. This context is the church as a community of the worship of God which interprets itself as being called to be a community of character, virtue and righteous action.[10] The approach which is implied in relating our discussion in this way to the church is one of conceptual reconstruction of the notion of God's goodness and of its implications for the understanding of human action asserted, presupposed and implied in the various practices in which this concept is present in the life of the church.

The practices which characterize the life of the church are in many ways related to a specific understanding of God and his agency. In Christian proclamation, which is based on the witness of Scripture, the action of God in Israel and in Jesus Christ functions as the paradigm for the interpretation of the present experience of Christian believers which determines their expectations for the future. In prayer God is addressed as a personal agent who is related to the world and humankind in a specific way that can - as Vincent Brümmer has shown[11] - be detected from the different forms in which prayer is practised. In confessions of faith believers express their faith as a community by professing their trust in God, Father, Son and Spirit. The confession of faith can be interpreted in such a way that the conditions for the possibility of the act of faith as an act of unconditional trust (fides *qua* creditur) are professed as the content of faith (fides *quae* creditur). The confessions of faith show that the agency of God which is seen as the ground of the possibility of trusting in him unconditionally has a specific structure which determines the relations in which the community of believers stands to God. The trinitarian form of the confessions of faith and the way in which specific types of action are appropriated as the work of the Father, the Son and the Spirit are intended to clarify the specific character of divine agency that is presupposed in the different forms of the expression of faith in the church.

I have suggested in chapter 1 that the conception of divine agency that seems to be presupposed in the expression of Christian faith in proclamation, prayer and confession of faith can be interpreted in terms of three internally related types of action. In this sense one can interpret the concept of divine agency as expressing the relationship of God's creative, revealing and inspiring agency. God's creative and sustaining action has to be characterised as the constitution of the existence of a finite and contingent world which depends for its being and structure on the agency of God as a sufficient condition for its existence and as a necessary condition for everything that happens in the world. In this conception God's agency in revelation has to be understood in terms of the disclosure experience in which God reveals himself in his creative relationship to the world and humankind and thereby discloses the truth about his relationship to his creation. God's inspiring action can in this framework be interpreted as the way in which God grants human persons the possibility of certainty concerning the

---

[10] Cf. the arguments for such an approach in Stanley Hauerwas' perceptive essay 'On Keeping Theological Ethics Theological', in: Hauerwas/MacIntyre (eds), *Revisions* (note 1), 16-42.

[11] Cf. Vincent Brümmer, *What Are We doing When We pray? A Philosophical Inquiry*, London 1984, especially chapters 5 and 6.

truth of his revelation as a true depiction of his relationship to the world and humanity and thereby motivates them to act in accordance with the truth of revelation.

It is one of the implications of this trinitarian conception of divine agency that the intentionality of divine action is not to be inferred from the structure of the world God has created, but has to be understood as grounded in the revelation in the Son. It is this paradigmatic action that is authenticated by the inspiration of the Spirit which then provides the framework for the interpretation of God's work in creation. In a similar way the characterization of the work of the Spirit as inspiration indicates how God involves human beings in the realization of his intentions. It is in the context of the interrelatedness of creation, revelation and inspiration that we can talk about God's action in terms of free, intentional action.

For any attempt of finding a foundation for the ascription of divine attributes such as goodness in the understanding of divine agency as it is expressed in the discourse of Christian faith the doctrine of the Trinity is of paramount importance. The theological thesis that forms the basis of all trinitarian theology is that the relatedness of God's triune being as Father, Son and Spirit is the condition for the possibility of his trinitarian relation to the world as Father, Son and Spirit. The trinitarian understanding of God provides, first of all, the possibility of understanding the unity of the divine economy in the three types of action we have distinguished. Secondly, it is the basis for ascribing a unitary intentionality to God's trinitarian action. Thirdly, it enables us to understand God's intentional action as expressive of his being and character.

Thomas F. Tracy has very fittingly described personal attributes that are predicated on the basis of intentional actions as 'character trait predicates'.[12] Such attributes can be predicated of a particular intentional action of a personal agent, and insofar as this action embodies the intention of the agent, it can also be predicated of the agent's intention. When the intentional actions of a personal agent exhibit a consistent pattern of orientation for the action of this agent, the attribute can also be predicated of the agent. It is obvious that this characterization of divine attributes as character trait predicates is particularly adequate for the so-called moral divine attributes. Our conception of divine agency requires however, that these attributes are carefully related to the types of action we have distinguished, since it is precisely this distinction which, by giving a central place to the notion of revelation, enables us to talk about character traits at all. Character trait attributes presuppose knowledge of a person's intentions, and according to Christian theology there is no other unambiguous access to God's intentions than his self-disclosure in Jesus Christ. Trinitarian theology makes this link even stronger, insofar as it claims that the

---

[12] Cf. Thomas F.Tracy, *God, Action and Embodiment*, Grand Rapids 1984, 3-20.

revelation in Jesus Christ is not an external expression of God's *will*, but the self-expression of God's *being* in the incarnate Son.

What would it mean to analyze the concept of God's goodness in this way? This would imply predicating goodness of God's actions, the intention that is realized in these actions and of the character of God that is expressed in the realization of these actions. With regard to the interpretation of God's agency as creative, revealing and inspiring agency this would mean that God's goodness is embodied in creating a good creation, in disclosing his intention in revelation and in motivating human agents to participate in the realization of his intention. In this sense the creation of a finite world with free personal agents, the revelation of the intention of this creative activity and thereby the disclosure of the relationship of this world to its creator, and the motivation of human agents to participate in the realization of God's purpose would have to be called good as an expression of God's being and character.

Interpreting goodness as a character trait predicate and relating it to the three types of divine action we have distinguished, has a number of important corollaries. First of all, it leads to an understanding of goodness where it is not conceived as an absolute value, or an abstract norm, but as the personal goodness of the tri-personal God that is ascribed to God on the basis of his actions. The fact that personal goodness is ascribed to God on the basis of his action in creation, revelation and inspiration points, secondly, to the categorical difference between the goodness of the infinite tri-personal God and the goodness of finite persons. In all three types of action the ontological status of God's agency is that of establishing and providing the conditions of the possibility of finite existence, knowledge and action. Confessing God as the creator who creates the world *ex nihilo* means ascribing the existence of a finite contingent world to the creative agency of God as the ground of its possibility and actuality. Talking about God's revelation in Christ refers to the self-disclosure of God as the condition for the 'knowability' of God in his relation to the world and of the world in its relation to God. Referring to the inspiration of the Spirit points to the authentification of this revelation in the Spirit as the condition for the possibility of faith which forms the basic orientation of human actions in accordance with God's relationship to the world. Discourse about God's agency in all three types refers to the *transcendental condition* of finite existence, finite knowledge and finite agency.

This transcendental character of God's agency applies also to the attributes that are predicated of God on the basis of his actions. It is the key to understanding the distinction and the relation between divine being and its attributes and finite being and its predicates. They are distinguished precisely by the nature of their relationship as a transcendental relation. On this view, the characterization of the relationship between God and his creation as a 'transcendental relation' is the attempt to indicate the onto-logical implications of belief in God the creator.[13] It

---

[13] Cf. Eilert Herms, 'Gottes Wirklichkeit', in: W. Härle/R.Preul (eds.), *Vom Handeln Gottes*, Marburger Jahrbuch Theologie I (1987), 82-101.

indicates the absolute dependence of all finite being, knowledge and action on God as the ground for its possibility. If this view of the relationship of God and the world is correct, it is also reflected in all divine attributes. The goodness of God the creator would therefore have to be interpreted as the condition for the possibility of all created goodness. The self-disclosure of God in revelation would have to be seen as the condition of the possibility of finite knowledge of goodness, and the inspiration of the Spirit as the motivation for the realization of goodness by finite agents.

The strongest objection against analyzing the goodness of God as a character trait predicate, ascribed on the basis of the view of divine agency expressed in the discourse of Christian faith, has always been that this would imply that moral rules, norms and values that regulate human behaviour cannot be applied in a similar fashion to God.[14] God has to be seen as his own standard of goodness, beyond any moral rule and utterly unimpeachable. Under the presupposition of the suggested interpretation of the transcendental character God's agency, this conclusion is indeed inevitable. It follows from belief in God as the creator who is the ground of the existence of everything there is. But this also implies that God is his own standard of goodness precisely insofar as he is the ultimate condition for the possibility of the existence, recognition and realization of goodness in creation. Therefore the very notion of moral rules, norms and values has a derivative character. But we can develop this argument a little further. The *prima facie* strength of this objection rests on the assumption that human righteousness and flourishing could come into conflict with God's goodness as the ultimate standard of all goodness. It is at this point that the significance of the trinitarian conception of divine agency expressed in the discourse of Christian faith can be recognized. The goodness of God should not be reduced to the goodness of a divine law-giver. It should be understood as the goodness of the triune God who does not only establish a standard of goodness in his relationship with his creation, but also overcomes the evil that results from the human contradiction against God's goodness in reconciling the world to himself in the Son and sanctifying it in the Spirit.

It could seem that the distinction between the goodness of God the creator and finite creatures would support the notion that goodness is necessarily beyond description and definition. This view of the 'indefinability' of goodness has a long and respectable history from classical Greek philosophy to G.E. Moore. And it is, of course, employed by Iris Murdoch in connection with her description of the transcendence and perfection of the Good.[15] Yet, there seems to be a sense in which this notion can be taken too far, i.e., where goodness is turned into a purely transcendent, non-representable and unattainable ideal which we can only

---

[14] For an interesting analysis of this problem cf. Thomas V.Morris, 'Duty and Divine Goodness, in: Thomas V.Morris (ed.), *The Concept of God*, Oxford Readings in Philosophy, Oxford 1987, 107-121.

[15] Cf. 'On "God" and "Good"' (note 9), 80.

contemplate. The thesis of the indefinability of goodness corresponds to a view of an essentially absolute and non-relational character of goodness. In a conception where goodness is understood as a divine attribute, rooted in God's trinitarian agency, goodness has to be understood as an essentially relational attribute, and the transcendence of God can consequently not be understood apart from the transcendental relationship of God to the world. Therefore an essential characteristic of goodness seems to be that goodness is that which enables, furthers and enhances goodness in others. This characteristic seems to be necessary for predicating goodness as a relational attribute of any intention, action or person. Furthermore, it can be applied, although in a different sense, to God, the creator, redeemer and saviour as well as to human beings. This is, of course, a condition for the possibility that God's goodness can become representable in the context of human experience. The crucial question is, however, how the sense in which goodness can be attributed to God as that which enables, furthers and enhances goodness in others and the sense in which it can be predicated of human beings is to be related? What is the relationship between goodness as an attribute of God the creator and the created goodness of human persons?

4 CREATED AND REDEEMED GOODNESS

The question of the relationship of God's goodness to the goodness of human persons is the central question for the attempt of determining the relationship between God's goodness and human morality. We have so far interpreted the concept of God's goodness as a character trait predicate based on God's trinitarian action in creation, revelation and inspiration which should be interpreted as the condition for the possibility of created goodness. For a more precise description of the way in which God's goodness is related to human morality we have to take a closer look at what is involved in the connection of creation, revelation and inspiration. Belief in God the creator whose free creative action is the condition for the possibility and actuality of everything there is implies a view of the world as creation. This does not only determine the understanding of the being of the world as finite and contingent, but also the view of the world as an ordered cosmos where everything is determined by its relationship to God the creator. It seems to me that this order has to be described as a network of relations, a structure of relatedness, in which the purpose of the creator for his creation finds its expression. This structure of relatedness is for human beings simply given. Human beings are relational beings and they exist in a specific relationship to God, to themselves, to other persons and to the cultural and natural world. The specific distinction of the human creatures is expressed in the traditional metaphor of the *imago Dei* which can be interpreted as consisting in the finite personal freedom of human beings to relate freely by intentional action to the structure of relatedness in which they exist. Human beings have the finite freedom to respond to the will of the creator. The goodness of God consists in this context in creating a good world in which human beings have the finite freedom to relate to the structure of relatedness either in accordance with the will of the creator or in contradiction to it. Human beings have the ability to recognize freely and gratefully God as their creator in relating to God and his creation in accordance with his will. And in this sense human beings are the images of God insofar as they have the freedom to realize created goodness as the appropriate response to the goodness of the creator. Human goodness is at the same time made possible and limited by God's goodness. The characteristic of goodness as enabling, furthering and enhancing goodness in others can, of course, not be ascribed to human beings in the radical sense in which God's goodness is the condition for the possibility of created goodness, but it nevertheless characterizes the way in which human beings should exercise their created freedom in relation to other human beings and to nature. The fact that God's goodness is seen as the condition for the possibility of human goodness implies that human goodness is with regard to its form and content not an absolute and autonomous goodness, but a relative and 'theonomous' goodness whose criterion is the goodness of God as the only standard of goodness.

According to the conviction of Christian faith we live in a situation where human beings have chosen not to use their freedom in accordance with the goodness of the creator but in contradiction to it. It is in this context highly significant that the story of the Fall describes the temptation of the serpent as consisting in the attempt at assuming the knowledge of good and evil that is characteristic of the creative and sovereign goodness of God the creator instead of accepting the created and derivative goodness of his images that is dependent and limited by God's commandment. The cosmic consequences of the Fall indicate that where human beings attempt to set their own standard of goodness, their actions lose the quality of enabling, furthering and enhancing goodness in others with regard to the human as well as to the non-human creation. Human goodness is only possible where it is based on the recognition of Gods' goodness as the condition for its possibility. Original sin which is so vividly and fittingly described by Iris Murdoch as selfishness, consists in the inability of human beings to restore their broken relationship to God by their own effort. Viewed in these relational terms, the universality of original sin is an implication of the fact that only the creator can restore the relationship to his human creatures.

It is the central message of the Christian Gospel that God has not left his human creatures in the state of selfishness where goodness either turns into an utterly transcendent and unattainable ideal or is turned into a function of human selfishness, but has restored his relationship to his fallen creatures. The revelation of God in Christ has traditionally been conceived in the notion of the Incarnation of God the Son in whom the true relationship of God to his creation is disclosed as well as the adequate relationship of humanity to God. Jesus Christ is the incarnation of God's goodness precisely in the sense in which his life is characterized by the goodness which enables, furthers and enhances goodness in others. Where goodness is understood as a personal attribute and not as a transcendent and non-representable ideal, it is representable as incarnate precisely in its essential characteristic, that of enabling goodness in others.[16]

The revelation of God's goodness in Jesus Christ is according to the convictions of Christian faith appropriated in the work of the Holy Spirit. It is perhaps significant that in confessions of faith like the Apostles' Creed, belief in the Holy Spirit is closely associated with ecclesiological and eschatological statements. The ecclesiological emphasis points to the fact that where the relationship to God is restored by the Incarnation of the Son and appropriated in the Spirit the relationship of the sinner to other persons and to nature is restored as well. The created sociality of humanity finds its restored expression as redeemed sociality in the community of the church.[17] The hallmark of that community is that it has its foundation in the promise of forgiveness of sin which indicates the way in which God's goodness is exercised by enabling the goodness of his creatures. When the mode in which that happens is seen as inspiration this can be interpreted to indicate that this does not happen by subjecting human persons under an alien law, but by reconstituting their finite, created freedom. Here Iris Murdoch's insistence on the moral content of realism points very accurately to the way in which this freedom is to be distinguished from the self-centred and deceptive freedom of sin in which human beings become prisoners of their possessive attachments. The reconstitution of created freedom through the appropriation of the revelation of God's goodness in Christ which is made possible in the Spirit is characterized by the acknowledgment of the limitations of human freedom that become evident where this freedom is no longer understood as self-produced, but as a gift of grace.[18] The liberation from the abortive attempt of the self-constitution of human freedom discloses the reality of the other person and of the non-human creation as the one to whom good action is directed. Human goodness is realized where it is acknowledged that it is not self-produced, but the result of God's creative, revealing and inspiring action. It reaches its fullest expression where this acknowledgment takes the form of good action precisely insofar as it consists in enhancing and furthering goodness in others.

This notion of human goodness receives its content from the recognition of the determination of the possibilities of human action in God's creative and sustaining action, from the acknowledgment of the revelation of God's goodness in Jesus Christ as the paradigm for human action, and from the acceptance that the certainty concerning the truth of revelation is the way in which God the Spirit motivates us to accept his intention of creating a community of love with his creatures as the framework for our intentions. It is based on the understanding of

---

[16] Cf. The illuminating discussion that comes to the opposite conclusion in Stewart R. Sutherland, *God, Jesus and Belief. The Legacy of Theism*, Oxford 1984, 150-162.

[17] Cf. Daniel Hardy's article 'Created and Redeemed Sociality, in C.E.Gunton, D.Hardy (eds.), *On Being the Church. Essays on the Christian Community*, Edinburgh 1989, 21-47.

[18] Cf. W.Härle, 'Werk Gottes - Werk des Menschen', *NThT* 34 (1980), 213-224.

divine goodness that is presupposed in the fundamental expressions of faith in the practices of the church and finds its social form in the community of believers as the reconstituted form of life of created and redeemed sociality. Yet, the form of human morality that is made possible by divine goodness as it is enacted in God's creative, revealing and inspiring action is far from ecclesiocentric. Since it is centred on the notion of goodness, it can only retain its character as long as it enables, furthers and enhances goodness in others. It is precisely the self-transcending character of goodness that implies that the church only remains the place where God's goodness is acknowledged as the constitution of human morality when it is able to become the catalyst of goodness for those outside the church.

In this connection it is necessary to remember that the paradigmatic confessions of faith continue their ecclesiological statements with eschatological statements which indicate that the church is not the ultimate purpose of God's agency. But insofar as the church is the place where God's goodness is gratefully acknowledged as the condition for human goodness and where the realization of this goodness is recognized as the purpose of God's agency for the whole of humanity, the church as the symbolic representation of God's Kingdom can become an instrument for the realization of God's purpose for the whole of his creation.

When we compare this sketch of a basic framework for human morality, based on the understanding of goodness as a divine attribute, with Iris Murdoch's reflections on 'God and Good', a number of obvious similarities and a number of crucial differences become clear. First of all, both accounts attempt to develop a realistic view of human morality and relate the moral task to the overcoming of the selfishness of the isolated will and to the ability of perceiving a reality separate of ourselves and our possessive attachments. Iris Murdoch's proposal concentrates on understanding 'the Good' on the analogy of 'God' as 'a single perfect non-representable and necessarily real object of attention' which as the focus of orientation for our morality provides the possibility of a moral vision and a subsequent moral conduct that is in accordance with what really is the case. The absoluteness and sovereignty of the Good is the warrant for the realism of human morality. In contrast to that our suggestion of understanding goodness as a divine attribute is centred on the relational being of God and the relational character of everything there is. On this view, the warrant for the realism of human morality is that human relationships to God, other human persons and to the world of nature and culture are in accordance with God's relationship to his creation. Since God is the creator of everything there is, his creative agency determines what is real. God's revelation of his relationship to the world has therefore to be seen as the foundation of true knowledge of what really is the case, and God's inspiring action motivates human beings to relate adequately to this reality by granting certainty concerning the truth of revelation. The fundamental issue for human morality comes to the fore in the question whether we relate to everything there is in accordance with the relationships God has established in his creative, revealing and inspiring action. The foundation of a realistic morality is therefore in this conception faith in God as the ground of all reality and of all knowledge of reality.

The second main point of contact between both views of goodness which also discloses significant differences, is the stress on specific practices where the orientation towards goodness is consciously exercised and appropriated. In Iris Murdoch's account this is the key for her emphasis on techniques, practices and concepts that were originally part of the religious life and are now 'reinvented' as part of the redirection of our awareness towards the Good as the object of our attention. In a conception which is based on the goodness of God as the focus for human morality these practices are fundamental expressions of faith in God, Father, Son and Spirit who is related to the world through his action in creation, revelation and inspiration. Miss Murdoch's emphasis on a specific form of life which mediates awareness of the Good is a forceful reminder of the ethical import of the practices that characterize the life of the church as a community of witness to God. The decisive difference between Iris Murdoch's conception and the life of faith in the Christian community is, however, that the goodness of God, understood as a character trait predicate of the tri-personal God, presupposes an understanding of God as actively and interactively relating to the world he has created. In this sense the practices of the life of faith are consistently characterized as a response to the agency of God. Therefore the life of faith in its concrete forms of proclamation, prayer, worship and sacramental action claims to offer more than techniques of purification and reorientation. It is the enactment of the relationship to the triune God as the basis for moral action. It is the concrete form of acknowledging the goodness of God as the condition for the possibility for created goodness by accepting the enablement and limitations of finite human freedom in God's creative action, by acknowledging the reconstitution of human freedom in Jesus Christ as the revelation of God's goodness and the paradigm for human goodness, and by accepting the reorientation of our will and action through the inspiration of the Spirit. The life of faith in the concrete community of the church is the enactment of the conviction that the triune God is the primary agent in creating the conformity with Christ that is the adequate response to God's goodness.

A third structural analogy appears when we consider the objective of Iris Murdoch's conception as providing the unitary focus for the framework of morality so that concepts of moral values, norms, obligations and virtues have to seen as being derived from the sovereignty of the Good. They can no longer claim absolute character, but have to be conceived in their relationship to the Good. In a similar way the goodness of God as the condition for the possibility of all created and redeemed goodness, provides the framework for the understanding of values, norms and virtues for Christian morality. But since goodness is not understood as an absolute value, but as a relational predicate that characterizes the way in which God's goodness is the condition for the possibility of created goodness and the way in which created goodness is realized in responding adequately to

God's goodness, the notions of values, norms and virtues have to be seen as relative to the relationship between God and the world.

This implies for the understanding of values that they are not characterized by absoluteness, but that God's action in creation, revelation and inspiration is seen as foundation for the being, recognition and active acknowledgment of all values. The paradigmatic case for these 'relative' values is expressed in the story of creation by the fact that God pronounces his creation good. Values are expressions of worth in virtue of the relationship of the creation to the goodness of its creator. Value-judgements place a being or an action in the relationship of God to his creation. Therefore they state neither an intrinsic worth nor pronounce extrinsic evaluations. They ascribe value, because it is intrinsic to the relationship of God to the world which is established and restored in his trinitarian agency. This conception can therefore very tentatively indicate a way in which the two major dilemmas of a theory of values can be overcome. First of all, it does not create a gulf between being and value, because both are seen as grounded in God's relationship to the world. Secondly, it does not raise the thorny questions of a hierarchy of values, because values and their order of priority are not defined with respect to one or more absolute values, but with regard to God's goodness as the condition for the possibility of all created goodness. Faith in God's goodness is the framework that provides unity for the perception and ascription of value.

This also applies to moral norms and obligations. In a conception of morality based on the notion of God's goodness, moral norms cannot claim an absolute status, but have to be seen in relation to the fundamental relationship between God and creation. They formulate the way in which human beings can relate to God, to other human beings and to nature in accordance with the relationship which God has established in creation and restored in Christ. The deontological norms and obligations presuppose the ontological structures which are the result of God's creative agency. Therefore all norms and duties are relative to the relationship between God and the world and to the will of the creator expressed in this relationship. This means, for instance, that the Ten Commandments should not be interpreted as the establishment of a relationship between the divine lawgiver and his human subjects. Rather, they already presuppose the relationship between God and humanity established in God's agency and formulate negatively which actions have to be avoided at all costs, if this relationship is to be upheld. Furthermore, this view of the 'relative' status of all norms and obligations would imply that the greatest commandment of love of God and of love of one's neighbour (Matthew 22: 37f.) should not be interpreted as the reduction of all norms of action to a fundamental normative principle of love. Rather, it would seem to indicate the dependence of all moral principles on the relationship of love between God and humanity which determines the human relationship to God and to humanity. This also implies that conflicts between moral norms and obligations have to be resolved by relating them to the goodness of God as it finds expression in the fundamental relationship between God and his creation.

In a similar sense, the virtues should on this account be understood as the basic orientation of our actions that is in accordance with the goodness of God as condition for the possibility of human goodness. Values are ascribed either to beings or actions that have a specific worth in virtue of their relation to the relational goodness of God. Norms and obligations formulate rules determining the choices of action in accordance with the nature of the relationship between God and his creation. The virtues express the over-all unity of a person's action- and value-orientation with his or her character. In a conception of human morality centred on the notion of God's goodness the concept of virtue expresses the comprehensive response of faith to the goodness of God the creator, redeemer and saviour. This conception of virtue is, however, 'excentric' insofar as it is constituted not by the autonomous moral effort of the agent, but refers to God's goodness as the unitary focus of human morality.

It is important to realize that the concept of the goodness of God does not only provide the constitutive notion for a conception of human morality. It also functions as its critical principle. With the help of this principle we can detect where suggested moral values, proposed norms of action and conceptions of virtue go wrong, when they are not based on the acknowledgment of God's goodness as the condition for the possibility of created goodness. This usually happens where values, norms and virtues are declared as absolute, so that their character and validity does not have to be understood in relation to the character and agency of God. The immediate consequence of this is that the unifying framework for our moral life is lost and moral practice as well as moral reflection turns into the battle-field of competing moral claims and justifications. Once the unifying framework is missing, the danger appears that precisely our moral endeavours become, if we follow Iris Murdoch's analysis, instruments of our 'natural' selfishness, and we ourselves become victims of our possessive attachments. In this context, it is important to be reminded of the fact, that the conception of morality based on the notion of God's goodness as the condition for the possibility of created goodness, is not an abstract moral theory, but is grounded in the expressions of faith in the practices of the church. This does not only provide the interpretative context for the conception of God's goodness. It is primarily the place where the fundamental orientation of human agency is established and restored. Repentance and forgiveness provide the possibility for the readjustment of our moral orientation to the relationship between God and the world which is the basis for our relation to God, to each other and to nature. The life of faith in the community of the church is therefore not only the context in which the constitutive role of God's goodness for human morality is proclaimed and gratefully acknowledged. It is also the form of life where we can receive assurance of God's forgiveness as the reconstitution of our moral agency.

The most serious objection against such a conception of morality is, of course, that its dependence on the practice of the life of faith in the church turns it into an utterly sectarian enterprise. From the perspective of this criticism, the price for treating the goodness of God as the condition for the possibility of created goodness and as the unifying framework for human morality, seems to be too high. It seems to cut off the ethics of the Christian community from the general context of moral practice and ethical reflection in society. Would it not be better to attempt to find a foundation for morality that is independent of the context of the church?

The first response to this criticism is, of course, that it is precisely the attempt of finding universal moral principles that has led to the present crisis of morality and moral reflection in Western culture. The effect of post-Enlightenment 'ethical foundationalism' which claims to be able to provide a universal set of moral principles and universally valid ethical justifications, had led to the situation where ethical justifications themselves have become the object of choice and where the absence of a unifying framework for our moral life is lamented by moral philosophers from different schools. All we seem to be left with seems to be an autonomous individual will that cannot be distinguished from the Freudian ego that is the victim of its possessive attachments. The only thing that is really universal, some might say, is our moral disorientation. While this view of the present situation in moral philosophy, if it is correct, might be sufficient as a motivation of trying to find a unifying framework of moral reflection based on the communal practice of the church, it is insufficient as a response to the challenge of sectarianism.

In order to provide a more adequate response to that challenge it is necessary to consider two crucial implications of our suggestion. The first concerns the conception of divine agency in terms of the interrelationship of the creative, revealing and inspiring action of the trinitarian God which is the basis for interpreting God's goodness as the condition for the possibility of created goodness. In this conception, the recognition of God's goodness as it is disclosed in Jesus Christ and authenticated in the Holy Spirit is inextricably connected to the particular revelation of God in Christ which is proclaimed and witnessed by the Christian community. But while the recognition of God's goodness as the foundation of human morality is dependent on the particularity of the self-disclosure of God in Christ as goodness incarnate, the content of this revelation is nevertheless the universal creative agency of God as the condition for the possibility of goodness. Our conception implies that there is only a particular mode of the recognition of God's goodness based on the particularity of his revelation in Christ, but this does not mean that the material content of a conception of morality based on God's self-disclosure is in any sense restricted to a particular form of Christian ethics. If the goodness of God the creator is the condition for the possibility of created goodness, then there is only one standard of morality and the created goodness restored and revealed in Christ through the Spirit is the moral destiny of all humanity.[19] The particularity of God's self-disclosure in Christ through the Spirit does not restrict the universality of God's goodness as the condition for the possibility of created goodness. Rather, it is the specific content of this particular revelation, that God's goodness is the universal condition of all created goodness. It is one of the central contents of Christian hope that the tension between the particularity of God's self-disclosure through the Son and in the Spirit will be overcome in the *eschaton* when God's creative, revealing and inspiring agency will be coextensive, so that God's creative agency will be universally disclosed as the inspiration of creation, and God's goodness will find the perfect response of created goodness. The Christian church as the context for the grateful acknowledgment and recognition of the universality of God's goodness as foundation and standard of all goodness, will only remain faithful to its message as long as it holds fast to this universal hope and witnesses to it by furthering and enhancing the goodness of the world. And precisely to this extent will it be able to respond adequately to the challenge of sectarianism.

The second implication of this conception is that the universality of the standard of morality depends on seeing goodness as an attribute of the triune God. The universality of goodness is entailed in its theological foundation. Therefore it would not make much sense to try to find a 'natural' and 'neutral' universal foundation for morality and then add the specifically Christian emphasis as an optional extra. From the perspective of this conception a 'natural law conception' of ethics is either an implication of the relationship between God's goodness and created goodness or an alternative proposal for understanding the nature of goodness. This would suggest a paradigm shift for the contemporary debate concerning the relationship between theological and secular ethics and between Christian morality and the moral conceptions of non-Christian views of life. We have started from the observation that the attempt to provide moral principles and justifications has led to a pluralism of competing ultimate principles neither of which can provide unity to our moral concerns. It would therefore seem justified to call for a shift from the search for common foundational principles to a dialogue of moral frameworks that do not claim to be able to provide universally acceptable moral principles, but recommend themselves by their internal coherence and ability to provide a unifying focus for human life.

Among the necessary conditions for a successful dialogue seem to be the mutual recognition of the distinctiveness and independence of the partners in dialogue, their ability to formulate a goal for their dialogue from their respective perspectives and a common medium of communication. The present chapter has been concerned with the first two of these conditions, to formulate an understand-

---

[19] Cf. Wilfried Härle's observations about the relationship between creation and moral law in his article 'Luther's Zwei-Regimentenlehre als Lehre vom Handeln Gottes', in *Marburger Jahrbuch Theologie I* (note 13), 12-32.

ing of goodness based on the goodness of God and to argue for God's goodness as the universal condition of the possibility of all created goodness. It may well be that the requirements of the third condition, the common medium of communication, can more easily be met on the basis and in the context of joint action in combating what different moral perspectives recognise as evil. As long as this pragmatic basis for joint moral action exists, the paradigm of moral dialogue can be said to be safe from the dangers of relativism that, ironically, seems to be the result of the search for common foundational principles in morality. If there is anything to recommend the view that the concept of goodness is not an alternative to the concept of God as the focus of our moral vision and action, but should be understood as an attribute of God, then it might be that moral reflection in the West has not only a theological past, but might also be said to have in some of its strands a theological future.

Part II
DIVINE REVELATION

4 'Revelation' and 'Experience': Reflections on their Relationship

1 'REVELATION' AND 'EXPERIENCE' AND THE CHANGING FASHIONS OF THEOLOGY

Theology can only be done in the medium of the thought of its time. Like all forms of cultural expression it is therefore subject to trends of fashion which in retrospect appear significant for the spirit of the times. These theological fashions are characterized by the concentration on certain topics, common elements of style and a shared preference for certain conceptualities. In all these features theological fashions reflect dominant tendencies in the cultural context of theology. Often there are also obvious parallels between fashions in theology and the issues hotly debated in the churches at a particular time. Within the common framework of such fashion trends there remain, of course, differences in the thematic foci and methods of particular theologians and theological groups, but they seem to indicate different accents and emphases within a common framework rather than totally different styles of doing theology. However, if theology wants to be more than a theological expression of its cultural milieu, it is necessary that theologians work not only as fashion designers or retailers of the theological 'trend setters'. They also have to attempt to relate as fashion critics the style preferences of the season to the perennial issues and questions of Christian theology.

The concepts of 'revelation' and 'experience' are not only key-concepts of the modern self-reflection of Christianity in the West, they can also be used to identify two dominant fashion trends in the theology of this century which have shaped theological debates for decades. These trends are particularly pronounced in Protestant theology in Continental Europe, but just as Paris, London, and Milan have a decisive influence on what fashion designers do all over the world, so Basel, Marburg and Heidelberg, among other places, have influenced the style of theological work in other countries and ecclesial settings. From the end of the first world war to the nineteen-sixties the concept of revelation can be seen as the common denominator of many debates in which central issues were discussed - from the new approach of 'dialectical theology' to the controversies about natural theology and general revelation in the thirties to the debates about Wolfhart Pannenberg's programme of 'revelation as history'. The common characteristics of theologies centred on revelation can be seen in the emphasis on the freedom, irreducibility and sovereignty of God's revelation and in the stress on the uniqueness and distinctiveness of revelation in contrast to all human expectations and cultural conditions. The conception of theology which corresponds to this understanding of revelation is one which emphasizes the autonomy and distinctiveness of theology over against all other forms of knowledge and distinctiveness of theology over against all other forms of knowledge and intellectual inquiry. One could easily show the effect of this concentration of theology on revelation as its foundational concept on the choice of relevant topics and preferred methods in all theological disciplines and on the practice and reflection of the work of the church. However, we also find pronounced tendencies of critical modification and self-critical qualification in the theologies of revelation - from the expressionist metaphors of the 'breakthrough' of revelation to the dialogical models of interpreting revelation and to Pannenberg's plea for a rational theology.

At the beginning of the nineteen-seventies the situation changed quite dramatically when the concept of experience became the key-word of a new fashion trend in theology. 'Experience and faith' was suddenly one of the standard themes of theological inquiry in all theological disciplines. At the same time a strong movement for the reception and appropriation of the results and methods of empirical sciences, especially of the social sciences, began. This necessitated a new phase of reflection on the foundations of theology in which the relationship of theology to the empirical sciences was explicitly considered. The new central concept of experience furthermore led to new reflections on the modern self-understanding of theology focussed on the foundational role of experience as a central feature of modernity. Common elements of style in this trend are the appeal to the experiential basis of theology which can be interpreted in various ways, the appropriations of patterns of theory-formation in the empirical sciences and the attempt at applying experiential or empirical strategies of validation to theological claims. At the same time attempts were made to find guidance for the work of the church in the results and methods provided by empirical research in the social sciences. We can also see that the initial consensus concerning the fundamental significance of experience as the basis and testing-ground of all theological statements soon made way for self-critical reflection on the structure and status of the concept of experience itself.

By referring to these different styles of doing theology as 'fashion trends' I want to indicate that changes in theological fashions have by no means the theoretical status of 'paradigm shifts' which Thomas Kuhn analyzed in the history of science.[1] The change of fashions in theology is, like the change of paradigms in the history of science, influenced by sociological, historical and cultural factors. However, to interpret the changing fashions of theology as paradigm shifts, which would include the incommensurability of their theoretical models and of what is regarded as the data for the formation of theories, would inhibit critical self-reflection on theological fashions. Understanding the change from concentration on the concept of revelation to concentration on the concept of experience as a change of fashion raises the question whether the different thematic focus is a genuine change of the subject-matter of theological reflection and the method of theological inquiry, or whether it is only a contingent emphasis on different aspects of a common problem. To ascribe to fashion trends

---

[1] Cf. Thomas S. Kuhn, *The Structure of Scientific Revolutions*, 2nd ed. Chicago 1970. For the discussion of Kuhn's theory of paradigm shifts see Wentzel van Huysteen, *Theology and the Justification of Faith*, Grand Rapids 1989, 47-67.

the status of paradigm shifts would mean that constructive theological work was only possible in the idiom of contemporary fashion, and it would reduce critical theological reflection to the description of the different models which parade on the catwalks of the different fashion houses of theology.

If we understand the theology of revelation and the theology of experience as alternative and mutually exclusive conceptions of theology, as seems to be suggested by the succession of theological fashions in this century, we can easily see the inherent perils of both approaches. Theological conceptions building on the concept of revelation stress that revelation cannot be deduced from or reduced to general principles of knowledge and they interpret the concept of revelation as signifying the completely contingent and irreducible event of divine self-disclosure. This concept of revelation is employed with the intention of safeguarding the sovereign freedom of God in his self-disclosure by ascribing a unique epistemic status to revelation. This special status is expressed in the claims that knowledge of God is only possible on the basis of God's self-disclosing action, and that this self-disclosure is therefore the basis of all assertions of Christian faith and their theological explication. Revelation is not subject to any conditions which are not contained in revelation itself and its validation is grounded solely in the being and action of God. This interpretation of the concept of revelation, including, as it does, a radical conception of the autonomy of theology can raise serious problems for Christian faith's claim to universal truth and for the Christian understanding of God. The content of God's revelation includes, according to this view, truth claims with a universal range of application. However, this universality seems to be called into question when the exclusive particularity of revelation is construed as an absolute contrast to all general principles of knowledge. If this is the case, then the view of God as universal creative, reconciling and saving love which is disclosed in revelation is in danger of being reduced to a subjective claim of the theologian who defends such a view. Furthermore, if the irreducibility of revelation is seen as contradicting all forms of human experience, then it seems that the certainty of faith which rests on the truth of revelation is stripped of all significance for human experience as a whole.

The different strands of a theology of experience can to some extent be seen as a reaction to the dangers and risks of a conception of theology of revelation which emphasizes the irreducibility of revelation in such a strong sense that it isolates revelation from all other pursuits of knowledge. They attempt to overcome the alleged isolationism of the theology of revelation with its emphasis on the autonomy of theology by finding, like the empirical sciences, the basis and testing-ground of theological statements in experience. If this approach is to lead beyond the threat to the universality of theological statements which we saw as one of the risks of a specific form of theology of revelation, then it must be based on a general concept of experience. This appears as a requirement for the compatibility of theological statements with statements in the empirical sciences and as a precondition of their potentially universal character. The problems which are raised by such a conception are intimately connected to the interpretation of the concept of experience which is seen as the foundation and testing-ground of theological statements. Where experience is interpreted as exclusively constituted by human subjectivity, the contents of theological discourse can only be seen as descriptions of attitudes and dispositions of human consciousness. Their function is interpreted as giving symbolic expression to a religious construction of reality. Finding the foundation of theology in the concept of experience with the aim of establishing in this way the universality of theological statements could result in putting the reality-content of its assertions at risk. These consequences are by no means restricted to approaches which subscribe to one of the forms of constructivism. They become apparent whenever the possibility of discourse about God is made dependent on the criteria of a non-theological epistemology which claims universal validity.[2] In such a framework the prevenient character of God's self-disclosure can no longer be maintained.

The task which seems to follow from these observations of the problematical character of a theology of revelation which excludes the concept of experience and of a theology of experience in which the concept of revelation has no place, consists in considering whether the alternative of seeing either revelation or experience as the foundational concept of theology is, in fact, justified. Are there possibilities of relating revelation and experience in such a way that we can avoid the risks we have indicated and can conceive of both concepts as signifying complementary aspects of a single phenomenon?

2 TOWARDS AN ANALYSIS OF THE CONCEPT OF REVELATION

The concept of revelation designates in Christian theology the event of God's self-disclosure in Jesus Christ for humanity which creates the condition for the possibility of faith in which the Christ event is acknowledged as the foundation of the true relationship of human beings to God, to the world and to themselves. The concept of revelation depicts revelation as the act of divine self-communication in which the triune God communicates himself through the medium of created reality as the ground and the author of creation, reconciliation and salvation of created being. This divine action enables human beings to respond to the prevenient relationship of God to his creation in their relationship to God, to the world and to themselves.

We can attempt to clarify the concept of revelation and the character of the disclosure event[3] it signifies by taking a closer look at the formal structure of the concept.[4] I want to suggest that we analyze 'revelation' as a relational

---

[2] For the critique of epistemological 'foundationalism' see Ronald F. Thiemann, *Revelation and Theology. The Gospel as Narrated Promise*, Notre Dame 1985.

[3] The expression disclosure event is derived from Ian Ramsey's notion of a 'disclosure situation', cf. I.T. Ramsey, *Religious Language*, London 1957, 11-54.

[4] The following proposal for the analysis of the concept of revelation owes important insights to Eilert Herms' phenomenological description of disclosure events, cf. E.Herms, 'Offenbarung', *Funkkolleg Religion*, Studienbegleitbrief 7, Weilheim-Basel 1984, 11-54. Our proposal offers a conceptual reconstruction of the second-order concept of revelation and therefore employs the traditional terminology of Christian dogmatics. All these concepts have, however, an experiential basis which can be phenomenologically described in the first-order language of discourse in religious situations.

concept in which the following five terms are set in relation: the author of revelation (A), the situation of revelation (B), the content of revelation (C), the recipient of revelation (D) and the result of revelation (E). The concept of revelation can consequently be construed in the following formula:

A discloses in the situation B the content C for the recipient D with the result E

The history of Christian thought offers many variations on how these formal terms can be substituted, especially with regard to the interpretation of the situation of revelation B, the content of revelation C and the result of revelation E. There is, however, in those strands of modern theology where the concept of revelation is regarded as theologically central a relatively wide-ranging, though sometimes implicit, consensus about the content of the formal terms of the relation expressed in the concept of revelation. I shall presuppose these points of consensus, which can be seen in the christological interpretation of the disclosure event and in the emphasis on the correlation between revelation and faith, and I will attempt to develop them constructively in the proposal for the analysis of the concept of revelation.[5]

[A] The *author* of revelation is interpreted as the triune God who relates in the disclosure event actively, directly and efficaciously to particular persons. The disclosure event itself is therefore understood as the result of the intentional action of God who as the sole author of revelation expresses his will and being in this event. The relation which characterizes the event of revelation is, because it has its ground in God's action, irreflexive and therefore asymmetrical. Consequently, no other reason can be given for the occurrence of the revelation than God's freedom. The revelation of God is therefore for its recipient completely contingent and cannot be derived or deduced from any antecedent conditions established in another context.

Interpreting the disclosure event of God's revelation in terms of divine action has a number of further implications which follow from the understanding of divine action in Christian theology. First of all, one cannot assume for the action of God, the creator, reconciler and perfecter of the world the limitations which apply to the actions of finite agents: the fact that the conditions for the agency of finite agents are not self-constituted; the restrictions which follow from the limitations of finite reason for the selection of aims of action; the restraints which are given by the bodily mode of existence of finite agents etc.[6] Since there are no external limitations imposed on divine agency there is no difference between God's intentions and the bringing about of these intentions in divine action in general and in God's revelatory action in particular. In interpreting the concept of divine agency the theological tradition has furthermore insisted that there is in God no conflict between being and will so that all God's actions are, as expressions of his will, also expressions of his being. If

---

[5] Cf. the concise exposition of the theological conception of revelation in I.U.Dalferth, *Theology and Philosophy*, Oxford 1988, 39-46, which is referred to at several points in the following discussion.

[6] For a more detailed comparison of divine and human agency cf. above chapter 1, 23-46.

there is no difference between intention and act, will and being in God, then God's action in revelation must be interpreted in such a way that it expresses the unity of divine action. This necessitates an analysis of the concept of revelation which adequately expresses the unity of divine action in creation, reconciliation and salvation while taking the internal differentiation of different modes of action into account. Christian theology has traditionally sought to formulate this insight in the doctrine of the Trinity: God's action is as the action of Father, Son and Spirit not uniform, but always unitary and in this way expresses the unity of intention and act, will and being of God.

[B] The *situation of revelation* B in which A discloses the content C for D with the result E has predominantly received in Christian theology a christological description. The Christ event is seen as the paradigmatic disclosure situation in which God communicates himself to particular persons. This implies that God discloses himself in created reality, including its historical structure and its capacity for semiotic interpretation. We summarize here in the expression 'disclosure situation' what has been discussed in traditional terminology as the medium of revelation. The Christ event is therefore a complex occurrence comprising a variety of different dimensions which becomes a disclosure situation only in the connection of its constituent dimensions.[7] This event includes, *first of all*, the historical dimension of Jesus' life, his message, his history and his fate, as well as its reception by those who followed him. Included in this historical dimension is the witness of Jesus to the coming of the Kingdom of God as the demonstration of the will of grace of God the Father for creation.

The Christ event is *secondly* characterized by the interpretation of the witness of Jesus' life by his followers as the actualisation of God's eschatological will and with that as the interpretation of Jesus of Nazareth as the Christ. The Christ event as the situation of revelation comprises therefore not only the *bruta facta* of the historical sequence of events, but also the claim coming to expression in this series of events (the words, deeds and suffering of Jesus) and the interpretation of both by Jesus' followers. The combination of both dimensions means that the self-interpretation of Jesus, as it is mediated by his message of God the Father and the present coming of the Kingdom, becomes part of the interpretation of his history and fate by his followers. Therefore the interpretation of the witness of Jesus' life by his followers not only asserts the truth of Jesus' self-interpretation, but also claims this truth as the truth for their own relationship to God, to the world and to themselves.

The *third* constitutive element for the Christ event as revelation becomes apparent where both elements, the self-interpretation of Jesus and the interpretation of Jesus by his followers are seen as enabled and validated by the action of God. The interpretation of Jesus as the Christ is seen as validated by God's action, where both the resurrection as the validation of Jesus' self-interpretation and the authorisation by the Spirit of the message of the

---

[7] Cf. Ingolf Dalferth's analysis of the 'Grundzüge der christlichen Anredeerfahrung' in *Religiöse Rede von Gott*, München 1981, 469-494.

resurrection of the one who was crucified are believed to be grounded in God's action.

Reference to God the Spirit points to the unity of the different dimensions of the Christ event as God's revelation. The Spirit who discloses God to Jesus as the Father who calls his human creatures into the community of salvation in the Kingdom of God, and the Spirit who enables the witness of Jesus' life as obedience to the Father and as *praxis* of the present coming of the Kingdom of God, is the same Spirit who discloses to Jesus' followers the witness of his life and validates it as the truth about their own lives and about all reality. The action of God the Spirit is therefore not only to be interpreted as consecutive upon the Christ event, but also as constitutive for it. Therefore God's action in the Spirit can be seen as the continuing presence of the revelation of Christ in the Christian community under the conditions of the absence of the earthly Jesus.

For the generations who no longer know Jesus 'according to the flesh' the Christ event becomes the Gospel of Christ, communicated in the word of proclamation, the word of Scripture and the visible words of the sacraments. This does not mean that the authority of revelation can be transferred to the medium of witnessing to revelation: neither the authority of Scripture, nor the authority of the church, nor the authority of the individual witness can replace or effectively represent the authority of revelation.[8] The message of the Gospel of Christ, is as the paradigmatic *witness* to the revelation of God, distinct from the self-disclosure of God. The truth claim of Christian proclamation is a truth claim which is witnessed is distinguished from the certainty of faith as long as this truth claim is not validated for the hearers of the Gospel of Christ by God's revelatory action. This happens where hearers of the message of Christ become convinced, or better, are convicted of its truth as the truth about all reality and therefore also as the truth for their own lives. The paradigmatic disclosure situation of the Christ event becomes as the Gospel of Christ a constitutive element in the disclosure situation by which those who no longer know Christ 'according to the flesh' are enabled to believe. It becomes the text whose truth is ascertained in the context of the life of believers. The validation of the Gospel of Christ through the *testimonium internum* of the Holy Spirit includes the validation of the claim of the Christian Gospel to be the witness of the self-disclosure of God in the Christ event.

Where God is believed as the ground of certainty with regard to the Gospel of Christ and where, consequently, the Christ event is acknowledged as the self-disclosure of God the creator in the reality of creation, there the truth of the Gospel of Christ that God reconciles his alienated creatures and leads them into salvation is also acknowledged in the community of God with his creation. Certainty concerning God's self-disclosure in the Christ event is certainty that the Christ event is the self-disclosure of God as the ground of the being, reconciliation and salvation of creation. From the perspective which is

---

[8] Eilert Herms has stressed the fundamental importance of this principle as an essential element of the Reformers' conception of revelation in *Einheit der Christen in der Gemeinschaft der Kirchen*, Göttingen 1984, 95-128, especially 100ff.

established where the Gospel of Christ becomes certain as the foundation of faith, created reality as a whole becomes a disclosure situation - *ubi et quando visum est Deo*. The personally disclosed truth about God's self-disclosure in the Christ event includes certainty about God as ground, meaning and end of all created reality and makes thereby the whole of created reality the context of validation for the truth of revelation.

[C] God's action in creation, reconciliation and salvation has in Protestant theology from the Reformation onwards been described as 'self-giving'.[9] Since Hegel this notion has been explicitly integrated into the conception of God's revelation as self-revelation. God does not reveal propositions about God, God reveals himself. This interpretation of revelation must immediately be safeguarded against a possible misunderstanding. Self-revelation of God does not mean that God's self as it is present to God himself becomes now accessible to his creatures. Against such misinterpretations we have to hold fast to the intention of the doctrine of the *ineffabilitas Dei* that assertions made on the basis of God's relationship to creation can have a definite truth value, but do not express what is said about God in the way it is present to God himself. The concept of God's self-revelation is therefore to be interpreted both as the condition and as a restriction of human discourse about God.

What the concept of self-revelation as interpretation of the disclosure event is intended to express is that God discloses *who* he is, and that this self-communication of God, Father, Son and Spirit is at the same time the authentic disclosure of *what* God is, i.e. of his being. The interpretation of the Christ event as self-revelation claims, more precisely, that this event is, firstly, an event of self-identification in which the author of the disclosure event identifies himself in created reality, and that it is, secondly, an event of self-predication in which God communicates himself as the creator, reconciler and perfecter of the world.[10]

---

[9] The notion of divine self-giving is a central feature of Luther's exposition of the Apostles' Creed in the *Greater Catechism*; with reference to the being and work of the Father:'Denn da sehen wir, wie sich der Vater uns gegeben hat sampt allen Kreaturen und aufs allerreichlichste in diesem Leben versorget, ohne daß er uns sonst auch mit unaussprechlichen ewigen Gütern durch seinen Sohn und heiligen Geist überschüttet...'(*BSELK* 650); with reference to the Son:"Hie lernen wir die andere Person der Gottheit kennen, daß wir sehen, was wir über den zeitlichen Gütern von Gott haben, nämlich wie er sich ganz und gar ausgeschüttet hat und nichts behalten, das er uns nicht gegeben habe.'(*BSELK* 651) We can find a summary in the exposition of the work of the Spirit in the interpretation of faith:'...denn durch diese Erkenntnis kriegen wir Lust und Liebe zu allen Gepoten Gottes, weil wir hie sehen, wie sich Gott ganz und gar mit allem, das er hat und vermag, uns gibt zu Hülfe und Steuer, die zehen Gepot zu halten: der Vater alle Kreaturn, Christus alle sein Werk, der heilige Geist alle seine Gaben.' (*BSELK* 661) For the notion of the identity of subject and object in revelation in German Idealism cf. W.Pannenberg, *Systematische Theologie* Bd.I, Göttingen 1988, 244ff.

[10] For an anlysis of the concept of self-identification cf. I.U.Dalferth, *Kombinatorische Theologie. Probleme theologischer Rationalität*, Freiburg 1991, 126-128; and by the same author *Theology and Philosophy*, Oxford 1988,188-192.

Self-identification is distinguished from identification by another by the fact that it establishes an asymmetrical reciprocal relationship between the one who identifies himself and the one he identifies himself to. This implies that self-identification is only successful when the addressee of this identification can identify the one who identifies himself on the basis of his self-identification. Self-identification is therefore 'identification of somebody as himself for us' which enables us to identify the author of this self-identification. The identification of persons is neither completely possible through ostension nor through predication. Persons can only be identified through an identity description which depicts them as intentional agents and describes their intentional actions as the actualization of their intentions and therefore as an expression of their character.[11] We can call those communicative actions of persons acts of self-identification which present their personal identity by so depicting them as the authors of their intentional actions and as the bearer of the attributes expressed in these actions that they can be identified by others. The identity description of personal agents and the self-identification of persons has therefore always a historical (e.g. biographical) structure. In the case of self-identification this historical structure comprises not only the connection between the intentions of a person and the actions actualizing these intentions but also the communicative representation of this connection for the addressees of this self-identification.

This is precisely the structure of God's self-disclosure as God's self-identification. The message of Christ is the story identifying God in which God appears in the history and fate of Jesus as the agent enabling and determining Jesus' actions and passion. In Jesus' relationship to God, which is characterized by free obedience to the will of the Father, the prevenient relationship of God to Jesus is disclosed as that which makes possible Jesus' relationship to God; and in the story of Jesus, as it is shaped by God's action, God discloses his will and being. Jesus' identification of the God of Israel as the Father is validated in the resurrection of Jesus as the self-identification of God the Father which, at the same time, identifies Jesus as the Son of God. The self-identification of God in Jesus becomes God's self-identification for us when we are convinced of the truth of the Gospel of Christ. This happens where the Holy Spirit re-presents the history of God's self-identification in Jesus to the believer and in this way integrates the believer's history into the history of God's actions. By being granted insight into the truth of the Gospel of Christ as the narrative of God's self-identification believers are thus enabled to identify God as Father, Son and Spirit.

This formal description of God's self-identification is as yet incomplete since it does not take into account that identification is only possible on the basis of a person's actions where the identity of an agent is determined through the connection between intention and action in intentional action and, consequently, the unity of an agent with his or her actions expressed in this way. Self-identification therefore always includes self-predication or self-interpretation. By

---

[11] Cf. Thomas F.Tracy, *God, Action and Embodiment*, Grand Rapids 1984, 1-44 and 98-107.

identifying themselves persons also interpret what they are. The formal structure of God's self-identification as Father, Son and Spirit is closely connected to the content of God's action by which God shows himself to be the creator, reconciler and saviour of the world. The content of the Gospel of Christ is the reconciliation of the fallen creation through God's grace, that is, God's contradiction of the contradiction of humanity against God's will, and therefore the recreation of the relationship between God and creation which had been broken by humanity. The content of this has been expressed in various metaphors - as the victory over the powers of a demonized creation, as the restoration of the justice of God's creation through God's judgement over sin and as the self-surrender of the Son of God for the life of the sinner[12] - and is promised to believers when the truth of the Gospel of Christ is made certain through God the Spirit as the truth about their existence and as God's promise for the whole of creation. The self-predication of God which is part of God's self-identification discloses God, Father, Son and Spirit as creator, reconciler and saviour of creation. Where insight is granted to sinners about the truth of the Gospel of Christ, God the reconciler is identified as the creator who brings about the perfection of creation. This content is not external to God's self-revelation. The point of the concept of self-revelation is that the self-disclosure of God is the unified mode of the actualization of God's creative, reconciling and perfecting action. God's revelation has no other content than his action in creation, reconciliation and salvation, and this unity of the content and the mode of the actualization of God's action is expressed in the trinitarian self-identification of God, Father, Son and Spirit.

[D] According to our structural formula of the disclosure event summarized in the concept of revelation D stands for the recipient of God's self-communication in revelation. The concept of self-communication characterizes revelation as a process of communication for which a recipient is as constitutive as an author [A], a content [C] and a disclosure situation [B]. The disclosure event is directed, asymmetrical and irreflexive, but without the reception of God's self-communication one could not talk about revelation. 'Revelation' is in this sense a 'success word' (G.Ryle) which presupposes the reception of the communication (not, however its acknowledgement - unless one regards the grace of God as irresistible[13]). Just as the self-disclosure of God has a particular author and content and happens in a particular disclosure situation, so it is also not directed at somebody in general and nobody in particular, but it is addressed to particular persons. The universal content of divine self-revelation (God's will of salvation for the whole creation) and the universal truth claim of the Gospel of Christ in which this content is expressed does not contradict this particularity. This content becomes effective only in such a way that its universal claim is

---

[12] A detailed and illuminating analysis of the central metaphors of reconciliation is provided in Colin E. Gunton, *The Actuality of Atonement. A Study of Metaphor, Rationality and the Christian Tradition*, Edinburgh 1988.

[13] Concerning the problem of the irresistibility of grace cf. Vincent Brümmer, *Over een persoonlijke God gesproken. Studies in de wijsgerige theologie*, Kampen 1988, 92-119.

vindicated for particular people as the truth about the personal reality of their lives and about the reality of creation as a whole. The mode of the actualisation of the universal truth of God's revelation is its personal particularization in the activity of the Holy Spirit.[14]

The particularity of specific people as recipients of revelation is closely connected to the personal character of God's self-communication. The trinitarian self-communication of God, Father, Son and Spirit reveals his being as creator, reconciler and saviour in the mode of personal self-identification and personal self-predication. As the personal self-communication of God it addresses the recipients in their personal being in the relational constitution of human existence as a relationship to God, to the world and as a self-relationship.[15] Human beings are personal relational beings in that their existence is passively constituted by its relatedness to God the creator, reconciler and saviour as the ground of their existence, its truth and its freedom, by its relatedness to the world as a part of creation and by their relatedness to themselves and other persons in the reflexivity and sociality of human existence as the medium of its personal constitution. The specific distinction of humans in creation which the tradition expressed in the doctrine of the *imago Dei* has to be seen in the fact that human beings can relate actively and in finite freedom to the relational constitution of their being, to the passively constituted structure of relatedness. Human person-hood is realized in the mode of actively relating to God, to the world, to itself and other human persons and is therefore characterized by finite freedom. Human beings therefore are the creatures who can correspond to their creator or contradict their creator.

In God's self-communication the recipient of revelation is made accountable with regard to the abuse of created freedom. This abuse consists in denying in the act of actively relating to God and the world the passive constitution of human freedom as it is given in the structures of relatedness. In this way human beings confuse their created freedom with the creative freedom of God, and thus claim for themselves the place of God as the source of the relationships in which they exist. In consequence, human beings are dislocated in the network of their relational existence, not only in their relationship to God, but also in their relationship to themselves and to the world. The contradiction of God is therefore always also self-contradiction, the contradiction of the created destiny of human beings to correspond in their created freedom to the will of the creator. It is furthermore also contradiction of the world, that is, contradiction of the fact that

---

[14] Luther's catechetical explanations of the Creed emphasize this aspect very strongly, cf. the analysis in E.Herms, *Luthers Auslegung des Dritten Artikels*, Tübingen 1988.

[15] For this relational conception of theological anthropology cf. W.Härle, 'Die Recht-fertigungslehre als Grundlegung der Anthropologie', in W.Härle/E.Herms, *Rechtferti-gung. Das Wirklichkeitsverständnis des christlichen Glaubens*, Göttingen 1979, 78-100, and I.U.Dalferth/E.Jüngel, 'Person und Gottebenbildlichkeit', in: *Christlicher Glaube in moderner Gesellschaft*, Teilband 24, Freiburg 1981, 57-99. Cf. also my essay 'Human Being as Relational Being. Twelve Theses for a Christian Anthropology', in C.Schwöbel-C.E.Gunton (eds.), *Persons: Divine and Human*, Edinburgh 1991, 141-165.

the existence and constitution of creation is grounded in God's creative action. It therefore has the character of contradiction of the solidarity of co-createdness in which humans share with the whole of creation. The self-deception of human beings in the abuse of created freedom includes the fact that this deception cannot be overcome by humans, since it consists in the denial of the passive constitution of human freedom which can neither be constituted nor reconstituted by human action. The fact that the human contradiction of God cannot be overcome by human beings is an implication of the asymmetrical relationship between creator and creature. Every attempt at autonomously restoring the relationship between God and humanity by means of human action radicalizes the human contradiction of God instead of overcoming it.

The self-disclosure of God is therefore for its recipients the judgement of God over the contradiction o God as abuse of created freedom, the unveiling of the deception of sin and the confrontation of humanity with the demands of the creative will of God. It is, however, also the assurance of the grace of God towards the alienated human creature and the promise of justification as the reconstruction of authentic created freedom. Both aspects of God's self-disclosure come together insofar as the self-identification of God, Father, Son and Spirit and the self-predication of God as creator, reconciler and saviour are received as aspects of the one self-revelation of God. The event of revelation is for its recipients the revelation of God the creator who lets creation be and gives human creatures the specific destiny of created freedom by which they can and ought to respond to his will. And it is the revelation of God the reconciler who overcomes by his self-disclosure in Christ the power of deception and alienation and so enables the fallen human creature to accept as the gift of grace its finite freedom and the commission of obedience to the will of God. In the process of divine self-communication in revelation both these aspects are not separate for the recipient of revelation, but are disclosed together. The *creator* who lets creation be and gives human beings the destiny of actualizing their freedom in correspondence to the will of God, is disclosed as the reconciler who unveils their failure in actualizing the human destiny and discloses anew to human beings in the Gospel of Christ the truth about their destiny and its foundation in God's grace. The *reconciler* who overcomes the contradiction of sin in the freedom of his grace is disclosed as the *creator* whose will is the salvation of his creation. Since the creator is disclosed as the reconciler and the reconciler as the creator it becomes clear that the unity of creation and reconciliation is grounded in God's will for the *perfection* of creation and that the action of God in revelation is the mode of the actualisation of creation, reconciliation and perfection as they have their ground in God's will.

Through the content of God's self-disclosure its recipients are confronted with the *commission* of created personal being to exercise their created freedom in obedience to the will of God and they receive the *promise* of created personhood that the actualization of this commission rests on no other condition than the acknowledgment of God's grace as the ground of the possibility of created freedom. In the confrontation with the demand of personhood and the encounter with the promise for personhood the self-failure of fallen humanity is unveiled as sin and the possibility of self-fulfilment is promised as gospel. The fact that the recipients of revelation are addressed in God's self-disclosure in commission and promise includes not only that humans are destined to be persons, but also that they can be held accountable for their destiny and are able to actualize this call to for personhood - in self-failure or self-fulfilment. It has to be noted in this context that the personal and particular character of divine self-disclosure which we have sketched here in the conceptuality of Christian dogmatics always includes its concreteness. The call to true personhood is always the disclosure of *my* failure to be a person in the concrete reality of *my* life. And in the same way the promise of created freedom is the offer of fulfilled life in the concreteness of relationships which constitute my life. What is made possible for the recipient of revelation in this mode of divine self-disclosure is the active acknowledgement of the self-communication of God in faith.

[E] Where the self-communication C of the triune God as the author of revelation A in the Christ event B is actively acknowledged as commission and promise of authentic personhood by the recipient of revelation D, there faith as the *result* E of God's self-disclosure is made possible. There are two extreme interpretations of the result of God's self-disclosure which are inherently problematical. One the one hand, the passive constitution of the condition of the possibility of faith in the divine self-disclosure ought not to be extended to a description of faith as a purely passive mode of existence. This is a deterministic distortion of the constitution of faith where faith is seen as the effect of the causal action of the eternal God which by-passes the created freedom of human beings. In this misinterpretation of the passive constitution of faith the conception of a determinist 'calvinist' doctrine of predestination (which mis-understands Calvin) and the conception of a quietist 'lutheran' view of the life of justification faith as *vita passiva* (which misinterprets Luther) are surprisingly close. At the same time we have to avoid the equally problematical versions of Arminianism which has found growing popularity - often inspite of explicit disclaimers - in many forms of evangelical Christianity. Here faith is reduced to an act of decision which effectively denies the passive constitution of the condition of its possibility. The rejection of these two extreme forms of interpreting faith either purely passively or purely actively does, however, not yet exclude the equally problematical notions of mediating between a passive and an active conception of faith which have dominated the doctrine of grace in Western Christianity for the longest time of its history. The difficulty lies here in the interpretation of God and humanity as interacting conscious substantial entities whose interaction takes the form of cooperation. In this connection the grace of God, and that includes revelation, is described as an *auxilium* (*gratia operans*) to intend the good and to act accordingly which creates in human beings the disposition (*habituale donum*) to act in accordance with the divine will (*gratia cooperans*).[16] This exposition of the relationship of divine and human action immediately raises the problem that divine and human action are interpreted as consecutive stages in the process of divine-human action whose unity must be

---

[16] The classical exposition of this conception can be found in Thomas Aquinas *STh* I-II,111, 2. For an illuminating discussion of the problem cf. Robert Jenson 'The Holy Spirit' in Carl E.Braaten, Robert W.Jenson (eds.), *Christian Dogmatics*, Philadelphia 1984, vol.II, 105-178, especially 125-142.

described as the cooperation between God's grace and the human will. Faith becomes an attitude which is to be described partly as a divine act and partly as a human disposition.

In contrast to the separation of divine and human activity in some forms of post-Reformation theology, and over against the risk of its conflation in pre-Reformation theology we have to hold fast to the original insight of Reformation theology that the distinction between divine and human agency is the presupposition of its relationship. In this sense we have to say that the constitution of faith as the result of divine self-disclosure is wholly the work of God inasfar as the ground of the possibility of faith is the self-communication of God in vindicating the truth of the Gospel of Christ which constitutes believers passively in their personal being. Faith as a human form of life is wholly a human act insofar as it is the active acceptance and acknowledgement of God's self-communication as ground, norm and end of human personhood. Faith is the act of acknowledging that the condition of its possibility cannot be constituted by human action; because it is constituted in God's self-disclosing action, it can only be received passively. Faith is therefore the active acknowledgement of its passive constitution in God's revelatory action. Faith is this acknowledgement as unconditional existential trust in God, Father, Son and Spirit as the creator, reconciler and perfecter of the world, that is, trust in God as God gives himself in his self-communication as the ground and 'object' of faith.

1. Characterized in this way faith can be understood as the *existential relation* of unconditional trust in God as he discloses himself in the medium of the Gospel of Christ.[17] This trust is made possible by the Spirit as faith in Jesus Christ in whom God the Father gives himself to be known as the creative ground of everything there is. In this trinitarian structure Christian faith is trust in God the saviour who reconciles the alienated creation and in this way actualizes his creative will for the perfection of his creation. In faith human personhood, in which the human person is called to be as *imago Dei* ,is recreated in its intended form. In this sense faith is to be interpreted as an internal, real, reciprocal, but asymmetrical relation between the believer and God[18] which is expressed in the recognition of the relationship of God, Father, Son and Spirit to the justified human creatures as it is disclosed in revelation. This relationship of God to humanity becomes the reconstruction of personal freedom where human beings acknowledge God's relationship to his reconciled creatures which is established in revelation as the foundation of the relationship of human beings to God, to themselves and to the world. The reconstitution of personal freedom in faith is therefore, on the one hand, the liberation *from* the self-misunderstanding of sin where human freedom is understood as sovereign and unrestricted freedom whose exercise brings about various forms of domination, alienation and exploitation. It is, on the other hand, liberation *for* a form of action that corresponds to the destiny of humanity disclosed in revelation, and which accepts

---

[17] Cf. W.Härle, 'Widerspruchsfreiheit.Überlegungen zum Verhältnis von Glauben und Denken', *NZSTh* 28 (1986), 223-237.

[18] Cf. I.U.Dalferth, *Existenz Gottes und christlicher Glaube. Skizzen zu einer eschatologischen Ontologie*, München 1984, 240-255.

God's revelation as the determination of the ground, norm and end of all human action.

Faith as existential trust in God must also be seen as the overcoming of the dislocation of sin in which human beings claim the place of God and deny their relatedness to God as the foundation of their relationship to God, the world and to themselves. The self-disclosure of God as creator, reconciler and perfecter is therefore the definite *relocation* of humanity to its appropriate place in the relational structure of creation: as the reconciled creature called to perfection which is enabled to use its finite freedom in obedience to the will of God.

2. When we understand faith ontologically as an asymmetrical real and internal relation, it becomes clear that faith is not a marginal theme of ontology, but rather the fundamental ontological *datum* which defines the perspective from which an ontology can be developed in the reflection of Christian faith. The classical themes of ontology are given their place in the perspective of Christian faith as the framework for the explication of general ontological categories. This has a number of far-reaching implications which we can only sketch here very briefly. *First of all*, concepts of being have to be analyzed in such a way that they denote in the case of contingent created being the results of divine action and in the case of God's being the ground of the constitution of finite being. From this follows that the concepts in which a fully-fledged ontology is to be developed (objects, events, change, space and time etc.) have no primitive status, but have to be explicated in relation to the foundational concept of divine action and to the relationship of God and faith which is based on God's self-disclosure. This excludes, for instance, an analysis of the relationship between God and humanity as a relationship between two self-sufficient causally interacting substances. *Secondly*, it follows from giving ontological reflection its basis in the relationship between God and faith which is constituted in God's self-disclosure that 'being' and 'consciousness' may not be regarded as two totally separate dimensions of reality. Both have their foundation in God's trinitarian action and come together in God's self-disclosure. Their connection consists precisely in the fact that God communicates himself as the one who is the ground of the existence of the world and who discloses himself in created reality in such a way that faith can acknowledge the truth of this self-disclosure. Inasfar as God is both the ground of created being and the ground of true consciousness of the constitution of being, both concepts are correlative. This excludes an interpretation either 'being' or 'consciousness' exclusively as a function of the other. *Thirdly*, there is, for an ontology which is developed from the relationship between God and faith, no final disjunction between 'being' and 'meaning' so that, for instance, a world which is in itself meaningless only receives meaning through the imposition of meaning by an interpreter of reality. Since the self-disclosure of God implies the unity of his trinitarian action, the meaning of being is precisely the actualisation of the will of the creator in creation. Only the contraction of God's will for creation - that is, sin and its effects in the dislocation of the human in the relational order of created being - appears as meaningless.

3. The epistemic dimension of faith, the certainty and knowledge of faith, is rooted in the specific ontological distinction of faith. The understanding of God, of the world and of human being which is based on God's self-disclosure is the

epistemic correlate of the relationship to God, to the world and to themselves which is made possible for human beings in God's self-communication. In its epistemic dimension faith is the passively constituted certainty with regard to the truth of the Gospel of Christ as the correct depiction of the reality not only of faith itself, but of everything which has its ground in God's creative action. This certainty is explicated by presenting knowledge of faith as the exposition of the view of reality of Christian faith which is shared in the Christian community.[19] Knowledge of faith therefore has the status of an epistemic explication of the certainty of faith. As a fallible form of human knowledge, knowledge of faith is not identical with faith itself nor with the certainty of faith. It is rather an attempt at presenting the content and constitution of the certainty of faith in the medium of the conceptualities of contemporary thought. In contrast to the certainty of faith the propositions of the knowledge of faith have the status of truth claims whose justification is attempted in the explication of the view of reality of Christian faith. The propositions of the knowledge of faith are therefore in need of permanent reassessment. This assessment proceeds by inquiring whether the knowledge of faith can be seen as an appropriate interpretation of the certainty of faith as it is grounded in God's self-disclosure.

The knowledge of faith is epistemologically not simply identical with one of the forms of factual knowledge (about contingent states of affairs), conceptual knowledge (about the operation of symbolic systems of signs for signifying and ordering states of affairs and about the rules of conceptual operations), normative knowledge (about the norms, values and virtues which guide human action and its evaluation) and knowledge of reflection (about the self-knowledge of human agents in dealing with factual, conceptual and normative knowledge). As ontological knowledge the knowledge of faith is the foundation of all these forms of knowledge and determines their function. The knowledge of faith is therefore not to be seen as one specific form of knowledge alongside other forms of knowledge, but as the basis for the unity of knowledge which is presupposed in every form of knowledge. It has this status as the exposition of the basic certainty of human agents with regard to their constitution as finite agents destined to be personally free and to exist in a world which is open to their interpretation and organisation. The types of human knowledge which can be distinguished as factual knowledge, conceptual knowledge, normative knowledge and knowledge of reflection are specific forms of the cognitive interaction of human beings with the world. In their different forms they express specific implications of the ontological convictions contained in the knowledge of faith as the explication of fundamental personal certainty. All these forms of knowledge presuppose quite specific ontological structures of the world and of personal agents who interact with the world and with one another in acts of interpretation and organisation. The knowledge of faith in which these ontological structures are expressed is therefore both the basis for the

---

[19] For the concept of 'knowledge of faith' and the distinction between different types of knowledge below cf. I.U.Dalferth, *Kombinatorische Theologie* (note 10), 102ff. and 108ff.

differentiation and the place of the integration of the different forms of knowledge.

In the knowledge of faith ontological beliefs concerning the world and personal agents in the world are seen as grounded in God's relationship to the world and to humanity. This applies to the existence and structure of finite being as well as to our knowledge of it. Insofar as God is seen as the creative ground of being and of the knowledge of being, Christian knowledge of faith presents a view of reality which is not a special form of knowledge alongside other forms of knowledge, but which provides the fundamental framework of interpretation for all forms of knowledge. Therefore it expresses the boundary conditions which regulate operations with the different forms of knowledge according to the view of reality of Christian faith. In this way it offers as a central aspect of human agency guide-lines for dealing with the different forms of knowledge.

We can illustrate this with regard to the different forms of knowledge we have distinguished. Let us first take a look at factual knowledge and conceptual knowledge. Belief in creation which is explicated in the knowledge of faith entails, for instance, that the world is a contingent nexus of events which is not grounded in itself but in God's creative action. This ontological conviction of the contingent status of the created being of the world implies, furthermore, that the sequences of events in the world are accessible to experience-based forms of knowledge which are appropriate to the contingent regularities of the structures of a contingent world. Belief in the self-communication of God in the medium of created reality in the Christ event implies moreover that the created media of communication are capable of communicating true insight through acts of signification. This, in turn, implies that human acts of signification are capable of being true, that is, of correctly signifying reality as it is in its contingent structure and dynamic as they are constituted in God's creative action.

Christian certainty of faith not only has important implications for a view of what is the case and why there can be be correct signification, it also sees what is always in connection with its destiny determined by the will of God. Being is in this view never value-neutral, but is always being which is destined by God's action to find its fulfilment in God's intention for it. The view of reality of Christian faith which is explicated in the propositions of the knowledge of faith therefore also contains convictions about the norms, values and virtues that must be observed in human action if it is to correspond to the will of the creator as it is disclosed in God's self-revelation. The knowledge of faith not only provides a normative framework within which the conditions and guide-lines of human agency are explicated; it also asserts an intrinsic connection between being and obligation, between 'is' and 'ought', insofar as both are seen as grounded in the will of the creator.

The knowledge of faith finally also defines the boundary conditions of an adequate self-interpretation in human knowledge of reflection. According to the knowledge of faith the active capacity of human beings for reflection is not regarded as a primordial self-constituted fact, but it is seen as passively constituted for active subjects of reflection in God's self-disclosure. This implies that the true self-interpretation of human beings in their acts of reflection, consisting, as it were, in the acknowledgement of their passive constitution, can be distinguished from false self-interpretation denying this passive constitution.

In this way true self-interpretation is described as an implication of faith, whereas false self-interpretation appears as a symptom of sin. The knowledge of faith explicates the content and constitution of faith insofar as faith is based on the truth of the relationship of human beings to God, to the world and to themselves as it is disclosed in God's self-revelation. This explication proceeds as the development of a view of reality which claims to integrate all other forms of human knowledge in a coherent framework which demonstrates their legitimacy and justifiability, but which also indicates their limitations.

This exposition of the concept of revelation in Christian theology as the conceptual description of God's self-communication in the constitution of faith shows that the concept is highly complex, because the disclosure event it describes has a number of internally related dimensions. It is essential for the explication of the concept of revelation that it can be construed in such a way that God as the one who vindicates the truth of the Gospel of Christ is also the reconciler who, in his self-identification and self-predication in the Christ event, discloses himself as the one who is the ground of the being of creation and who by overcoming the alienation of created being leads it to perfection. The process of God's self-disclosure can receive a clear conceptual expression in the interpretation of the concept of revelation only if it can be shown that divine self-disclosure as the self-identification of God, Father, Son and Spirit is the self-interpretation of God as creator, reconciler and perfecter of creation. Only in this way it is possible to understand God's self-disclosure as the communication of his unitary will and to see this as an expression of his being. This opens up the possibility of understanding the essential unity of the content and the mode of actualisation of divine self-revelation.

In the doctrinal tradition of the Western church it is to a large extent customary to construe the unity of God's trinitarian action as its uniformity so that there is no functional difference between the work of the Father, the Son and the Spirit - a view which is often sanctioned by appeals to the slogan of the Augustinian tradition *opera trinitatis ad extra sunt indivisa*.[20] Apart from the Incarnation which was interpreted as solely the work of the Son, divine agency was seen as an, in principle, one-dimensional simple form of agency. Certain aspects could be appropriated to one of the trinitarian persons *de dicto*, but this did not signify the functional particularity of the action of this person in God's uniform agency. This has not only in many cases relegated the doctrine of the Trinity to an appendix of the doctrine of the one God, which is left to the austere speculation of experts or to the language of worship; it has also reduced the understanding of divine action to an understanding of agency based on the model

---

[20] Cf. R.W.Jenson, 'The Triune God', in C.E.Braaten/R.W. Jenson, *Christian Dogmatics* (note 16) vol.I, 79-191, especially 149ff. For a decisive critique of Augustine's interpretation of the Trinity and its consequences cf. 'Augustine, the Trinity and the Theological Crisis of the West', in: C.E.Gunton, *The Promise of Trinitarian Theology*, Edinburgh 1991, 31-57.

of efficient causality which led to manifold problems in connection with the mechanistic interpretation of reality in the Enlightenment.[21]

In contrast to this conception of the unity of divine action as uniformity, which abolishes the differentiation between the work of the Father, the Son and the Spirit, our reflections on the concept of revelation have a led to an understanding of the unity of divine action which does not eliminate the particularities of the work of the Father, the Son and the Spirit, but interprets them as constitutive aspects of divine action.[22] When creation is interpreted as a trinitarian act, the creative action of God is not only the bringing about of created being (according to the tradition the work of the Father in God's trinitarian action), but also the ordering of creation through the rationality of the Logos-Son, which is the ground of the rational structure of creation, and the energizing of creation through the life-giving power of the Holy Spirit. This is interpreted as the ground of the processual self-transcendence of life as well as the foundation of the capacity of creation, which is concentrated in humanity, to correspond to the will of the Father as it is mediated through the rational structure of creation. Where the Christ event is interpreted as a trinitarian act, it is asserted that it has its ground in the creative will of the Father. By being interpreted as the Incarnation of the Son, the Christ event is seen as the embodiment and 'inhistorisization' of the rationality which gives creation its structure from the beginning. The Incarnation appears in this way as the historical appearance of the rational order of creation in the medium of created reality. The work of the Spirit in the Christ event is emphasized where the Incarnation of the Son is interpreted as the overcoming of the powers of death rooted in the alienation of created life from God through the gift of eternal life in the Spirit. Through the Spirit created life is moved to correspond to the will of God the Father by the disclosure of the order and purpose of creation in the Son. The vindication of the truth of the Gospel of Christ through the Spirit is therefore the process in which the disclosure of the order and destiny of creation in the Incarnation of the Son, which reveals the Father as the creative ground of all being, becomes certain as

---

[21] An excellent illustration of these problems is Jonathan Edward's critique of the mechanistic interpretation of the metaphysics of substance in the Enlightenment, cf. R.W.Jenson, *America's Theologian. A Recommendation of Jonathan Edwards*, New York-Oxford 1988, especially 23-34.

[22] In contrast to the Augustinian thesis of the functional indiscriminateness of the three persons of the Trinity in divine action the Cappadocian founders of the doctrine of Trinity have insisted that each of the three trinitarian persons contributes to the unitary divine action in accordance with its personal particularity as it is constituted in the inner-trinitarian relatedness. In this sense, Basil distinguishes between the originating cause of everything there is, the Father, the creative cause, the Son, and the perfecting cause, the Spirit. (*De Spir.* XV,38) Calvin, who rediscovered many of the original insights of the Cappa-docians for the theology of the Reformation, has developed this distinction in his trinitarian theory of divine action in such a way that he ascribed to the Father the particular aspect of the origin of all action, to the Son the characteristic of wisdom, in which all occurrences are arranged in their rational order, and to the Spirit the effectiveness, power or energy of all action. (*Inst.* I,13,18)

foundation of the personal life of believers. They are in this way included in the victory of eternal life over the deadly effects of alienation from God. The self-disclosure of God the Father through the Son in the Spirit comprehends in this way the dimensions identified in the trinitarian description of God's agency: the disclosure of the Father as the creative ground of all being, the revelation of the Son as the Incarnation of the Logos in whom the rationality which determines creation from the beginning appears in created reality, and the disclosure of the Spirit who in vindicating the truth of the Gospel of Christ constitutes human existence as the form of life which can correspond to the revealed truth of its order and purpose and is in this way included in the eschatological perfection of creation.

The unity of the content and the mode of actualization of revelation which we characterized in the context of a trinitarian understanding of divine agency determines the systematic place of the concept of revelation in the context of Christian dogmatics. On the one hand, the explication of the concept of revelation presupposes the concepts of material dogmatics (as they are presented in the doctrine of creation, anthropology, Christology etc.), since revelation has no other content than the trinitarian God, the creator, reconciler and perfecter of the world. On the other hand, the explication of the concepts of material dogmatics presupposes the concept of revelation, since God's action in creation, reconciliation and perfection becomes the content of faith only through God's self-disclosure. The most appropriate way of doing justice to this interrelationship which follows from the unity of the content and the process of God's self-disclosure is not to discuss the concept of revelation in the prolegomena of Christian dogmatics, but to give it its systematic place in the doctrine of God, more precisely in the theory of divine action.[23] The justification of the concept of revelation in Christian theology should not therefore proceed by offering reasons for the *possibility* of revelation on the basis of already established epistemological principles. The preferred way of justifying the concept of revelation seems to be the rational reconstruction of the view of reality of Christian faith as the description of the relationship between human

---

[23] This proposal has already been made by Ronald F.Thiemann. 'Theology would be well advised to follow the logic of Matthew's identifying description by locating its justificatory account of God's prevenience neither in the *prolegomena* to theology nor in a separate doctrine of "God's Word" but within its account of God's identity. *The doctrine of revelation ought to be a subtheme within the doctrine of God.*' *Revelation and Theology* (note 2) 137. The reference to Matthew's gospel in the context of which Thiemann develops his narrative identity description of God indicates the restrictions of Thiemann's arguments for his proposal. The narrative identification of God on the basis of a paradigmatic biblical text and the subsequent interpretation of the Gospel as 'narrated promise' is insufficient for the interpretation of the concept of revelation in the framework of a 'non-foundationalist theology' as long as the ontological implications of such a conception are not developed. In this respect Thiemann's conception - in spite of its fundamental correctness and in spite of all its valuable insights - remains below the level of critical reflection found in those theological thinkers he accuses of 'foundationalism' (Locke, Schleiermacher, T.F.Torrance).

and divine action which presupposes the *actuality* of revelation as its basis. In considering the relationship of revelation and experience Christian theology therefore reflects on the relationship between the constitution and the content of the view of reality of Christian faith.

3 TOWARDS AN ANALYSIS OF THE CONCEPT OF EXPERIENCE

The concept of experience has, like the concept of revelation, a complex structure. The tendency to ignore this complexity and to reduce it by proposing a simplified conception of experience is one of the main reasons for the manifold difficulties which have accompanied reflection on the concept of experience in modern theology. Ever since John Locke proclaimed experience to be the foundation of all knowledge and all true beliefs,[24] a claim which seems to have been amply validated by the establishment and progress of the empirical sciences, the theme of experience has become the central arena in which theology is called to justify critically and constructively its claims to knowledge and its claims concerning the plausibility of its propositions. This does not imply that theology has to provide a justification of its claims to knowledge within the framework of a presupposed non-theological epistemology. The history of modern endeavours to develop an appropriate conception of revelation offers ample evidence - starting from Locke himself - for the failure of attempts to secure a place for revelation in epistemological conceptions whose reductionist concepts of experience cause such attempts to founder. This should not have the consequence of circumventing the theme of experience in reflecting on problems of theological epistemology. Theological conceptions which refrain from engaging with the problems of the concept of experience are not only unable to meet the challenge of their intellectual milieu. They also pay for their abstinence with regard to experience with the epistemological and, in the last resort, ontological opacity of their conceptions. I will try in this section to sketch the complex structure of experience in an analysis of the concept of experience, in order to provide a foundation for reflecting on the relationship between experience and revelation. Our approach is to develop the complex structure of experience from an analysis of elementary aspects of the act of experience. This procedure has the aim of overcoming common reductionist conceptions of experience by demonstrating that they are partial aspects of the complex structure of experience which is expressed in the concept of experience.

Prima facie the concept of experience seems to have a very simple structure, i.e. that of a relation between the two terms of the subject of experience A and the object of experience x:

A experiences x

---

[24] Cf. the famous passage in Locke's *An Essay Concerning Human Understanding* (1690) where Locke summarizes the answer to the question 'whence the understanding may get all the ideas it has' in the emphatic expression 'from EXPERIENCE'. (New York 1959, Vol.I, 121f.). For a systematic analysis of the history of philosophical reflection on the concept of experience cf. the concise exposition in E.Herms' article 'Erfahrung II. Philosophisch', *TRE* X (1982) 89-109.

However, both of the terms of the relation, the experiencing subject and the object of experience cannot be understood as 'simple' entities related by experience. Even superficial consideration shows the object of experience to be a complex 'object': 'Something' becomes an object of experience by being interpreted as something, which involves that it is structured according to specific guiding criteria by the subject of experience.[25] In basic processes of perception a certain bundle of sensory stimuli which affect our sensory apparatus is isolated and becomes the object of our perceptual attention in the context of our 'holistic' bodily indwelling of our environment. This process is an interaction between our being passively affected by the stimuli of the object of perception and our active isolation of this particular 'something' by directing our attention at it. In this process our comprehensive bodily interaction with the world which comprises conscious as well as preconscious dimensions functions as the backdrop against which we select a specific object of attention as a response to being affected by it.[26] This whole process is characterized by irreducible individuality, both with regard to the individual 'something' which is the perceptual 'object' as well as with regard to myself as the individual perceiving subject. Perceptions are always individual. This specific individual character of perceptions presupposes our general involvement in and interaction with our environment which includes the possibility of being affected by sensory stimuli and the capacity for focussing our attention by isolating particular, relatively coherent units of perception. Even the most basic processes of perception presuppose the fundamental accessibility of the world for experiencing subjects and the openness of subjects of experience for being affected by the world which is presupposed in perception.

If the concept of experience were to be reduced to these basic processes of perception, it could in no way function as the foundational organizing concept for all human knowledge. The basic situation of perception as we have described it is not an exemplary case of our 'normal' experience which is usually far more complex. In fact, we have to create such simple situations of perception artificially by excluding the complexity of experience in a controlled environment as in certain types of scientific experiments or in optometric or

---

[25] The thesis that all experience can be analyzed as 'experiencing-as' has been developed by John Hick on the basis of Wittgenstein's analysis of 'seeing-as' in ambiguous situations of perception (Jastrow's famous duck-rabbit) and it forms the basis for Hick's interpretation of faith as the interpretative element in religious experience. Cf. *Faith and Knowledge,* 2nd. ed. Ithaca 1966, Glasgow 1974, especially 95-148. In Hick's epistemological theory this thesis is bound up with an extreme kantian disjunction of *phenomena* and *noumena,* of experience and things-in-themselves which in its application to the concept of God (the Real, Ultimate Reality etc.) forms the foundation of his theory of religious pluralism. In this respect the reflections in this chapter are directly opposed to Hick's conception.

[26] The integration of the subconscious and pre-conscious dimensions of our indwelling of our environment into the epistemological debate is one of the great achievements of Michael Polanyi's 'Theory of Tacit Knowing'. Cf. Andy F.Sanders, *Michael Polanyi's Post-Critical Epistemology. A Reconstruction of Some Aspects of Tacit Knowing',* Amsterdam 1988.

audiometric tests. However, the concept of experience can only function as the foundational concept for understanding our epistemic interaction with the world if it can depict its factual complexity. The attempt to reduce experience to perception, which is a feature of certain types of empiricism and which has the consequence that neither the objectivity of the objects of experience nor the subjectivity of the experiencing subject can be conceptualized in its factual complexity, is a classic example of a 'revisionary' metaphysics which prescribes what can be the case instead of attempting to reconstruct our factual interaction with reality.[27]

Our 'normal' situation of experience is, however, not limited to isolating something which can then be signified and described. It usually consists of interpreting something 'as something' in basic acts of predication so that we come to the structural formula:

A *experiences x as y*

In this process of conceiving 'something' 'as something' the set of sense data which we have isolated as a particular object of perception is constituted as an object of experience by the use of general predicates. The paradigmatic case for such basic synthetic acts of predication is the classification where the object of perception x is subsumed as an element under the class y and thereby acquires object status. Viewed formally, this process functions according to specific rules which can be formulated in a table of categories. In this synthesis of experience a specific object of perception is signified, not, however, by an individual name, but by a general predicate. The synthesis of experience can therefore be expressed as a proposition which follows the logical form f(x): This x is a y.

General concepts which function as predicates, however, do not exist in an isolated manner for themselves, but form part of a complex network of predicates and other interpretative concepts which is constituted by specific rules of predication and interpretation. The relation of experience can therefore be expressed as the process of integrating a specific object of perception into an interpretative framework by interpreting it as something:

· A *experiences x as y by integrating x through the predication as y*
 into the interpretative framework I

The function of such an interpretative framework is to provide certain general concepts such as predicates, to offer a structured order for the predicates it contains and to present specific rules for the synthesis of individuals and general predicates.[28] This framework of interpretation is constitutive for experience, insofar as it brings the atomistic particularity of objects of perception into forms of ordered generality. This applies both to the object and the subject of perception. The object of perception is integrated through the synthesis of experience into the objectivity of the world of experience and the subject of experience takes part in the trans-individual structuring of sense experience in a

---

[27] For the term 'revisionary metaphysics' cf. P.F.Strawson, *Individuals. An Essay in Descriptive Metaphysics*, London (1959) 1974, 9ff. Strawson's general distinction between 'revisionary' and 'descriptive' metaphysics is very illuminating, but his classification of particular philosophies as 'descriptive' or 'revisionary' is debatable.

[28] Cf. I.U.Dalferth, *Religiöse Rede von Gott* (note 7), 460ff.

community of interpretation. The linguistic, or, at least, semiotic character of the synthesis of experience points to the fact that this synthesis is made possible through the social communicative action of persons.

It is possible to analyze the function of this frame of interpretation in purely formal terms with regard to the formal characteristics of the operations which can be performed by means of general concepts as predicates. This attempt would lead to a table of categories or one of its functional equivalents. In real situations of experience these formal characteristics are, however, always part of a material interpretative framework which comprises specific interpretative models and paradigms which are themselves expressions of the belief-systems that are dominant in a specific socio-cultural context at a particular time. This framework of interpretation is therefore always historically concrete. It confronts us as a tradition of interpretation which is shaped by the cultural, social and scientific presuppositions of its origin and its contemporary application. In a tradition of interpretation we find that certain ways of organizing predicates in models and of summarizing them in comprehensive paradigms are provided which constitute the material conditions of the synthesis of experience. The interpretative models of modern particle physics, post-Freudian psychoanalysis or modern medicine offer different conditions of interpretation and therefore different conditions for the synthesis of experience than Lavater's physiognomy or Galen's art of healing - even though they follow formally identical categorical conditions for this synthesis.

This interpretative framework can comprise in itself several regional frameworks of interpretation which are specifically designed to meet the requirements of aspects of a highly differentiated culture. It provides with its predicates and structuring models for our experience the conditions for the interpretation of reality and, with that, the conditions for our active organisation of reality. It therefore shapes the total situation of human action in the world. Although the synthesis of experience which is made possible through the social, cultural and semiotic framework of interpretation in a particular community of interpretation is an active and constructive process - we make experiences, we do not receive them - it is, nevertheless not arbitrary. Both the success of acts of the synthesis of experience and of the theoretical constructs based upon them and their failure indicates that there remains a difference between what is claimed as experience and reality as the sum of what can be experienced. The propositional structure of experience in every act of the synthesis of experience therefore implies that each synthesis is confronted with the alternative of 'true' or 'false'. The act of predication can either correctly interpret reality or it can fail to do so. And this does not only apply to individual cases of the synthesis of experience, but also to whole sections of the interpretative framework, and perhaps even to the interpretative framework in its entirety. This shows that the question of truth cannot be elided simply by declaring that truth and falsity are always intra-systematic. The success of the natural sciences, the fact of real progress in our knowledge of the world, could not be explained if truth and falsity were not real alternatives for our acts of experience and interpretation.

So far we have not looked directly at the subject of experience. The type of empiricism that restricts the concept of experience to sense-experience of 'external' sense data elevates this abstraction from the subject of experience to a methodological principle which leads to the virtual equation of experience and perception. Where, however, experience is described as the active synthesis of objects of perception and general predicates which are provided by an interpretative framework, inquiry into the status and role of the subject of experience cannot be circumvented. Experience is thereby not only regarded as the process of the constitution of 'objects', it is also the process in which the possibility of experience as it is given to human subjects is actualized. It cannot be denied that in the complex processes of the synthesis of experience the subject of experience develops as an agent of acts of interpretation with increasing competence in the practice of interpretation. If one describes this process from the observer's perspective as the evolution of cognitive competence, this can create the impression that this process should be interpreted directly as the genesis of the subject of experience. This, however, confronts us with the difficulty that the genesis of the subject of experience is derived from certain experiences so that experiences are interpreted as the condition of the possibility of experience. In order to avoid this contradiction it is advisable to distinguish the question of the condition of the possibility of experience from the question of the development of cognitive and interpretative competence in the complex processes of the synthesis of experience. The achievement of cognitive competence as the genesis of a complex structure of the subject of experience is the actualization of the possibility for experience which is given for the subject of experience. It belongs to the field of developmental psychology, whereas the question of the constitution of the subject of experience as the question of the condition for the possibility of experience has its place in philosophical epistemology.

When we inquire about the subject of experience not from the observer's perspective of empirical research, but from the perspective of the subject of experience, it becomes clear that the act of the synthesis of experience does not occur automatically according to fixed and necessary rules. We are capable of employing the predicates and models of the interpretative framework selectively and creatively. The subject of experience is therefore to be interpreted as an agent of intentional actions, i.e. as a self-conscious personal subject. It is therefore inevitable to assume that reflexive self-experience can accompany all acts of the synthesis of experience. In consequence, we have to expand our formula for the structure of the concept of experience:

(A experiences) A experiences x as y, insofar as x is integrated
into the interpretative framework I by interpreting it as y

Self-experience is present in all acts of the synthesis of experience. Therefore we have to say that the interpretative framework is not only communicated in the medium of social communication and interaction, it also exists only in the form of personal appropriation. The social tradition of interpretation is represented for the subject of experience as the connection between remembered practice of interpretation and action in the past and the expectation which this elicits for the future practice of interpretation. Subjects of experience are temporally present to themselves insofar as their present practice is shaped by memory and expectation of interpretative acts in the past and in the future. This continuity of self-experience is one of the determinative factors for the constitution of the world of experience for experiencing subjects. In this continuity of their self-experience subjects of experience are also subjects of reflection because they consciously and reflectively select from their memory of the past experience of interpretation elements which shape their expectations for their present and future practice of interpretation. In the reflective synthesis of experience the act of interpretation becomes an act of freedom, of the intentional selection of predicates and models for the practice of experience. This freedom in the interpretation of experience turns the practice of experiential interpretation into an act of conveying meaning by constituting the coherence of the world of objects of experience as well as the coherence of the practice of of interpretation.

Freedom and meaning as constitutive elements of the self-experience of subjects of experience provide important insights into personal experience and interaction. Reflective self-experience not only discloses to the subject of experience its own capacity for the interpretation and interaction with its environment in free intentional action; it also discloses its ability to enter into personal relations with other personal agents who demand acknowledgement as self-experiencing personal subjects of experience. In our life-story this happens when other persons relate to us as personal agents and challenge us by means of their personal interaction with us to respond to them in personal communication. Personal interaction is distinguished from other modes of interaction with non-personal entities in that it presupposes the mutual acknowledgement of the partners of communication as self-experiencing agents. This mutual acknowledgement finds expression in the mutuality of receptivity and spontaneity in personal relations. Personal interaction is therefore for self-experiencing agents the context where they experience their own personal freedom as being provoked and elicited as well as being shaped and limited by the personal freedom of others. Personal experience implies therefore not only the experience of A in self-experience as a subject of experience, it also presupposes the acknowledgement of B as a self-experiencing subject of experience.

A experiences B

implies therefore

(A experiences) A experiences x as y by integrating x through the
predication as y into the interpretative framework I

and it presupposes

(B experiences) B experiences x as y by integrating x through the
predication as y into the interpretative framework I

so that we arrive at the full structural formula

A[=(A experiences) A experiences x as y by integrating x through
the predication as y into the interpretative framework I] ex-
experiences
B[=(B experiences) B experiences x as y by integrating x through
the predication as y into the interpretative framework I]

The awareness of ourselves and others as agents of personal freedom accompanies our practice of interpretation in the synthesis of experience across the whole range of our activity. It is important to note that this self-consciousness of freedom is only given in the sociality of human life where our freedom is elicited and restricted by other personal agents. Only in this context do we experience the mutuality of receptivity and spontaneity which constitutes personal freedom and the the social communication that underlies our practice of experience. The interchange with other persons in personal communication also illustrates one essential element of our free and intentional agency in all process of experience. The constitutive mutuality and reciprocity of personal relations presupposes that neither my own freedom nor the freedom of the other is self-created or self-produced. Furthermore, it is impossible to conceive of ourselves as creators of the freedom of others or the other person as the creator of my freedom without denying the free reciprocity of personal relations. In personal relations my freedom and the freedom of the other person is therefore exercised, recognized and acknowledged as something that is already there, that is not constituted in personal relations, although it is perhaps actualized and reconstructed.

This points to a crucial element in the make-up of self-conscious personal agents of acts of experience: our freedom is not something that is constituted in our free intentional action. It has to be presupposed as already given. As we have seen, freedom implies not only the capacity for free intentional action and personal communication, but also self-experience as the underlying reflexive awareness of ourselves as free experiencing subjects. The condition for the possibility of self-experience appears in the personal experience of freedom as something that is given in, with and under all acts of experience, but not as constituted by the subject of reflection. Post-Kantian philosophy has identified this condition for the possibility of freedom therefore as the reflexivity of which the subject of experience is aware in immediate self-consciousness as the necessary condition for the possibility of experience. This insight has important ontological implications. It entails that for all subjects of experience there is a difference between what is constituted for the experiencing subject and what is constituted by the experiencing subject. And this difference is interpreted as a transcendental relation: what is constituted for the experiencing subject is the condition of the possibility of what is constituted by the experiencing subject in all acts of the synthesis of experience.[29]

Here we are at the crucial point of all modern theories of experience. The fact that reality can be experienced by actively reflecting and interpreting subjects of experience is in itself an essential element of its ontological constitution. This fundamental openness of reality for the active processes of interpretation which constitute experience implies that experience and reality can no longer be contrasted as entirely separate entities. Reality itself has to be understood as the sum of what can be experienced, as the sum of all possible experience. Reality can therefore be interpreted as the experience of reality in the reality of experience. On this view, experience becomes an ontological concept, and this we can see in a veritable tradition of modern thought from Berkeley to Hegel, to

---

[29] Eilert Herms has in this connection spoken of the 'two layers' of the constitution of experience ('Zweischichtigkeit' der Erfahrungskonstitution). This is intended as a critique of both an epistemology which describes the constitution of experience exclusively as a result of human activity and an approach which reduces human activity to mere receptivity in the constitution of experience in the 'disclosure of being' (Heidegger). Cf. *Theologie - eine Erfahrungswissenschaft*, München 1978, 44ff.

Charles Sanders Peirce, Josiah Royce and Alfred North Whitehead.[30] The fundamental upshot of this is that the constitution of experience has to be understood as proceeding on two levels: on the level of what is constituted for the experiencing subject as the condition of the possibility of what is constituted by the experiencing subject on the second level. The crucial difficulty of modern theories of experience is to try to keep these two levels together: neither to deny the active constitution of experience in the interpretative reflective acts of the synthesis of experience nor to deny the passive constitution of this active capacity of experience. Many strands of modern epistemological reflection are dominated by an unrestricted absolutism of human action in the constitution of experience, others, like Heidegger's later philosophy, emphasize the contingent and for human subjects purely passive disclosure of truth as an event of being which is essentially unrelated to the human practice of experience.

It seems that this is a highly unsatisfactory state of affairs which obscures the task of adequately relating the two levels of the constitution of experience. The self-experience of freedom can again be a help in approaching this task. The ground of freedom and its constitution for free agents is something that is not self-produced by the free agents themselves. It can only be passively received, but it is received as the condition for the possibility of the active exercise of freedom. Because human freedom excludes the possibility of self-constitution it is never absolute and infinite, but always relative and finite. The active exercise of freedom in the acts of the synthesis of experience is therefore never arbitrary. The active determination of the content of experience in our acts of interpretation and reflection and our acts of self-determination are confronted with the alternative of either being in accordance with what reality is in and for itself as what can be experienced or in contradiction to it. The free act of the synthesis of experience is always confronted with the question of truth as the correspondence between what is constituted for the subject of experience and what is constituted by the subject of experience. Our experience is always fallible, precisely because the condition for its possibility is not self-produced and because our freedom of interpretation and action is not absolute and infinite, but relative and finite. Our experience as the active synthesis of experience has the capacity for truth which consists in the correspondence of our determination of particular being as something with the determination of this particular being in itself and for itself.[31] There is ample evidence for this capacity for truth in the real progress of knowledge which we see, for instance, in the sciences. But together with this,

---

[30] According to Herms the development of the concept from an epistemological to an ontological concept is the result of its modern history of reflection and can be seen as an interpretation of the conception of revelation in the theology of the Reformers. 'Die ontologischen und kosmologischen Entwürfe of Berkeley, Schleiermacher, Hegel, Peirce, Royce können sämtlich als - jeweils auf ihre Sachgemäßheit hin kritisch zu überprüfende - Versuche einer begrifflichen Explikation des reformatorischen Verständnisses von Welt als Selbstwort ihres Schöpfers gelesen werden." (art. 'Erfahrung IV. Systematisch-theologisch', *TRE* X 1982, 128-136.)

[31] With regard to the relationship between the concept of truth, criteria of truth and procedures of verification cf. my article 'Wahrheit', in *Taschenlexikon Religion und Theologie*, 4th ed. 1983 V, 283-289.

there is also ample evidence for error and falsity from the history of our interaction with the world. The fact that we can (eventually) distinguish between them shows both the basic correctness of a realist conception of truth as well as the, at least partial, success of some of our methods of validation.

We have arrived at an interpretation of the concept of experience where experience is understood as the determination of reality as an object of experience and certainty by interpreting and organising subjects on the basis of the disclosedness of reality for the signifying acts of self-experiencing subjects of perception and interpretation. By construing the concept of experience as an ontological concept we have reached the stage where the full complexity of the concept which we have attempted to sketch becomes apparent. I do not claim that the concept of experience can only be construed in this way. However, I have tried to show that a theory of experience must be able to offer a reconstruction of the different structures and layers of experience if it is to do justice to the complexity of the concept of experience.

We can retrace our steps briefly by going through the successive stages of developing the multi-layered structure of the concept of experience. When experience is identified with perception, the active structuring of experience by the subject of experience is ignored, and the understanding of reality is reduced to the exposition of a mechanism of stimulus and response. The object-structure of reality and the contingent regularities of events in reality cannot be adequately conceived. When experience is interpreted as the synthesis of the object of perception and general predicates, the concept of experience can elucidate the structure of perceived reality and can explain reality as the 'objective' reality of commensurable events whose connections can be described in general empirical statements. What can be grasped in this way is the object-structure of reality within the bounds of sense. It is construed as the result of the synthesis of experience. The active ordering of reality by the subject of experience is interpreted as the condition for the possibility of the 'objective' order of reality, but this activity is not in itself accessible to human knowledge. The active ordering of reality only becomes accessible in the self-experience of the subject of experience where reflection is experienced as the condition for the possibility of experience. The view of reality can now comprehend both the structure of reality and the process of the structuring of reality in the self-conscious free action of the subject of experience. The interpretative activity of personal subjects can itself be conceived as part of reality and as the key to its object-structure. Together with the self-experience of the experiencing subject the horizon opens for the personal experience of other persons as self-experiencing subjects who communicate with us in personal communication. With that we gain insight into the constitution of the practice of interpretation in the personal communication of reflecting subjects which is presupposed in the acts of predication in the synthesis of experience. The experience of other persons as free subjects of reflection and experience illustrates the basic aspect of the self-experience of the subject of reflection, that the activity of reflection as the basis of the intentional synthesis of experience presupposes reflexivity as the condition of its possibility. This enables us to understand reality as the sum of possible experience which is in its different layers open for the acts of signification, interpretation and judgement by subjects of experience. The determinateness of reality in and for itself is the condition for the possibility of its correct determination by subjects of experience.

When we present the concept of experience in this hierarchical structure of different layers it becomes clear that experience should be conceived as the foundational concept of a theory of human agency which does not only explicate epistemic acts, but the totality of human agency. The relationship between the disclosedness of reality in its determinateness in and for itself and the determination of reality in the acts of interpretation and organisation of free agents comprises all dimensions of human action in all spheres of culture. At the same time it becomes clear that human agency in all spheres of action presupposes as the condition of its possibility the existence of reality (including the agent) as an in itself and for itself meaningfully ordered field of the exercise of finite freedom in meaningful acts of interpretation and organisation, which is passively given to the agent. We have now reached the interface between the concept of experience and the concept of revelation. Their relationship can be stated in the following thesis: the concept of revelation as the basic concept of a theory of divine action explicates what is passively given as the condition of its possibility for experience which can be conceived as the basic concept of a theory human action: the disclosedness of reality for the interpretation and organisation of human subjects of experience which is capable of expressing truth. Theologically the disclosedness of reality which is presupposed in experience as the ground of its possibility is interpreted as grounded in the free and contingent revelatory action of God.[32]

4 THE RELATIONSHIP BETWEEN 'REVELATION' AND 'EXPERIENCE'

We have arrived at the thesis that the concept of revelation (as the basic concept of a theory of divine agency) expresses the event of disclosure which is the condition of the possibility of experience (as the basic concept of a theory of human agency) by explicating the complex structure of both concepts. Now it has to be shown that this conceptual analysis can be confirmed by reflection on the concrete content of Christian revelation. Only in this way can the fruitfulness of an approach from the analysis of both concepts be validated. The test for systematic-theological reflection is whether the proposals concerning the analysis of 'revelation' and 'experience' can claim to offer - at least in important respects - a reconstruction of what is expressed in the context of the practice of Christian faith with 'experience' and 'revelation'.

---

[32] According to Herms the ontological conception of experience as the total situation of the exercise of finite freedom enables us to see revelation and experience characterized by their different relationship to *one* subject-matter:'...dieser Begriff von Erfahrung und der theologische Begriff von Offenbarung haben denselben Gegenstand - die Existenz von Welt als Praxissituation -, den sie nur unter verschiedenen, aber gleichursprünglichen Aspekten bestimmen: unter dem Aspekt seines unverfügbaren Konstituiertwerdens als offenbarendes Handeln Gottes; und unter dem Aspekt des durch dieses Handeln Gottes gesetzten Werkes: eben der Praxissituation endlicher Freiheit. ('Offenbarung und Erfahrung' [Ms.] 21)

When we now attempt to explicate the understanding of revelation in Christian theology in the context of the concept of experience and, conversely, the concept of experience in the context of the Christian conception of revelation, it seems appropriate to start from the Christ event as the fundamental disclosure event for Christian faith. In this way we can present important elements of the revelation of Christ in their relationship to the structure of the concept of experience. The different strands of the proclamation, interpretation and explication of the Gospel of Christ in the New Testament show that the Christ event is presented as a particular experience in the light of which the universal truth about God's relationship to humanity and the world is disclosed. This particular experience includes all aspects which we have tried to develop in the analysis of the concept of experience. The testimonies of Jesus' history and fate emphasize in their different forms the perceptual basis of the interpretative experience of Jesus in the exposition of his historical appearance as it is perceived by concrete witnesses. This emphasis on the aspect of perception in the Christ event which already characterizes the earliest forms of the Gospel of Christ relates everything that can be said about Jesus to the perception of historical existence. This applies both to Jesus and to the witnesses of his appearance. For all christological statements in which the Gospel of Christ is presented the perceived historical existence of Jesus is a necessary, but not sufficient, condition of their truth.

The basic forms of christological statements follow the pattern of all predication as the synthesis of experience by predicating particular title-terms of Jesus. The concrete individual, x, who can be identified by the proper name Jesus, is predicated as y through the christological title-terms. These predications refer to the whole impression of the proclamation, activity, suffering, death and resurrection of Jesus. They presuppose the message of Jesus of the coming of the Kingdom of God, his *praxis* which witnesses to the coming of the Kingdom in the present, his testimony of God as the loving Father, his self-surrender to the will of the Father in the obedience of the death on the cross and the event of his being raised from death. All these intrinsically connected aspects of Jesus' story are interpreted in the predication of particular title terms of Jesus in such a way that his history and fate is integrated into a specific framework of interpretation which relates Jesus to God, to humanity and to the world. The integration of the Christ event into the already existing interpretative framework of the faith of Israel indicates the decisive role of contemporary beliefs and convictions of faith for the Christ event as a particular experience, and points to the essential connection between Christian faith and the faith of Israel. These beliefs and convictions of faith include the fundamental assertions about the relationship between God, world and humanity which determine as the interpretative framework the possibilities for the interpretation of the Christ event.

These common convictions which form the interpretative framework of christological predications and which could be very differently conceived in different traditions and religious groups can be summarized in the following way:[33]

God is seen as the creator, reconciler and perfecter of the world who calls the world as a contingent creation into being and brings it to perfection in the revelation of his righteousness.

The world is ordered by God in a specific way and is entrusted to humanity for its care so that human beings can in their actions do the will of the creator in acting in accordance with the order of creation. The world is therefore an ordered structure in which the deeds of humans have their appropriate consequences and can lead to salvation or perdition. However, this world order is disrupted and violated by the abuse of finite human freedom so that the world as a whole is in need of salvation through God's action.

Human beings have the created destiny to do the will of the creator and maintain as God's representatives the integrity of creation. In its contradiction against God and, with that, against the world order which makes righteousness and salvation possible, humanity is constantly threatened by the consequences of this contradiction. Orientation is provided only by trusting in the faithfulness of the creator in granting Israel as his covenant people through his commandments insight into his will of the creator and the order of creation. The self-understanding of humans is therefore fundamentally determined by the question of how it is possible to do God's will for creation in righteous works which can be acknowledged by God in judgement and enable those who follow the commandments to participate in God's righteousness.

These basic convictions can be developed and emphasized in various ways. For the specific material interpretation of the Christ event in the New Testament the radicalization of these beliefs in Apocalypticism are very significant. Apocalypticism in its various strands radicalized, on the one hand, the consequences of the fall of humans by describing it as universal cosmic catastrophe which negatively prejudges any attempt to do God's will in this aeon and in this way disqualifies this world as the place of the actualization of God's will. On the other hand, Apocalypticism stresses the universality of the revelation of God's righteousness for the whole of creation in the judgement of this aeon and in the break-through of the new aeon.

These convictions of the interpretative framework of christological predication contain particular beliefs about the relationship between God, world and humanity, its intended order and its distortion. The interpretative framework, furthermore, comprises beliefs about the victory of the righteousness God and about the way in which the contradiction of humanity against the will of the creator is overcome when the righteousness of God is made victorious. These

---

33 This exposition of the basic convictions presupposed in the predication of Jesus as the Christ can only indicate the formal structure of believers' understanding of God, the world and of themselves. Their particular material interpretation differs in particular groups of texts and religious communities und would require in each case a far more detailed analysis. For Pauline theology as a representative case of the interaction between interpretative framework and disclosure even cf. 'Grundriß der paulinischen Rechtfertigungslehre' in W.Härle/E.Herms, *Rechtfertigung* (note 15), 16-40.

beliefs form the matrix of christological predication. When these traditional notions are applied to the witness of Jesus' life, his death on the cross and his resurrection, in christological predications, certain fundamental statements of the interpretative framework are explicitly affirmed in the synthesis of experience, while others are radically corrected in the light of the story of Jesus of Nazareth.[34] Explicitly affirmed is the understanding of the creative power of God who is the sole ground of being, righteousness and salvation. Expressly affirmed is also the understanding of the bondage of humanity in the power of sin. However, both notions are now radicalized in such a way that God who is seen as the exclusive ground of creation is also interpreted as the exclusive ground of a righteousness which excludes the possibility that human beings could offer their own and independent contribution to the victory of the righteousness of God by keeping the commandments. This radicalization has both negative and positive implications. The negative aspect can be seen in the resurrection of the *crucified one* who is sentenced according to the law, and whose resurrection and exaltation represents the judgement of God over the use of the law as the way of salvation. The positive aspect is also expressed in the message of the *resurrection* of the crucified one: that God has restored in the cross and resurrection of Jesus Christ the broken relationship between creator and creation so that faith in Jesus Christ is confirmed as the true way of salvation.

The dialectics between the interpretative framework which is presupposed in christological predication and the christological predication itself and which, in turn, leads to the modification of the interpretative framework, illustrates the relationship between the particular experience of the Christ event and the general interpretative framework. The revision of the basic assumptions of the interpretative framework becomes necessary because the core of the christological predication, certainty with regard to the acknowledgement of Jesus as the Christ or certainty with regard to the resurrection of the crucified one, is neither inductively inferred from the data of the history and fate of Jesus nor deduced as the conclusion from the premises of the interpretative framework. It is the result of a particular disclosure event, and God (very soon in the history of Christian thought it is stated more specifically: God the Spirit) is identified as the author of this disclosure event.[35] This specific character of the revelation of Christ not only gives it a special status compared to all possible inferences or deductions, but also elucidates its content: just as God is the sole ground of the certainty of faith, so he is also the sole ground of salvation and the sole ground of the being of the world.

The particular experience of Jesus as the Christ becomes, as the disclosure event effected by God, the key to the reconstruction of the whole interpretative framework of human experience. The common structural element which makes this reconstruction possible is the prevenience of God's action which

---

[34] Cf. Härle/Herms op.cit. 26-32.

[35] All these elements are exemplified in the narrative of Peter's confession of Christ at Caesarea Philippi Mark 8.27-32; cf. the careful analysis in C.H.Ratschow, *Der angefochtene Glaube. Anfangs- und Grundprobleme der Dogmatik*, 3rd. ed. Gütersloh 1967, 31-67.

distinguishes the disclosure event from other cognitive actions and which is disclosed as the determinative characteristic of God's creative, reconciling and perfecting agency. The correspondence between the event and the content of revelation leads to the recognition of the universality of the constitution of reality which is experienced in it and which as a whole presupposes God's action as its ground and destiny. It is this insight which leads the theology which is based on the experience of Christ to the development of the doctrine of the Trinity, which expresses the unity of God's action in its differentiation.

The particular experience of the Christ event does not remain external to human existence in such a way that the certainty concerning the predication of Jesus as the Christ which is created by the disclosure experience leaves human self-understanding untouched. Since this predication has the recognition of the resurrection of the crucified one as the reconciling action of God the creator as its content, it disqualifies any form of human self-understanding which ascribes to humanity partial independence over against the claim of God the creator. At the same time the revelation of Christ opens up a new self-understanding which has as its content the acknowledgement of the reality of God as it is disclosed in Christ. This new form of self-understanding is faith understood as the relationship to God in which God is acknowledged as the ground of human being as the sole ground of salvation and as the author of his disclosure as the ground of being and salvation. This new self-understanding includes the reconstruction of the past from the perspective on the future which is opened up in the present. The past appears as a misguided and deceived self-relationship which was determined by the error of actualising created existence independent from the creator which, however, was in spite of this self-contradiction maintained as created existence by God.[36] In the self-understanding of faith not only does the self-experience which accompanies all acts of experience become manifest, but it also becomes clear how this self-experience is determined by what is acknowledged as the content of the self-disclosure of God in the Christ event. Faith is the form of life in which what is disclosed through the experience of Christ for the self-experience of the believer is actively acknowledged as passively constituted truth and so becomes the fundamental orientation of life. The specific characteristic of this truth is that it is *ontological* truth which, because it applies to all created being, also applies to the personal life of the believer. The process in which this certainty is constituted validates its content: the prevenience of God as the ground of being, the source of its salvation and the author of the disclosure of the truth about created existence and so as the condition of the possibility of appropriate human action.

Although the vindication of the experience of Christ happens as a personal disclosure experience for particular persons and although this personal vindication cannot be replaced by the report of reliable witnesses, it nevertheless creates for those persons who experience the Christ event as revelation a new form of community. Its distinctive feature is that in this community the

---

[36] This relationship between discontinuity and continuity determines not only the individual life story, it is also the basis for the conception of the unity of history as the New Testament documents in various forms.

revelation of Christ is professed as its one foundation. The truth of the revelation of Christ becomes in this community the subject-matter of the communication of believers and the guide-line of their communal and personal actions. In the medium of the personal communication of believers the certainty about the truth of God's self-disclosure is developed to a view of reality which provides the framework for the interpretation of all reality and formulates the guide-lines for a policy of action which is in accordance with this view of reality. This view of reality comprises the revisions of the framework of interpretation of the faith of Israel which is presupposed in the experience of Christ. They are occasioned by the vindication of the experience of Christ as the self-disclosure of God in personal certainty. These revisions comprehend both the affirmation of fundamental assumption of the underlying framework of interpretation as well as their modification in the light of the experience of Christ. The integration of discontinuity and continuity with regard to the understanding of God is again expressed in the doctrine of the Trinity which interprets the historically contingent experience of Christ and its vindication in the contingent operation of the Spirit as rooted in the eternal being of the triune God.

For our considerations about the relationship of revelation and experience we can see that the Christ event corresponds as a particular experience to the general structure of experience which we have sketched in our analysis of the concept of experience. The experience of Christ comprises the perceptual element of the history and fate of Jesus. This is interpreted within the framework of the faith of Israel as the event of the reconciliation of God with his fallen creation and as the beginning of the fulfilment of the promise of the perfection of creation. This experiential judgement which is expressed in the predication of Jesus as the Christ includes a new self-understanding of human beings who can now understand their actions no longer as the creation of righteousness which is to be recognized by God, but as obedience to the will of God who will bring about righteousness and salvation. Through the vindication of the truth of the Gospel of Christ as the self-disclosure of God the constitution of the certainty of faith validates its content: God's action in creation, reconciliation and salvation is, as it is made manifest in the experience of Christ as God's self-disclosure, the condition for the possibility of created freedom for human action. Therefore human action can correspond in the interpretation and organisation of the world to its constitution and so realize the destiny of humanity by obeying the will of God.

The specific characteristic of the experience of Christ is therefore that the self-disclosure of God is vindicated as the condition of the possibility of all experience, insofar as the constitution of the certainty of this experience validates its content. The experience of Christ has this special status because the Christ event discloses in the reality of experience the action of God as the condition of the possibility of all human experience. Human experience is therefore confronted in the vindication of the Gospel of Christ with its truth as the correspondence between the determination of reality by the will of God and its consequent and dependent determination in the interpretative acts of human experience. On the basis of the particular experience of the vindication of the Gospel of Christ the general structure of experience is illuminated as one which presupposes the disclosure of reality through God's action. The fact that reality

117

can be experienced is both with respect to the object of experience as well as with respect to the subject of experience not an independent property which could be ascribed to the subject or object of experience, but is grounded in God's action as the ground of its possibility. On the basis of the experience of Christ the relationship between revelation and experience is clarified as the relationship between the constitution of the existence of reality which is capable of interpretation and organisation and its active interpretation and organisation by human subjects of experience. Revelation is therefore not a special realm alongside or above experience, but it is the ground of its possibility and the condition for the possibility of its truth.

This view of the relationship of experience as the fundamental concept of human action and revelation as the expression of the unity of God's action in creation, reconciliation and perfection has a number of implications for the understanding of revelation as well as for the conception of experience. From the description of the relationship between revelation and experience we can reformulate the traditional distinction between 'natural' general revelation and 'supernatural' special revelation. 'Natural' and general revelation refers from the perspective of this proposal to the openness of reality for human experience, which includes the insight that human experience is not the condition of its own possibility. 'Supernatural' and special revelation signifies on this view the particular disclosure event of the self-communication of God as the self-disclosure of Father, Son and Spirit which identifies the openness of the world for human experience as the work of God and illuminates for human experience the actuality of its truth in faith.

The relationship between 'experience' and 'religious experience' or 'experience of faith' can be described in a similar way. All experience indicates on the basis of its specific structure that it presupposes the openness of reality for acts of reflection and interpretation in the synthesis of experience as the condition for its possibility. In religious experience we do not have access to a particular object of experience which existed in a separate sphere of experience alongside or above the general realm of experience. In religious experience divine action as the condition of the possibility of all human experience becomes thematic in its connection to all forms of human experience. On the basis of the insight into the enabling of all human action through divine action and into the constitution of human experience in God's revelation which can be gained from the particular experience of the Christ event, all experience is open for insight into the underlying conditions of its possibility. There is therefore no specific epistemological privilege of certain forms and types of experience in relation to others which would thereby be devalued in their significance.

For the theological justification of this description of the relationship of general and special revelation and experience in general and specifically religious experience we can again refer to the doctrine of the Trinity. It is one of the crucial emphases of trinitarian theology that the Spirit who as the Spirit of truth makes certainty of faith with regard to the truth of the Gospel Christ possible is none other than the creator Spirit who invests creation with the energy of life which is the basis of created existence and the condition for the possibility of creation's response to the will of the creator. Furthermore it is one of the central insights of trinitarian theology that Christ as the Son in whom the Father reveals through the Spirit his will and his being is none other than the Logos who gives creation its rational structure and order. Moreover, trinitarian theology insists that the Father with whom believers enter into a relationship as God's daughters and sons through the Spirit and in Christ is none other than the Father who is the ultimate source of all being. The trinitarian explication of the concept of revelation as the conceptual exposition of the self-disclosure of the triune God is therefore the basis for an attempt at relating revelation and experience in such a way that the emphasis on the irreducibility and freedom of God's self-disclosure is reconciled with its universality as the condition of the possibility of all experience.

5 THEOLOGY OF REVELATION AND THEOLOGY OF EXPERIENCE

Our reflections on the relationship of revelation and experience have attempted to show that both concepts should not be seen as expressions of two separate and unconnected themes, but that they have their common reference point in the relationship between divine divine and human action. The self-communication of the triune God as the disclosure of the determination of reality through God's action in creation, reconciliation and perfection is the condition for the possibility of human experience as it is practised in the determination of reality in acts of interpretation and organisation. It is, furthermore, the foundation for the truth of human experience in the correspondence between the human determination of reality and its determination through God. Both concepts, 'revelation' and 'experience' have an ontological status. The concept of revelation expresses the constitution of reality as reality for experience in God's action. And the concept of experience expresses on this foundation the fact that reality can be determined by human subjects in acts of interpretation and organisation as a fundamental feature of the constitution of reality. On the basis of this description of the relationship between both concepts we have tried to show that the insight into the relationship of both concepts is rooted in the Christ event which discloses as a particular experience the general structure of experience.

This interpretation of the relationship between revelation and experience has a number of significant implications for the theological assessment of the way in which the concepts of revelation and experience have been presented in the fashion trends of the theology of this century as key concepts for alternative conceptions of theology. Our reflections confirm the central place which theologies of revelation give to the emphasis on the irreducibility of revelation and the emphasis on God's freedom in revelation. We can furthermore agree with the insistence of these theological conceptions that the epistemic character of faith and, consequently, of theology does not need to be justified before the forum and on the basis of the presuppositions of a non-theological epistemology. However, there seem to be good reasons for the critical question whether revelation is conceived with sufficient radicality in those conception which give it a central place in Christian theology. Has the epistemic and epistemological significance of revelation not often been understood in such a re-stricted sense that the constitutive role of revelation for all experience has been ignored? This can lead to the risk that the constitutive role of revelation for all human action is insufficiently clarified.

On the basis of our considerations we can agree with the theologies of experience which followed the theologies of revelation in their emphasis on the concept of experience as the foundational notion for the understanding of all forms of human action, and emphasis which has brought theology into new contact with the experiential and empirical orientation of the sciences and arts in modernity. However, there also seem to be good reasons to ask whether the concept of experience is conceived radically enough in this new experience-oriented strand of theology. Only if theological engagement with the concept of experience includes the question of conditions of the possibility of experience can the theological import of the new orientation towards experience be adequately considered. Where this is not the case we are confronted not only with the risk that non-theological concepts of experience will rule over the theological enterprise, but also that fundamental theological concepts will be only considered with regard to their functional capacities for the interpretation of reality, without elucidating the theological reasons why theological concepts can function in this way. Where this radical theological reflection on experience is ignored we can easily be left with a reductionist conception of theology which can no longer give authentic expression to the view of reality of Christian faith.

With regard to both fashion trends it has to be critically remarked that the concentration on the concept of revelation over against the concept of experience or the concentration on the concept of experience in contrast to the dominance of the concept of revelation can in both cases obscure the fundamental connection of experience and revelation which can only become apparent on the basis of their distinction. This leads to a situation where God's action which is theologically interpreted on the basis of God's self-disclosure is not understood as the ground and criterion of human action in judgement and grace, or, *vice versa*, to a situation where human action as it is summarized in the concept of experience cannot be considered in its connection to divine action as its ground and as the criterion of its truth. The consequences can in both cases be seen in an insufficient mediation between dogmatics and ethics and in the contradictions which arise between the content of Christian proclamation and the social and political *praxis* of Christian communities. In such a situation theology finds its task in critical dialogue with the dominant fashion trends of the day in pointing to the fundamental and perennial relationship between divine and human action as it becomes apparent in the relationship between revelation and experience and in constructively developing insights gained in this fundamental theological reflection with regard to the relevant issues of the time. It should have become clear that the relationship between revelation and experience is by no means a marginal theological topic that could be ignored without serious repercussions. In their reflections on this central theme over against the changing the fashions of the theological scene it should become obvious that theologians are neither in the business of the fraudulent dress-makers of fabricating fashionable illusions nor are they called to parade in the role of the fashion-conscious emperor their nakedness which is only too quickly revealed to the unclouded view.

5 Faith and Personal Experience

1 RELATING EXPERIENCE AND FAITH

In the previous chapter we have attempted to offer a description of the relationship between revelation and experience in the framework of a theoretical reconstruction of both concepts. The theoretical character of the analysis should, however, not disguise the fact that the correctness of our description of the relationship between both concepts depends on whether it can be shown that they are rooted in the concrete practice of Christian faith and in the concrete forms of human experience. We will therefore try in this chapter to relate these theoretical considerations to their practical foundations in the life of Christian believers.

The notion of faith of paramount importance for such an enterprise, because faith is the interface between God's revelatory action and human action as experience. On the one hand, we have to say that the constitution of faith is entirely God's work in us. Faith is created by the vindication of the Gospel of Christ in the Spirit. And this authentification of God's self-disclosure enables believers to turn to God as the ground and end of their lives in the act of existential trust. In this way they find orientation for their actions in the certainty of faith concerning the truth of the Gospel of Christ. On the other hand, we have to maintain that faith as a form of life is a human work, because faith is practised in the active recognition of the truth of the Gospel of Christ as the basis for all acts of human experience. Faith is therefore the form of life in which the passive constitution of the certainty of faith is actively acknowledged as the condition of the possibility of human experience in the interpretation and organisation of reality. For believers this acknowledgement is implicitly presupposed in all acts of human experience. Consequently, we can describe faith as the form of life in which human experience becomes transparent for itself as being rooted in God's self-disclosure. According to the self-understanding of faith, faith itself is a representative case of reality as a whole, because like all reality it is grounded in God's creative action and destined to find fulfilment in God's perfecting action. The reality of faith has, however, the special distinction that it is characterized by the explicit acknowledgment of the divine ground and destiny it shares with all other reality. In this way, faith comprises both the distinction and the relationship of human and divine action, since the truth of faith is constituted by the correspondence between divine and human action, between God's self-disclosure and human faith. The contents of Christian faith can therefore become the framework for the interpretation and organisation of reality, including the reality of faith itself.

In a similar way we can give the notion of personal experience a central place in a person's active life of experience. I use the expression 'personal experience' in a similar sense in which word *Lebenserfahrung* is used in German. Literally translated it means 'experience of life' and it signifies the totality of a person's experience as it is consciously appropriated by that person. The term 'personal experience' should therefore not just express the truism that all experience is person-relative. It should also denote the self-experience of experiencing subjects as persons. 'Personal experience' can in this way describe the conscious reconstruction of the past experience of a person which structures the particular experiences of the past in such a way that it forms the horizon for the expectation of future experience.[1] Personal experience is therefore the mode of the self-presence of persons, both with regard to their memory of the past and with regard to their expectation of the future, which opens up the present for a person as a space for experience. In consequence, personal experience integrates the experience of persons concerning the consequences of their own actions with the experience of the actions of others in such a way that this process of integration determines their factual possibilities of experience. This applies both to the possibilities of interpreting as well as to the possibilities of organizing the world.

Furthermore, personal experience comprehends the different relationships which are constitutive for human existence. It expresses in the relationship of persons to themselves the sum of their views of their relationship to other people and their involvement as bodily beings in the processes of nature. Therefore personal experience determines the way in which persons take part in processes of social interaction and cultural organisation. We can also say that personal experience gives concrete expression to the intersubjective reality of experience of a particular person. Personal experience therefore provides the reflective horizon of the personal appropriation of the different forms of knowledge, from factual knowledge to knowledge of meaning and knowledge of norms and values. Personal experience is, moreover, the context in which personal agents acquire insight into their possibilities and aims of action, because it represents for an agent a framework which gives meaning to acts of interpretation and organisation. It is therefore in personal experience that a person's beliefs about acts and their consequences, about receptivity and spontaneity and about freedom and dependence take shape for the formation of a this particular person's possibilities of action. Personal experience is, of course, not static. It is a dynamic process which is understood by the experiencing person as an increase of insight and so shapes the capacity for distinguishing between fact and fantasy and between good and evil which determines our possibilities of action.

There are two questions which are particularly relevant in the discussion of the relationship between faith and personal experience. The first question is, how the view of reality of Christian faith enables believers to interpret their personal experience in such a way that the revelation of God becomes the criterion for the truth of the interpretation of their experience. The second question, and the converse of the first, is, how the fundamental assertions of Christian faith are interpreted in the context of the personal experience of believers so that they can provide the interpretative framework for the reality of their lives. The first question concerns the interpretation of personal experience by faith, the second the interpretation of faith by personal experience.

Faith in the triune God which is made possible through the self-disclosure of God in the vindication of the truth of the Gospel of Christ locates the personal experience of believers in the context of God's action as the creator, reconciler

---

[1] Cf. the instructive analysis of 'Lebenserfahrung' as a process in Reiner Preul, 'Lebenserfahrung und Glaube', in: W.Härle, R.Preul (eds.), *Lebenserfahrung. Marburger Jahrbuch Theologie III*, Marburg 1990, 1-22.

and perfecter of creation. The experiences of a person are from this perspective interpreted as the reality of a contingent creature with finite freedom which is called into the community of the creation with its creator. Faith as the framework for the self-interpretation of persons confronts them therefore with the relativization of their own freedom as creaturely self-determination and with the relativization of all absolute claims of finite entities, be they persons or institutions, through the power of the creator who is the unconditioned ground of all being. Faith in God the creator therefore defines the possibilities of action of believers and determines the overall aim of their actions as correspondence with the will of the creator in accordance with the contingent order of creation.

Faith in God the creator discloses the ground and limitation of human action in God's creative action in such a way that it reveals, together with the destiny of finite created freedom, also its failure. The common denominator of the many forms of failing to realize the destiny of finite created freedom is the confusion of the relative finite freedom of the human creature with the absolute infinite freedom of the creator. The consequences of this confusion are known in human experience, because personal experience reflects the effects of actions which are misguided because the agents are in a state of self-deception about their possibilities and aims of action. What, however, is not known independent of God's self-disclosure is the rootedness of these actions in the human contradiction against God by assuming divine freedom. The self-disclosure of God as the reconciler, as God's judgement over the assumption of divine freedom by the human creature, unveils the root of the failure of finite freedom, and as the assurance of God's grace it reveals that God overcomes this contradiction against his creative will. Through this revelation human freedom is again given the possibility of corresponding to the freedom of God in doing the will of the creator and in acknowledging the grace of the reconciler. The Gospel of reconciliation therefore enables believers to integrate their own failures and their consequences in their lives into the reconstruction of the perspective for the interpretation of their personal experience. The experience of failure is in this way incorporated into personal experience from the perspective of forgiveness, the overcoming of failure in God's grace.

When the Gospel of God's reconciliation with the alienated creation is vindicated for Christian faith, a new way of dealing with experience is opened up in which personal experience is reconstructed from the perspective of faith. This occurs where the self-awareness of believers is reconstituted as the self-experience of creatures who are reconciled with God by God and therefore reconciled with themselves. The appropriation of the message of God's grace as the foundation for the self-awareness of believers includes the acknowledgement that becoming convinced of the truth of the Gospel of Christ is itself part of God's perfecting action, which consists in bringing about the perfected community between the creator and creation. What is in this way established as the content of the self-awareness of the believer and as the foundation for the reconstruction of personal experience is the reconstitution of the finite freedom of reconciled creatures whose ground and norm is the revelation of the will of the creator in Jesus Christ. Where this is acknowledged in faith as the basis for the orientation of the life of the believer, a perspective on the perfection of creation is opened up, which as the hope of faith, enables believers to hold fast to the certainty of faith even where it is challenged by experiences which seem to contradict it.

The content of faith becomes in the process we have described the interpretative framework for personal experience. This includes the fact that personal experience as orientational import of the sum of particular experiences becomes in this process the subject-matter of new experience. This 'experience with experience'[2] consists in the integration of personal experience into the interpretative framework of faith. The personal experience of the believer is in this way interpreted as part of the history of God's action as it is disclosed in God's self-revelation as the unity of creation, reconciliation and perfection. The message of Christ becomes the ultimate framework for the interpretation of personal experience which is in this way brought to its truth. The foundation for this reconstruction of personal experience is the certainty of faith as the conviction that the truth of God's self-revelation is the condition for the possibility of the truth of human experience.

The unity of the action of the triune God is expressed in Christian faith as love. This is interpreted in such a way that love is seen as the determinative characteristic of God's triune being which, since God's agency is the expression of God's being, unifies all aspects of divine action in their distinctive particularity.[3] Love is therefore, first of all, understood as creative love which calls a contingent creation into being in order to lead it into a community of love with the creator. Love appears, secondly, as reconciling love which overcomes even the contradiction of the human creature against the creator and so enables human beings to lead a life of love of God and of their neighbours. Finally, God's love has the form of perfecting love which comes to expression in the perfected fellowship of the reconciled creation with God the creator. For the reconstruction of personal experience from the perspective of faith, love is therefore the organizing centre of the different forms of divine action (creation, reconciliation and perfection) and in this way becomes the material focus of the Christian understanding of reality. God's love is both the heart of the interpretation and of the organisation of reality in Christian faith. The claim of Christian faith to express universal truth for the whole of creation can therefore with regard to its content only be justified on the basis of the universal character of God's love.

2 THE SOCIAL SHAPE OF CHRISTIAN FAITH

The place where Christian faith is appropriated as the subject-matter of social communication for the interpretation of the whole of reality and of personal experience is the church.[4] As a human organisation the church is the community

---

[2] The expression 'experience with experience' was, of course, coined by Gerhard Ebeling and Eberhard Jüngel, cf. E.Jüngel, *Gott als Geheimnis der Welt*, Tübingen 1977, 40f., where Jüngel refers to Ebeling's essay 'Die Klage über das Erfahrungsdefizit in der Theologie'.

[3] Cf. I.U.Dalferth, *Theology and Philosophy*, Oxford 1988, 213ff.

[4] For the exposition of the relationship between the concept of revelation and the concept of the church cf. E.Herms, *Einheit der Christen in der Gemeinschaft der*

of witness to God's revelation which understands itself as being constituted by this self-disclosure and as being commissioned to witness to its truth. As a community of witness the church has the specific social function that in its processes of interaction God's self-disclosure is explicitly made the subject-matter of communication as the condition for the possibility of human action which corresponds to the truth of revelation. This is based on the conviction of faith that God's action as it is disclosed for faith in revelation is not only the foundation of a special sphere of religious or ecclesial activity, but the ground of all human *praxis* of experience.

In the *proclamation* of the church the Gospel of Christ is communicated on the basis of the witness of the biblical traditions as the truth about the destiny of the world. It is proclaimed both as the promise of salvation and as the call to freedom and is in this way presented as the fundamental interpretative framework for the view of reality of Christian faith. The proclamation of the Gospel is based on the confidence that the message of God's action as the foundation of human life which corresponds to its created destiny is vindicated for its hearers by God the Spirit as the truth about their own lives.

In the *sacramental praxis* of the church the reality of God's creative, reconciling and perfecting action is expressed in the semiotic acts of baptism and holy communion as the determination of human life in its personal and social dimensions. These acts express the constitution of the life of believers through their incorporation into God's covenant people, and so into community with God himself, and the reconstitution of human life through the promise of forgiveness with regard to the abuse of finite human freedom. These semiotic acts which are located in the context of the proclamation of the Gospel are performed in the confidence that the truth of the Gospel on which they are founded is vindicated by God in such a way that he employs the human acts of sacramental praxis as the instruments through which God brings about his purposes.

The *spiritual praxis* of the church which comes to expression in its life of prayer is based on the witness of the Gospel of Christ about the truth of God's relationship to humanity and the world and the corresponding relationship of humanity to God. In Christian spirituality the relationship between God and humanity is not only proclaimed, it is enacted by addressing God in praise, thanksgiving, petition, repentance and lamentation as the ground of human life in all its relationships[5] The prayer of the church is therefore the place where the communication about God leads to communication with God. The spiritual life of the church therefore focuses the whole reality of the life of believers in the world so that it is brought before God as the ground of being and salvation.

The view of reality of Christian faith which is the subject-matter of communication in the church's acts of proclamation in its sacramental and spiritual *praxis*,

---

Kirchen, Göttingen 1984, 95-128, especially 100ff; W.Härle, art. 'Kirche', *TRE* XVIII (1988), 277-317, especially 281-293. Cf. also my paper 'The Creature of the Word. Recovering the Ecclesiology of the Reformers', in: Colin E.Gunton/Daniel W.Hardy (eds.), *On Being the Church. Essays on the Christian Community*, Edinburgh 1989, 110-115.

[5] Cf. Vincent Brümmer, *What Are We Doing When We Pray? A Philosophical Inquiry*, London 1988.

becomes in the *teaching* of the church the subject-matter of processes of learning in which the potential of the traditions of Christian faith for the interpretation of reality is explicated. The potential of faith for the elucidation of reality is in the pastoral work of the church explicitly applied to the personal experience of individual people. The aim of this process of application, as it is, for instance, enacted in the practice of pastoral counselling, is to restore the possibility of life in the truth by offering and exploring ways of reconstructing personal experience in the light of faith.

The work of the church in the field of social ethics is devoted to the attempt to translate the insight of faith into God's action as the ground and norm of human action into forms of communal *praxis* whose norms, values and virtues are determined by the relationship between divine and human action as it is grasped in faith. The policy of action which is based on the insight of faith does not simply abolish the personal experience of agents as the reflective memory of past actions and their consequences. Rather, this experience is integrated into the perspective of faith in which the agent's competence to act is determined by love since love as the ground, end and mode of God's action shapes the aims and modes of human action so that it can correspond to God's actions. The church acts in the social arena often in cooperation with people who do not acknowledge the truth of the Gospel of Christ as the foundation for their actions and who would justify their policy of action in quite different terms. From the perspective of faith this cooperation is based on the confidence that the will of God can also be done where it is not recognised and acknowledged as such.

3 THE PERSONAL REALITY OF FAITH: THE ORDER OF SALVATION

The process of the elucidation of personal experience in the light of God's revelation which we have described as the reconstruction of personal experience from the perspective of faith is in traditional Protestant dogmatics discussed under the heading of 'the order of salvation'.[6] The alleged intention and the various forms of expression of this doctrine have been extensively criticized in modern theology.[7] The criticism is mainly directed at a conception of this doctrine which

---

[6] Cf. the instructive historical and systematic analysis in Manfred Marquardt's essay 'Die Vorstellung des "ordo salutis" in ihrer Funktion für die Glaubenden', in: W.Härle/R.Preul (eds.), *Lebenserfahrung* (note 1), 29-53.

[7] A particular drastic example of this criticism can be found in Martin Rade's *Glaubenslehre, Zweiter Band, Drittes Buch:"Vom Geist"*, Gotha 1927, 181f.:'An diesem Kapitel von der Heilsordnung kann man den Unsegen einer Mechanisierung und Schematisierung in Glaubenssachen als an einem klassischen Beispiel aufs beste studieren. Und wie ist es zu solchem Unfug gekommen? Gehorsam gegen den Bibelbuchstaben ist doch der Ausgang gewesen. Denn da fand man nun eben diese Ausdrücke "berufen", "erleuchten" usw., und die mußten in all ihrer Synonymität differenziert und in ihrer Nuanziertheit rubriziert werden (man kann hier schon nur in Fremdwörtern reden) - und wenn sie nun in glatter Reihe vor und hinter einander standen, siehe so war alles sehr gut...Damit soll nicht geleugnet werden, daß in jenen abwüagenden und definierenden Untersuchungen unserer Väter auch viel Ernst und Erfahrung mit unterläuft. Der Spezialist wird sich dem Studium ihrer Logik,

interprets it as a psychological description of the effects of God's grace or as the process of the cooperation of divine grace and human decision. In this connection the criticism is often made that justification by faith is depicted as one stage in the process of the order of salvation, so that God's judgement over sin and the assurance of forgiveness to the sinner becomes a stage in the development of faith. However, this criticism affirms the necessity of a doctrine of the order of salvation more than it denies it: not as a psychological description of the cooperation of divine grace and human feeling and decision but as an exposition of the personal reality of Christian faith from the perspective of the relationship of divine and human action, which may not be conflated but should be strictly distinguished in their relationship. The point of this exposition should then be how God's revelation is appropriated in faith as the condition for the possibility of experience and how it becomes through the reconstruction of personal experience the orientational framework for reflective individual and social human action.

The different concepts in which the doctrine of the *ordo salutis* is developed should therefore not primarily be interpreted as denoting a temporal sequence, but as signifying the structural elements of the constitution of faith. By describing the structure of faith they enable us to structure the biographical life-story as the reconstruction of personal experience from the perspective of faith. This approach can also interpret all aspects of the order of salvation as structural elements of the event of justification as the summary expression of the relationship of divine and human action so that justification is not described as merely one stage in the order of salvation. The series of concepts which are employed by individual theologians for the exposition of the order of salvation vary. However, they also concur in essential elements of the reality of salvation. They describe the connection between the constitution of faith, the practice of faith, the structure of faith, the conservation and vindication of faith and the final destiny of faith.

We can clarify these particular elements with the help of the concepts which the Lutheran theologian David Hollaz (1648-1713) employed in his *Examen theologicum acroamaticum* (1707)[8] for the exposition of the *ordo salutis*. His presentation of the process of the appropriation of salvation begins with the concept of *vocatio* (vocation).[9] It occurs where the proclamation of the Gospel of Christ which is exercised in the preaching of the church is understood as an address to the hearer, not by the preacher, but an address through the witness of Christian proclamation. Vocation presupposes that Christian proclamation witnesses to the action of God in creation, reconciliation and perfection and to the fact that the truth of this witness is presented as an address to the hearer. It furthermore presupposes that this message can be understood by the listener as an

---

Psychologie und Praxis nicht ohne Interesse und Gewinn hingeben. Aber irgend Etwas, das *gilt*, können wir in dieser *Ordnungs*tafel nicht finden. So mag auch der junge Theologe, der Glaubenslehre studiert, Zeit und Schweiß lieber auf andere Dinge wenden."

[8] Reprint Darmstadt 1971.

[9] Cf. F.Wagner, art. 'Berufung III. Dogmatisch', *TRE* V (1980), 668-713.

address by God, more precisely, as a call into community with God, mediated through the human word of proclamation. This implies that through the claim to truth which is presented in proclamation its content as witness to God's self-disclosure is received by the hearer. The truth claim of the proclamation of the Gospel of Christ is vindicated in the *illuminatio* (illumination or enlightenment)[10] as the certainty of faith which determines the life of the hearer of the message. This includes the affirmation that in vindicating the truth of the Gospel of Christ God identifies himself as the author of this self-communication. At the same time the hearer is identified as the addressee of this message insofar as the truth of the Gospel of Christ appears as the truth for the hearer's personal life. The certainty of faith which is constituted by the Spirit's vindication of the Gospel of Christ has as its content a self-understanding of the person who is called and 'enlightened' as a creature reconciled with God and called to do God's will. The concepts of *vocatio* and *illuminatio* describe together the process of the constitution of faith through the self-disclosure of God in the vindication of the Gospel of Christ. They can therefore be seen as applications of dimensions of the fundamental content of the Christian doctrine of creation to the interpretation of the individual existence of the believer and to the interpretation of the communal life of believers in the church as the *creatura verbi divini*.

The *illuminatio* as the creation of the certainty of faith discloses through the truth of God's self-communication the character of reality as determined by divine action and as open for human action in the interpretative activity of experience and the organising activities based on it. Reality appears as that which can be formed by finite human freedom as it is enabled and limited in God's action. Through the reconstitution of created freedom which is included in the vindication of the Gospel of Christ the possibility of actualizing this freedom in doing the will of God is restored to human beings. It is this fundamental notion of freedom which is expressed in the next concept in Hollaz' order of salvation, the concept of *conversio* (conversion).[11] This concept denotes the conscious turning to God as the act of freedom which is reconstituted in the certainty of faith. The concept of *conversio* therefore describes faith as the act of fundamental existential trust in God which is the active acknowledgement of the truth of God's revelation as it is passively disclosed for the believer in the *illuminatio*. The opposite of *conversio* is the Fall of human beings which consists as contradiction against God in the assumption of God's creative freedom. In contrast, *conversio* is the acknowledgement of created human freedom which is properly exercised in doing the will of God. As the fundamental concept of the *praxis* of faith *conversio* has its paradigm no longer in Adam, but in the humanity of Christ, so that *confor-*

---

10 Hollaz:'Die Erleuchtung ist ein Akt der zueignenden Gnade, durch den der hl. Geist den Menschen als Sünder, der zur Kirche berufen ist, durch das Amt des Wortes unterrichtet und infolge aufrichtigen Verlangens mehr und mehr belehrt, daß ihm die Kenntnis des Wortes Gottes in Abwehr der aus Unwissenheit und Irrtum resultierenden Finsternis zuteil wird, und ihm so die Erkenntnis eingießt, die aus dem Gesetz durch das Wissen um die Sünde und aus dem Evangelium aufgrund der im Verdienst Christi begründeten Barmherzigkeit folgt." Cit. in H.Schmid, *Die Dogmatik der evangelisch-lutherischen Kirche*, 9th edn. Gütersloh 1979, 288.

11 Cf. F.Wagner, art. 'Bekehrung II.III", *TRE* V(1980), 459-480.

mitas Christi becomes the guide-line for the *praxis* of faith. With the concept of *conversio* the basic contents of Christian anthropology are brought to bear from a christological perspective on the description of *new humanity* in the reality of faith.

The fundamental orientation of existential trust in God in the act of *conversio* is not a unique act which happens only once. Because of the fact that human beings remain exposed to and susceptible to temptation it is the fundamental decision of faith which has to be renewed over and over again. Its structure includes the notion that believers can correspond in the active shaping of the relationships in which they exist to the fundamental relatedness which determines the life of believers as reconciled human creatures called to perfection in community with God. In this way unconditional trust in God as active relationship to God corresponds to the prevenient relatedness of human beings to God as their creator. The concept of *regeneratio*[12] which follows the concept of *conversio* in Hollaz' exposition can be interpreted in such a way that it describes the way in which human beings are in faith conformed to their destiny so that the relationship of human beings to God, to themselves and to the world corresponds to the truth of their destiny which is disclosed and vindicated in faith. What is in this way expressed in the concept of *regeneration* is the reconstitution of the relational structure of human being on the basis of the certainty of faith about its constitution. This reconstitution has to be interpreted as the active shaping of all relationships of human life according to its destiny as it is disclosed in faith. The created sociality of human beings is in this way actively restored as reconciled sociality[13], and the relationship of human beings to nature can as co-createdness become the guide-line of a responsible interaction with nature which respects the world of nature as God's creation. The claim which underlies the concept of *regeneratio* is that in this reconstitution of human being as relational being the potential of humanity is restored to find fulfilment in doing the will of God the creator. The concept of *regeneratio* describes in this way the reconstitution of the image of God in humanity. It consists in the distinction of the human person to correspond in freedom to its relational destiny in its active relationship to God, to other human beings and to the world of nature. The character of this restoration is interpreted by the metaphor of *regeneration* (with its connotations of rebirth) as acceptance into the relationship of daughters and sons to God, as the participation in the Spirit in the relationship of Christ to God the Father which is granted to believers as a gift of grace.

The concepts of *conservatio fidei* and *sanctificatio*[14] which follow in Hollaz' scheme are intended to do justice to the fact that faith is not yet the full possession of the perfection of creation in eternal life, but that it continues to be susceptible to temptation and exposed to the tribulations of life. This raises the question how faith as a form of life can be sustained in time in view of the con-

---

[12] Still rewarding is W.Elert's exposition in *Morphologie des Luthertums I*, München 1931 (3rd. edn. 1965), 123-135.

[13] Cf. Daniel W.Hardy, 'Created and Redeemed Sociality', in: Gunton/Hardy (eds.), *On Being the Church* (note 4), 21-47.

[14] Cf. E.Herms, *Einheit der Christen* (note 4), 121ff.

tingent occurrences which confront human life. The conservation of faith is interpreted in this connection as a work of God who represents the truth of the revelation of Christ anew to faith and preserves faith by vindicating it in the concrete experiences of life. It is significant that the two concepts of *conservatio fidei* and *sanctificatio* are discussed together by Hollaz: the preservation of faith through the vindication of the Gospel of Christ in the changing scenes of life is the sanctification of believers by God who are in this way incorporated in the process in which God's will becomes victorious against the counter-forces of sin and evil. This aspect of the *locus* is intended to make clear that the whole existence of faith, its beginning, its conservation in time and its perfection are enabled by the action of the triune God. There is therefore for faith no sphere of life which is excluded from God's agency. The conservation of faith in temptations and tribulations occurs therefore where God the Spirit re-presents the unity of God's action in creation, reconciliation and perfection to believers. This whole process appears therefore as the sanctification of creation by God, the process in which creation is transformed to conform to God's holiness. An existential crisis in life can from this perspective be interpreted as part of the process of the actualization of God's will for creation, and it is this insight which invests faith with the perseverance which can hold fast to faith in crises without ignoring them. We can note that the doctrine of election has its place in this existential context of the preservation of faith since it gives believers the assurance and comfort for their conscience that their salvation is grounded in nothing else but the will of grace of the triune God, and that there is therefore no being or power which could ultimately extinguish this certainty.

When faith apprehends its conservation in time as made possible through the re-presentation of God's actions by God it can grasp at the same time the ultimate end of the life of faith: *glorificatio* as participation in the perfection of God's creative and reconciling action. This makes clear that the relationship in which faith exist in time as it is made possible through the *vocatio* and *illuminatio* for the believer, which is actively acknowledged by the believer in the *conversio*, and whose character is the *regeneratio* of the relational being of the *imago Dei*, has eschatological ultimacy. The *conservatio fidei* in time as the incorporation of the believer into God's sanctifying action has its end in the perfected community of God and creation in eternity. This gives the human practice of experience on the basis of the certainty of faith about God's self-disclosure its particular validity and responsibility. It consists in the confidence that its awareness of truth will not be superseded, but will be validated in the process of the perfection of God's creation. Faith as a form of life can in this way be understood as a process which is directed towards its goal in perfect community with God, a process in which faith is transformed but not superseded so that all prior stages would appear as irrelevant from its end. The basis of this hope is the unity of God's trinitarian action as the condition of the possibility of faith.

Although this brief sketch is better suited to illustrate the task of a detailed development of the doctrine of the *ordo salutis* than to fulfil this task, it nevertheless can indicate the significance this *locus* has for theological reflection on the relationship between revelation and experience and between faith and personal experience. Since this doctrine has as its focus the exposition of Christian faith as a form of life which we have described as the reconstruction of personal experience from the perspective of faith, it stands at the interface between dogmatics and ethics. It has this peculiar place because it applies the fundamental assertions of Christian dogmatics to the description of the personal and social life of faith. In this way it presents the content of Christian faith in the mode of its appropriation in personal experience. It can therefore depict Christian faith as a comprehensive policy of action with regard to its constitution, its structure and its form as a process in time and with regard to its ultimate destiny. This doctrine therefore offers a concrete account of the contents of Christian faith in the form of a description of the Christian life and in this way provides a concrete account of human personal experience from the perspective of the relationship between divine and human action as it is disclosed in revelation. It can therefore provide important orientation, not only for the task of Christian ethics, but also for the *praxis* of the church.

Postscript
On Being Rational in Theology

1 THE RATIONAL ROOTS OF THEOLOGY
AND THE THEOLOGICAL GROUNDS OF RATIONALITY

In the modern era the relationship between theology and rationality is often seen as deeply problematical. There seem to be two extreme positions which - with only slight exaggeration - can be seen as defining the perimeters of the debate. On the one hand, there are some self-appointed guardians of rationality who hold that theology, especially in its Christian variety, is incompatible with the requirements of rationality. They urge Christian theologians either to prove the rational feasibility of their enterprise or to give up any claim that theology could be pursued as a rational activity. On the other hand, there are some custodians of faith who argue that it belongs to the very nature of faith to be foolishness to the Greeks and that faith has essentially the character of a leap which leaves the requirements of reason behind. They recommend that theology should accept its irrational character and resign as an intellectual discipline which in any case had confused rather than aided believers by its rational pretensions. Between these two extremes we find various positions which reflect in different ways the uneasiness of the relationship between rationality and theology. This uneasiness is, not least, increased by the fact that the understanding of rationality and of the task of theology are far from clear and therefore provide an additional source of misunderstanding about the nature of the agreement or disagreement between the different positions.

The problematical relationship between rationality and theology in modern times conceals the fact that theology and rationality are, in fact, intricately related through a long common history in the West, compared to which the view of the problematical nature of their relationship appears as a recent and, at least so far, comparatively brief episode. In its Greek origins the intellectual enterprise of theology was first inaugurated as the rational critique of what was seen as an intellectually and morally irresponsible way of depicting the Divine in the mythologies of the poets and of popular piety.[1] For Plato theology is the rational reflection on the nature of the Divine which is in accordance with the conceptual, metaphysical and moral requirements of discourse about the Divine as the highest instantiation of goodness and reason. One of the reasons for casting theo-logy in this role becomes apparent from the *Nomoi* (X, 896e-898d) where god is conceived as the one perfectly good soul which is the principle of being of the forms and the ground of the participation of the sensible world in the rational being of the forms. Since god as the world-soul is thus conceived as the ground of the being, order and intelligibility of the cosmos, the Divine cannot be described in forms which call its goodness and intelligibility into question. However, god is not only conceived as the ground of rationality, but also as the

---

[1] Cf. Wolfhart Pannenberg's instructive exposition of the Greek origins of 'natural theology' in *Systematische Theologie* Bd.I, Göttingen 1988, 87ff.

boundary of finite rationality. According to the *Republic* (509b) and the *Seventh Letter* (341c-402) god as the suprarational principle of all rational being is beyond being and intelligibility and can, in principle, not be fully known. Therefore god's being can only be expressed apophatically and in mythical language. This, however, by no means indicates by a return to the traditional mythologies which in Plato's view deny rationality and morality. Mythological language is introduced in order to express, however incompletely and inadequately, that which by its very nature is suprarational.[2] In Aristotle the connection between God and rationality is decisively strengthened by the replacement of Plato's conception of an independently existing realm of forms (whose relation to the Divine remains ambiguous in many of his writings) by a conception of forms underlying things. The achievement of Aristotles' philosophical theology is a unified picture of reality which is seen as anchored in the 'Unmoved Mover', the First Principle which is absolutely self-existent, changeless and self-explanatory and therefore the ground of all existence, change and explanation. This sole wholly self-explanatory being is, with regard to its mode of being, characterized as the *noesis noeseos* (*Parts of Animals* IV 10, 686a 29) the pure self-contemplation of absolute intelligence.[3] The place which the notion of god holds in this metaphysical conception as the ground of being and rationality determines the organization of subsequent philosophical world-views. The *logos* (in some authors: *pneuma*) theory of the Stoics which replaces Plato' s conception of the *psuche* and Aristoteles' conception of the *nous* is notably different from the preceding conceptions. It emphasizes the dynamic activity of the *logos* as the ordering force of reality which is conceived as permeating and shaping all reality. Though the Divine is no longer understood as pure changeless intelligence, it functions nevertheless as the ultimate reference-point for all being and rationality.[4]

When Christian faith moved from its Palestinian homeland into the cultural world of the Mediterranean which was saturated by philosophical and religious fusions of the main types of Greek philosophical theology, enriched with the various types of religiosity that flourished in this multicultural milieu, it was challenged to develop its own universal claims in dialogue with these existing

---

[2] Cf. the excellent account of the Greek origins of theology in I.U.Dalferth, *Theology and Philosophy*, Oxford 1988. The classic treatment of the beginnings of theology in Greek thought is still Werner Jaeger, *The Theology of Early Greek Philosophers*, Oxford 1947.

[3] In Aristotle this is a limiting concept the positive content of which cannot be clearly determined. It is, however, clear that for Aristotle the Unmoved Mover is the only being able to follow the recommendation of the Delphic oracle 'Know Thyself'. Cf. the brief summary of Aristotle's theology in the context of a comprehensive account of his thought in Olof Gigon, art. 'Aristoteles/Aristotelismus I' in *TRE* III (1978), 726-768, especially 748-750.

[4] Cf. Max Pohlenz, *Die Stoa. Geschichte einer geistigen Bewegung*, Göttingen 1959.

views of reality.[5] This synthesis was not only a requirement of the cultural and intellectual context in which Christianity had to learn to survive and flourish, it was also necessitated by the claims of Christian faith itself that the God who is believed as the source of salvation through Christ in the Spirit is the creator and consummator of the whole of creation. The ingredients of the synthesis that was eventually achieved, even if only in fragmentary form, were, however, not easily compatible. The background of hellenistic philosophy presented god, understood as the ground of being and of all rationality and goodness, as an impersonal principle or force, either absolutely transcendent as in Platonism and Aristotelianism, or universally immanent as in the Stoics' view of the world as god's body. The principle of rationality that is the corollary of this understanding of God is predominantly one where the universal scope of rational order is equated with necessary immutable and atemporal principles. In contrast to that, Christian faith claimed that God acts in the temporality of the history of Israel, becomes personally present to the created order in the life, cross and resurrection of Jesus Christ and brings the temporal order of creation to fulfilment by taking the historical and material up into community with the everlasting God. If this faith was to be defended rationally, a model of rationality was required that integrated the emphasis on the personal, contingent, temporal and material without relegating it to a subordinate realm of rationality.

The development of Christian theology in the patristic era can be interpreted as presenting the groundwork of such an integrated view of reality which combined the stress on the comprehensive character of rationality with an understanding of reality which conceived the whole created order as grounded in God's free action. The whole of creation is therefore conceived as a contingent rational order with human beings as personal agents of finite freedom and rationality in which God becomes personally present in the particularity of temporal events to overcome the alienation of his human creatures and bring the whole of creation to its fulfilment in community with its creator, saviour and consummator. The coping-stone of this synthesis is the doctrine of the Trinity which asserts the ultimate compatibility of the one and the many, of the personal and the metaphysically ultimate in expressing the being of God as constituted in the personal communion of Father, Son and Holy Spirit. The result of this revolution in the understanding of reality is a new conception of rationality which radicalizes the comprehensiveness of rationality: God is seen as the creative ground of all being, meaning and truth, so that the rational order of the world and the rational capacities of human beings are understood as being conveyed to them by the free will of the creator. This understanding of rationality also embraces the personal, contingent, material and temporal. Since the eternal Word of God in whom the whole of the created order is established in the beginning becomes incarnate in the contingent materiality and temporality of a human life, and since the Spirit

---

[5] Cf. the comprehensive exposition of the problems raised by the reception of the Greek philosophical conception of God into the doctrinal scheme of Christian beliefs in W.Pannenberg, 'Die Aufnahme des philosophischen Gottesbegriffs als dogmatisches problem der frühchristlichen Theologie', in: *Grundfragen systematischer Theologie*, 3rd. ed. Göttingen, 296-346.

is active as the source of the dynamic capacity of creation to respond to the creator in the contingent temporal and material processes of life the contingent order of time and space can no longer be seen as excluded from the realm of rationality and can no longer be regarded as an inferior form of being which is necessarily lacking in rationality. God is in this radical sense seen as the ground of all contingent rationality, freedom and goodness in creation. This established, on the one hand a strong conception of the unity of rationality and, on the other hand, a necessary connection between the understanding of rationality and the conception of God. This interrelationship shapes the discussions of rationality throughout the medieval period: every new conception of rationality is accompanied by correlative modifications in the understanding of God, and every modification in the understanding of God leads to correlative modifications in the understanding of rationality. Even where a plurality of conceptions of rationality is postulated or even where philosophers and theologians experimented with the notion of a twofold truth, God remained the ground of the ultimate unity of what was thus distinguished in the realm of finite rationality.

Throughout this period the underlying tensions of the elements which formed parts of the original synthesis of the convictions of Christian faith and the conceptuality of Greek metaphysical thought led to a flourishing in the technical development of the means of rational enquiry and investigation, from the invention of semiotics as the theory of correct signification to the elaboration of complex systems of modal logic. The eclipse of the synthesis which characterized the *Corpus Christianum* in the Enlightenment is a complex process which cannot be explained in simplistic fashion. For our theme we can concentrate on two aspects of the dissolution of the synthesis. The first is the denial of the derivative character of human rationality, goodness and freedom which are now conceived in terms of human autonomy. Human reason or human experience become the sole origin and seat of rationality, freedom and goodness. Secondly, and as a consequence of the first development, we see the segmentation of the notion of rationality, at least partly caused by the rejection of God as the unitive ground of all rationality. Different aspects of rationality which had been developed within the comprehensive framework of a theological understanding of rationality in the Middle Ages now become autonomous and are claimed to serve as the paradigmatic model for rationality. The intellectual history of the West after the Enlightenment can almost be described as the succession of different autonomous forms of rationality, intricately connected with one particular sphere of culture, all claiming to provide the unitary framework for the whole of rationality. The last of these candidates for a new synthesis on the basis of one specific form of rationality is the idea of the logical positivists of an *Einheitswissenschaft* as the ultimate paradigm of what can count as rationality. During the course of this development we can see a succession of candidates for the normative and comprehensive model of rationality: the model of self-evident and incorrigible principles of reason in rationalism, the model of evidential support in the empiricist traditions, the model of the organic unity of the imagination in Romantic thought, the model of deductive systems proceeding from axiomatic foundations in logics, the model of the inductive validation of observation in the empirical sciences and so on. The very plurality of these candidates for the normative model of rationality became one of the stimuli for the self-critical investigation of rationality in epistemology and the philosophy of science, which itself claimed to be able to assess the validity of these different models and to offer a normative notion of what can count as rational. The advent of post-modernism marks the provisional end of this contest for domination in the realm of the mind, since it is characterized by the conscious embrace of a plurality, if not relativism, of multiple forms of rationality - 'anything goes' - even with respect to the interpretation of the diffuse notion of post-modernism.

This situation has led to a variety of widely diverging notions of rationality - from maximalist to minimalist conceptions - which seem to offer a creative playground for philosophers and, sometimes, theologians with a taste for conceptual puzzles. However, as long as some of these conceptions play an important role in the formation of the attitudes people adopt towards Christian faith and theology, theologians cannot simply enjoy the debate from a safe seat in the audience, but have to enter the discussion. Quite apart from this apologetic motivation - can theologians simply surrender the insight that created the Western synthesis of theology and philosophy, that God and rationality are intricately related, and that, not least, for the sake of our rationality, reflection on God and rationality must continue? Does not the legacy of the intellectual history of the West, which provides evidence both for the rational motivation in the development of theology and as examples for various attempts to understand rationality itself in theological terms, at least provide strong reasons for not discarding the relationship between rationality and theology as an obsolete problem?

Many of the ways in which theologians often tended to deal with the problem of theology and rationality would seem to be quite problematical in themselves. Very often their discussions have consisted in an attempt to apply the available notions of rationality to theology in order to show that theology as an intellectual discipline could, at least in some way, satisfy the criteria of some models of rationality. In this way reflection on the nature of rationality has in many cases remained external to theology, so that the issue is discussed in the form of whether theology can meet already externally established standards of rationality. Theologians who felt unable to follow this route have often insisted that theology has its own notion of rationality, but have, at least in most cases, not taken the trouble of showing how this notion relates to the understanding of rationality outside theology.[6]

In order to avoid the pitfalls of either importing standards of rationality from outside theology or of isolating a supposedly purely theological conception of rationality, I shall take the rather unfashionable route of first enquiring whether there is, if not a unified concept of rationality, at least a series of characteristics which we would in everyday life, if not in philosophy, associate with being rational. Then I shall consider how these findings can be related to theology, and

---

[6] This dilemma is at the heart of the controversy between Heinrich Scholz and Karl Barth about the scientific character of theology cf. H.Scholz, 'Wie ist eine Theologie als Wissenschaft möglich?' (1931) in: G.Sauter (ed.), *Theologie als Wissenschaft*, München 1971, 221-265; and 'Was ist unter einer theologischen Aussage zu verstehen?' (1936), in: Sauter (ed.), loc.cit, 265-278. Cf. the instructive discussion in Wentzel van Huysteen, *Theology and the Justification of Faith. Constructing Theories in Systematic Theology*, Grand Rapids 1989, 11-23.

finally I will conclude with a few remarks about what it means to be rational in theology.

2 SOME MARKS OF RATIONALITY

In his book *Minimal Rationality* Christopher Cherniak relates an interesting example from the stories about a fictional character who (because or in spite of his fictional status?) is probably considered by most as an example of maximal rationality.[7]

In 'A Scandal in Bohemia' Sherlock Holmes's opponent has hidden a very important photograph in a room, and Holmes wants to find out where it is. Holmes has Watson throw a smoke bomb into the room and yell 'Fire!' when Holmes' opponent is in the next room, while Holmes watches. Then, as one would expect, the opponent runs into the room and takes the photograph from its hiding place. Not everyone would have devised such an ingenious plan for manipulating an opponent's behaviour; but once the conditions are described, it seems easy to predict the opponent's actions. Prima facie, we predict the actions not as commonsense behaviourists or neurophysiologists, but by assuming that the opponent possesses a large set of beliefs and desires - including the desire to preserve the photograph, and the belief that where there's smoke there's fire, the belief that fire will destroy the photograph, and so on - and that the opponent will act appropriately for those beliefs and desires.

This brief example makes a number of important points for our analysis of the understanding of rationality. *First of all*, the notion of rationality as the intelligent pursuit of appropriate ends[8] is according to our operative everyday practice and understanding of rationality to be located in the context of action.[9] Rationality is not primarily to be seen as an attribute of theories and beliefs, but as a quality of our actions. More precisely, the primary context for our understanding of rationality are intentional actions of free personal agents who are capable of ordering their actions in such a way that they can be seen as following from their intentions as they are actualized on the basis of their beliefs and desires in a given situation. *Secondly*, in this primary application the concept of rationality is always perspectival, it is construed from the perspective of specific agents and their intentions and beliefs. The ordering of intentional actions as following from intentions, beliefs, desires and the knowledge of a given situation enables the observer to predict the probable behaviour of an agent in a given situation, provided the observer has sufficient knowledge of the agent's intentions, beliefs and desires. The fundamental rule 'no rationality, no agent' is therefore one which refers both to the personal freedom of agents to organize their actions and to the social situation of recognizing the pattern of an agent's act because they are rationally organized. *Thirdly*, the rationality of beliefs and theories depends

---

[7] C.Cherniak, *Minimal Rationality*, Cambridge, Mass./London 1986, 3f.

[8] This is Nicholas Rescher's basic definition of rationality, cf. *Rationality*, Oxford 1989,1.

[9] Cf. in this context Nicholas Rescher, *The Primacy of Practice. Essays towards a Pragmatically Kantian Theory of Empirical Knowledge*, Oxford 1973.

on their capacity to organize an agent's actions and on the way in which agents hold their beliefs and convictions, that is whether they are able to offer good grounds for holding them. No belief is in itself, apart from its relation to a specific agent, rational. It becomes rational in being employed for the ordering of an agent's actions and by being entertained in a rational way.

Let me illustrate that with a short example. I might believe that the theory of relativity is correct because when I first came across it, it was written on a blue piece of paper, and blue being my favourite colour I tend to believe everything that is written on blue paper. Furthermore, I have a liking for moustaches and Einstein's moustache has always impressed me as a particularly monumental example of its kind. Although the theory of relativity can be held on rational grounds, and might therefore be called a rational belief, my way of entertaining that belief is - most would say - completely irrational, and therefore I will not be able to apply the theory of relativity in any rational and successful way for the understanding of certain phenomena in astronomy. To be able to apply the theory in some way requires that my reasons for accepting it are in some way connected with the reasoning that supports the theory, so that I will be able to employ the theory in some context of action. This again points to the social constitution of beliefs: my reasons for holding the belief must in some way accord with the reasons supporting the theory which I have not devised and developed. Briefly: there is a distinction between grounds for accepting a belief and reasons which support the belief itself, and one condition for applying the belief in the ordering of activities is that the practical justification for holding the belief and the theoretical reasons which support the belief or theory itself must conform in some way.

After this brief consideration about the fundamental connection between the understanding of rationality and the conception of free personal agency in the sociality of human life, we can look a little more closely at what can be regarded as basic conditions for rationality. The *first* mark of rationality I would like to dub the *consequence criterion*. By this I mean the connection between two things in such a way that B can be seen as following in some way from A provided that this connection is the result of the act of an agent. In this way a certain state of affairs B can be seen as the consequence of the action, belief or desire A of a given agent. The consequence criterion can only function as a criterion of rationality if it is related to the intentional action of an agent who can be seen as the principal condition for the bringing about of the consequence B. The landing of a piece of paper in the waste paper basket can thus be seen as the result of the execution of my intention of throwing away a discarded piece of the argument of this paper, whereas my dropping my pencil while falling asleep at my desk does not satisfy the consequence criterion of rational action, because I did not intend to drop my pencil. However, both events can be analyzed by the use of the consequence criterion by an observer who, in the first case, assumes that I have sufficient practical knowledge of the laws of physical motion to execute an intentional aimed throwing action and furthermore subscribe to the belief that wastepaper belongs into the wastepaperbasket. In the second case, the observer can establish a connection between the relaxation of the muscles in my fingers as a result of having fallen asleep and the pencil falling to the ground. This however, is only a natural regularity since it excludes my intentional action, but it becomes an example of rationality as the *observer's* explanation of the event which is in itself an intentional act performed on the basis of a certain knowledge of the regularities of the physical world.

The most basic form of irrationality is to be found where the consequence criterion cannot be applied at all, so that a certain event cannot be related to any antecedents. If this occurs in the context of action we would perceive such an event as mere behaviour, that is as not qualifying as intentional action at all. In the context of our reflection on rationality the consequence criterion can also not be applied where an apparent connection between A and B (as in the case of the dropping pencil) cannot or should not be explained with reference to an agent's intentions or beliefs, but simply to a mechanism of stimulus and response. The criterion by which to make this distinction is whether agents would be able to give an account of their behaviour which included reference to their beliefs, since observers base their explanation of an event as action on the assumption that there are beliefs regulating the actions of an agent. This already points to the second criterion without which the first remains ambiguous.

The *second* mark of rationality can be called the *inference criterion*. It states that it is condition for the rationality of an action that the action could be explained or justified by reference to certain beliefs and the inferences that can be drawn from them. The simple existence of beliefs is not enough to deem an act rational, if it cannot be presupposed that agents are able to draw inferences from their beliefs which connect their beliefs to specific contexts of action. The complex set of inferences which are, for example, required in the Sherlock Holmes story for the prediction of the villain's behaviour is that he can infer from the belief 'no smoke without fire' that the fire in the study threatens to destroy the photograph that will render his whole policy of action - in this case: blackmail - unsuccessful. A belief A can be seen as a rational ground for the action B, if this belief includes inferences about the application of a general principle to a particular situation of action. Perhaps we could say more generally, that a rational way of entertaining a belief is one that presupposes the ability to draw inferences from the belief in such a way that the belief can regulate the actions of the agent. Very often the rationality of entertaining a specific belief can be tested by assessing the possible inferences that can be drawn from it in the situation in which the agent has to act. Conversely, many of the justifications for our holding certain beliefs will consist of possible or, better, probable inferences that can be drawn from it. In analyzing the actions of agents observers will therefore assume that they possess certain beliefs and have the capacity for drawing inferences from them, and that both in conjunction organize their actions.

On this view, an action is irrational if it contradicts the valid inferences that can be drawn from the beliefs the agent possesses. It is also irrational, if no significant connection can be made between the action an agent performs and the beliefs, convictions and desires the agent entertains. This second case already borders on the irrationality that can be detected on the basis of the fundamental consequence criterion, where no connection can be established between an action and its antecedents.

The *third* mark of rationality is already presupposed in the first two criteria. I shall dub this criterion, which is in many ways the central criterion for the analysis of rationality, the *semiotic criterion*. All rational acts whether they are physical acts or mental acts presuppose the basic rules of *semiosis*, the process of signification. For the application of the consequence criterion it is, for example, necessary that we are able to identify something as something, and in this way distinguish and relate it to other things. It would not be possible to see B as a consequence of A, if one could not reliably distinguish B from A and then establish the nature of their connection. Every intentional act presupposes basic forms of signification. The basic condition for the ability of intentional agents to order their actions in such a way that they are not merely unintentional behaviour but free personal action is identical with one of the basic conditions for communicating about actions and for communicative actions: the presence of a process of signification. The basic condition of every act of communication is already present in every intentional action. In justifying an act agents make the considerations explicit which already regulate their actions.

The semiotic process is regulated by the two fundamental conditions which have axiomatic status for every system of logics: the principle of identity and the principle of freedom from contradiction. The principle of identity $A = A$ states that every sign is always identical with itself, and the *principium contradictionis*, which states A non-A can be interpreted in this context as expressing the rule that one and the same sign cannot be affirmed and denied as the signification of one and the same thing at the same time and in the same respect. These two axioms constitute our semiotic universe and describe the basic conditions of all communication. Without them not only rationality, but communication itself becomes impossible.[10] Our intentional agency always presupposes the validity of these two principles - even where they remain tacit in the process of action. Without these two principles even a distinction between rationality and irrationality becomes impossible and communication about anything becomes a futile exercise. Rationality is therefore only possible where the two conditions expressed in the principle of identity and in the principle of contradiction are observed.

The semiotic process comprises according to conventional analysis three dimensions: the pragmatic dimension which concerns the relations between signs and sign-users, the syntactic dimension which refers to the relationships between signs, and the semantic dimension which is concerned with the relationship between signs and the things signified.[11] This three-dimensional structure leads to three more marks of rationality. The *fourth* mark of rationality is the *communicability* of the grounds that support a specific action or course of actions or the

---

10 W.Härle has summarized this fundamental role of the *principium contradictionis* in the following way:'*Verständigung durch Zeichen und folglich Kommunikation basieren auf dem Prinzip des ausgeschlossenen Widerspruchs oder sie finden überhaupt nicht statt. Das heißt: Das Widerspruchsprinzip (wie auch das Identitätsprinzip - Gleiches gilt m.E. nicht notwendig für das Prinzip vom ausgeschlossenen Dritten) bringt nur Implikationen auf den Begriff, die mit jedem Sprach-, Kommunikations- oder Zeichengeschehen notwendigerweise gegeben sind, weil sie dessen Sinn ausmachen. Die Bestreitung des Widerspruchsprinzips ist darum konsequent allenfalls durch die Verweigerung von Kommunikation möglich.*" 'Widerspruchsfreiheit. Überlegung zum Verhältnis von Glauben und Denken', *NZSTh* 28 (1986), 223-237, 228f.
11 Cf. W.Härle, *Systematische Philosophie*, München-Mainz 1982, 50ff.

grounds for specific beliefs. Although beliefs are, on the one hand, always person-relative - my way of entertaining a specific belief might be different from yours - they are, on the other hand, if they are claimed to be rational, never entirely private. Our knowledge and our beliefs are a social product which is socially acquired and socially exercized. Rationality which is essentially semiotic in character therefore always presupposes a community of sign-users. In this community exist specific conventions for the use of signs which are a fundamental part of traditions. The standards of rationality are therefore always dependent on the traditions and conventions of a specific community of sign-users.The communicability of sign-systems and with them of the traditions and conventions for their correct use makes, for instance, education and training in the use of signs possible. This communicability can be employed self-referentially so that the correct use of signs itself can become the subject-matter of communication. This self-referential character of sign-systems is a distinguishing characteristic of linguistic sign-systems. In this sense language is the medium for the self-referential reflection of rationality where the rational ordering of actions becomes in itself the subject-matter of rational inquiry. This social and public dimension of rationality follows from the social character of all acts of signification and is summarized in the pragmatic dimension of all semiotic acts. What is, in principle, incapable of being communicated cannot count as a rational ground for a belief or an action. Communicability is therefore a criterion of all rationality.

From this view-point the incommunicable defies rationality and sociality. What cannot be communicated, however fragmentarily, cannot be shared in a community of people and it is therefore not accessible to rational scrutiny.

The *fifth* criterion which follows from the *syntactic* dimension of the semiotic process is that of *coherence* or *consistency*. This criterion regulates the relationship between signs so that different signs and sets of signs such as propositions, arguments and theories are connected in such a way that their relationship can be justified according to rules which underlie the use of propositions, arguments and theories in the community of sign-users and are adequate to the specific areas of semiotic practice. The rules which constitute coherence in belief-systems are apart from the two principles of identity and non-contradiction those which are used in logics to regulate the relations between propositions (such as conjunction, disjunction, implication and equivalence) and which determine the range of application of any given predicate (quantifiers). These are formal means which are employed for the analysis of predications, propositions and arguments which form belief-systems and determine the rules for the application of such belief systems in the concrete situation of human action in the world. Coherence which can be specified in this sense can function as a criterion of rationality, because it enables agents to order their actions in such a way that their policy of action is informed by a formally coherent belief-system which helps to increase the competence of the performance of their actions and the justifiability of their reasons for specific actions. This criterion of coherence can take several forms, it applies to the formal consistency of the belief-system of an individual as well as to those shared by groups, and it applies to personal beliefs just as much as to public and semi-institutional forms of the organisation of knowledge, such as scientific paradigms.

Incoherence and inconsistency, on the other hand, indicate lack of rationality. It is, however, in this case necessary to specify precisely what this lack of rationality consists in. Whereas a violation of the consequence criterion or the absence of the semiotic criterion indicates total absence of rationality, inconsistencies can occur on different levels. The former irrationalities are fundamental denials of rationality, the latter are often mistakes in the application of criteria of rationality which are otherwise accepted. Inconsistencies are therefore intra-systematic mistakes within the semiotic system. Examples are, for instance, mistakes concerning the logical relationship of propositions or concerning the compatibility of theories.

The *sixth* criterion which follows from the semiotic process is that of *corrigibility*. It is based on the semantic relation between a signifier and the thing signified. The semantic dimension of the semiotic process relates the system of signs to the reality it is intended to signify where something is signified as something. This semantic dimension has two aspects, one concerns the set, class or number of things signified which define the extension or reference of the sign, the other the meaning, or intension, of the sign, 'as what' it signifies something. This criterion could also be dubbed the *reality criterion* or the *truth criterion* of rationality. Rationality and truth are by no means simply identical, it is perfectly possible to hold false beliefs in a *prima facie* rational way, and to entertain true beliefs in an irrational manner. This does not, however, permit us to treat the questions of rationality and truth as completely separate issues. Rather, it is necessary to indicate the point where the two questions overlap, and this seems to me to be the semantic dimension of the semiotic process which underlies all rational operations. It is at this point, that the corrigibility of our beliefs and of the grounds justifying them in the context of action must be introduced as a criterion of rationality. Where this criterion is missing, we may be able to identify mistakes in the use of signs and sets of signs in a specific community of sign-users and we may be able to identify logical mistakes in the syntax of belief-systems, but we will not be able to satisfy referential criteria of truth. This criterion identifies fundamental mistakes and errors concerning the possibilities of action in the situation in which we act which are neither due to pragmatic mistakes in our strategy of intentional action nor due to syntactic mistakes in our use of signs to regulate our action. This criterion therefore acknowledges the fallibility of our rationality in its most fundamental respect of being in accordance with reality or of contradicting it. This criterion of corrigibility functions therefore as an important qualifier for the criteria of coherence and communicability. It points to the fact that communicability and coherence are both necessary, but never sufficient, criteria of rationality, because they might sanction a use of rationality which because it is incorrible is not distinguishable from irrationality.

Irrational are on this view all beliefs which are treated as in principle incorrigible, perhaps because of the high degree of communicability and coherence they promise. Irrational are therefore all ideals of rationality which do not allow for the possibility of their being wrong - at least in some respects - and for the subsequent necessity to introduce corrections.

The *seventh* criterion is that of the adequacy of the methods of rational inquiry, validation and justification to their respective subject-matter. This criterion has played a significant role in recent debates about the nature of rationality where, especially with regard to religious belief, the influence of Wittgensteinian philosophy has led to the introduction of the distinction between internal and external rationality.[12] This criterion attempts to take into account the diversity of contexts in which we act in specific ways and where our grounds for doing so depend very much on the 'internal logic' of the 'language games' and 'forms of life' we are dealing with. In this respect the criterion represents in my view a plausible and valid suggestion. It is obviously unsatisfactory to settle logical problems by referring to empirical evidence or to decide the correct result of an empirical experiment on the basis of a logical theorem. In its application to theology this view of a rationality whose criteria are internal to a religious form of life has helped to end the predominance of the model of scientific rationality as the only one which could provide valid and reliable criteria of rationality. The emphasis on internal rationality has, however, also led to certain isolationist tendencies in which one form of life with its own rationality seems to exist as a self-sufficient and relatively self-contained system, which as a whole is incorrigible, side by side with other forms of life with their separate internal logics. This suggestion, however, seems to overlook that in our highly differentiated societies, with their compartmentalized systems of rationality, we are constantly challenged to act in different cultural spheres and forms of life so that we are required to form strategies of dealing with this differentiation of our universe of meaning. One of the principal policies we adopt is to develop 'second-order beliefs' - as Ingolf Dalferth calls them[13] - which provide orientation for our actions in the diverse fields in which we are required to act. These 'second-order beliefs' do not necessarily provide criteria of rationality which transcend the internal criteria of rationality in every field, rather we tend to adopt one particular field of culture and reconstruct from this perspective the range of applicability and the degree of validity of the other fields.

We conclude that apart from the formal requirements of rationality as they have been developed in the first six criteria there are material criteria which are internal to certain activities, forms of life or spheres of culture, so that the formal criteria of rationality are materially applied in a way that is adequate to its respective context. It would consequently appear irrational to demand that one specific set of material criteria of rationality be normative for all different spheres of activity at the expense of ignoring the specific internal forms of rationality that are operative in the respective forms of life. It would seem that it is this form of irrationality which unites such divergent ideologies as scientism and creationism. To reject such an imperialist notion of the universal applicability of one set of criteria of rationality, however, does not mean to reject the notion of the unity of rationality altogether, since our situation as agents who have to act in various fields requires some kind of unitary framework for the correlation of our actions and beliefs. Otherwise our notions of rationality will either

---

[12] Cf. I.U. Dalferth, *Kombinatorische Theologie. Probleme theologischer Rationalität*, Freiburg 1991, 65-71.

[13] Op. cit. 68.

be relativistic or favour the heteronomous determination of all spheres of rational action by the criteria of one particular field.

The *eighth* requirement of rationality is therefore the *ability to integrate* the different internal criteria of material rationality in one comprehensive framework where second-order beliefs define our orientation in the different fields of action in which we exist. This criterion rests on the assumption that the rationality of personal agents is enhanced and not restricted or curtailed if they have an integrated view of their possibilities of action and the criteria and norms which would define competent and successful action. Such an integration would require that the whole set of criteria of rationality, including the different internal, criteria could be seen as part of one criteriological framework. Alvin Plantinga has recently suggested that this unity of rationality should be seen as the problem of foundationalism.[14] According to this view a belief is rational if it is evident with respect to the beliefs that form a foundation for a person's 'noetic structure'. On this view, a belief can be seen as rational in two ways. First of all, a belief can be rational since it is evidently supported by beliefs which make up a person's set of foundational beliefs. Secondly, a belief may be rational as a belief *defining* the foundational set without being supported from 'neutral' evidence since all possible evidence already presupposes the foundational belief-set. This second group of beliefs can be seen as rational not because they are supported by evidence, but because they belong to what can be seen as 'properly basic beliefs' which make up a person's noetic structure. For Plantinga beliefs about God's existence and his actions, such as 'God created the universe' are to be regarded as rational in the sense of being properly basic for a person's noetic structure. The problem that is presented with this view is: How are we to define 'proper basicality' and will our view be able to avoid the relativistic consequences of postulating different basic beliefs for different persons?

The suggestion I want to make for this *eighth* criterion of rationality, the *criterion of integration*, is that our criteria of rationality should be rooted in fundamental beliefs which comprise our whole personal being as agents in the world and which therefore can provide us with orientational beliefs about our possibilities of action, both with regard to the world as our field of action and with regard to our capacities as agents, about our goals of action and about our norms of action. From this criterion it would follow that a belief can be seen as rational if our grounds for entertaining this belief can be based on such fundamental orientational beliefs. A belief would appear to be a candidate for an irrational belief if it contradicts the orientational beliefs which we regard as fundamental in normal circumstances of action.

From the criterion of integration follows a *ninth* criterion which concerns the relationship of the criteria of rationality to other criteria which shape our orientational beliefs. The set of orientational beliefs can only provide comprehensive orientation if is not only fundamental for our rational criteria, but also for our moral and aesthetic criteria. By integrating the criteria of rationality into a com-

---

[14] Cf. A.Plantinga, 'Is Belief in God Rational?' in: C.F.Delaney (ed.), *Rationality and Religious Belief*, Notre Dame 1979, 7-27; and 'Is Belief in God Basic?', *Nous* 15 (1981), 41-51.

prehensive framework based on orientational beliefs we thereby also relate the criteria of rationality to the values of goodness and beauty. Relating the criteria of rationality in this way to criteria of goodness and beauty implies, on the one hand, a limitation of rationality, because we deny in this way the claim that the criteria of rationality are the only or even the primary criteria regulating our actions. On the other hand, since the degree of rationality is increased and not diminished by relating the criteria to a wider set of orientational beliefs, relating the criteria of rationality in this way to the criteria of goodness and beauty promises a higher and not lesser degree of rationality. The final point in this discussion of the marks of rationality is therefore the thesis that the criteria of rationality should be based on a *view of reality* which provides the fundamental beliefs with regard to which the different material internal rationalities in their formal characteristics can be integrated. Only on the basis of such a view of reality is it possible to maintain the unity of rationality in the diversity of its criteria.

3 CHRISTIAN FAITH AND FUNDAMENTAL BELIEFS

The summary of the marks of rationality I have attempted to develop describes rationality as a complex phenomenon of interrelated characteristics. On the basis of this description it is possible to distinguish between forms of rationality which satisfy only some of the basic criteria and could therefore be seen as types of minimal rationality and forms of rationality which could be described as approaching types of maximal rationality because of their capacity to integrate most or perhaps even all of the outlined criteria. The underlying thesis of this description is, of course, that meeting the requirements of more than just the basic rationality conditions leads to an increase in rationality. To strive for an ideal of rationality which can embrace both the criterion of integration and the requirement of adequacy to particular contexts of application would therefore appear as an inherently more rational course of action than to rest content with a more limited conception. Ultimately an understanding of rationality is, in my view, an important aspect of a view of reality, because only within such a framework is it possible to integrate human rationality in a complex of beliefs which can relate the requirements of truth, goodness and beauty in a comprehensive orientational framework. The demands of rationality and the task of metaphysics are therefore, in spite of impressive counter-evidence, by no means contradictory, but mutually complementary.

The question that is raised by this discussion for Christian theology is whether Christian theology can provide a comprehensive view of reality which can serve as the foundation and the orientational framework for the understanding and exercise of human rationality. What I will attempt to show is that Christian theology does indeed offer such a framework within which the criteria of rationality can be seen as implications of a Christian view of reality.

One way of describing Christian theology is to interpret it as the self-explication of Christian faith. The different disciplines of theology therefore have to be seen as rooted in specific aspects of the structure of Christian faith. If we follow the lead given by the Reformers we can understand faith as the relationship of unconditional trust in God, Father, Son and Spirit as the ground of being, meaning and truth of everything there is, including the life of the believer. This relationship has to be seen as all-encompassing and normative for all other relationships in which human life is lived. According to Christian understanding, faith is the basic orientation for all human action, whether it be intellectual, moral or aesthetic activity. There exists therefore a close correlation between faith as the act of unconditional trust and the beliefs in which the presuppositions and implications of this faith are expressed. The act of faith as ultimate trust is for Christians an appropriate (indeed the only appropriate) orientation for life in all its dimensions, because God as the object of faith is believed as the ground of all being, meaning and truth, as the creator, redeemer and saviour of the world. But also the converse is claimed to be true: since God is the ground of all being, the source of redemption and salvation, it is appropriate to have faith in God as unconditional trust. Because God is believed as the creative source of all being meaning and truth, Christian faith as absolute trust in God is the fundamental orientation for all human action and therefore presupposes and implies a comprehensive view of reality.

We have in this way arrived at a conception of what can theologically be seen as fundamental - or, in analogy to Plantinga, as properly basic - beliefs. These fundamental beliefs, however, are dependent on faith as the basic orientation for all human action. In the tradition of Reformation theology it is claimed that this is, in fact, a universally valid description of the basic orientation of human life and therefore of the fundamental beliefs that form a view of life. Luther writes in his explanation of the first commandment in the Greater Catechism: 'whatever...thy heart clings to...and relies upon, that is properly thy God'[15], and he offers an extensive description of the things people hang their hearts on and which in this way form the basic orientation for their lives. Faith is therefore quite generally seen as the fundamental orientation towards something or someone that becomes the focus of value, meaning and reality in a view of life. The beliefs which express this fundamental orientation can therefore be regarded as fundamental beliefs, and they function as fundamental beliefs because of their orientational capacities for organizing people's actions. The criterion of their fundamental status is consequently the extent to which they can be shown to be directly implied or presupposed in faith as the fundamental orientation for human life. This basic orientation and the basic beliefs it entails can, if we follow Luther, now either appear in the form of 'superstition' or of 'right' or 'real' faith. As 'superstition' appear all forms of faith where someone invests unconditional and absolute trust in a finite and conditioned entity. This attitude, however, appears self-contradictory, because unconditional trust can only rationally be directed at something or someone that is itself unconditioned and infinite. Therefore only a form of faith can without contradiction be unconditional faith if its 'object' is indeed the unconditional ground of all being, meaning and truth, and

---

15 *Luther's Primary Works together with his Shorter and Larger Catechisms.* Translated into English. Edited with theological and historical essays by H.Wace and C.A.Buchheim, London 1896, 34. Cf. the interpretation of this passage in I.U.Dalferth, 'The Visible and the Invisible: Luther's Legacy of a theological Theology', in: S.W.Sykes (ed.), *England and Germany. Studies in Theological Diplomacy*, Bern-Frankfurt/M 1982, 15-44, 26-37.

this, Christians claim, is only God as the creator, redeemer and saviour of the world. Unconditional trust is the right faith, the right basic orientation for human life, because it is in relationship to God as the ground of being, meaning and salvation that human life finds its fundamental orientation.

This account of faith not only offers us an account of what can count as the fundamental orientation for human life, it also provides us with a criterion for what can be seen as fundamental beliefs, namely, those beliefs which are implied and presupposed by the fundamental orientation of life. The distinctive feature of these beliefs is that they have an orientational capacity for determining the possibilities, norms and ends of action for human agents. Such beliefs therefore combine ontological beliefs about reality as grounded in and determined by the object of faith as the creative source and end of all reality, with axiological and normative beliefs about the moral and aesthetic goods, values and norms that should provide orientation and the opportunity for flourishing in human life. It is to be noted that this account of faith and of basic beliefs has in its distinction between inappropriate faith and right or real faith an 'in-built' rationality criterion: that it is contradictory to invest ultimate trust in a finite and conditioned entity and that only the unconditioned ground, norm and end of finite existence can be the appropriate 'object' of faith as ultimate trust.

It is one central aspect of this understanding of faith that faith itself is seen as constituted by the 'object' of faith, that it is grounded in the self-disclosure of God. This is by no means a sudden escape into irrationalism, but only a radical implication of the understanding of God as the creator. If God is radically understood as the ground of all being, meaning and truth, then he must also be the ground of all knowledge of being meaning and truth and the one who makes faith as the response to this self-disclosure possible. Faith is therefore understood as the active acknowledgement of its passive constitution in the self-disclosure of God. The reality of faith is the exemplary case of all created reality, insofar as it owes its existence to God and ascribes also the awareness of this dependence to the activity of God. If one wants to avoid the pitfalls of isolating faith from the other dimensions of human life and of setting the knowledge of faith against all other forms of knowledge, one has to interpret this relationship of divine and human agency in this radical sense. God's self-disclosure is the condition for the possibility of all human knowledge, not only of theological knowledge, but also of our knowledge of the world and of ourselves. This applies also to the understanding of rationality: a theological understanding of rationality cannot be restricted to a conception of rationality in theology or of rational knowledge of God, but must refer to all forms of rationality in whichever area they are applied. A theological account of rationality is therefore an account of human rationality in its entirety, including the conditions for its possibility.

The fundamental beliefs which summarize the view of reality that is presupposed and implied in faith as the basic orientation of human agency are expressed in the creeds and confessions of faith of the Christian tradition. The fact that they are not (and, perhaps, cannot be) summarized in a neat handbook of Christian theology called 'The Christian *Weltanschauung*', but are placed within the context of communal worship and religious instruction is in itself quite significant. It points to the social and historical dimension of the fundamental beliefs of the Christian community and to the integration of the different dimensions of life in the dialogical enactment of the liturgy in worship. The fundamental beliefs of the Christian view of reality are therefore not only professed, but they are also contextualized by the proclamation of the Gospel, prayer, praise and the celebration of the sacraments which integrates the epistemic and intellectual dimension with the affective life of embodied personal beings. This integration illustrates their orientational function in connection with the life of faith. These fundamental beliefs, as they are expressed in creeds and confessions of faith, are nevertheless not seen as independent of the witness of Scripture, but as summaries of and guide-lines for the interpretation of Scripture.

In order to illustrate the orientational function of these basic beliefs for a view of reality which is the foundation and the context for the theological understanding of rationality, we can concentrate on some crucial points. Christian faith includes fundamentally belief in God the creator. Creation has traditionally been interpreted through the two formulae *creatio ex nihilo* and *creatio continua* or *continuata*. These conceptual reconstructions of what is implied in Christian faith are much less explanations about the process of bringing the world into existence than ontological expressions of God's creative activity on the one hand, and of the status of created being on the other hand. Creation is seen as a free personal act which has no presuppositions apart from God's creativity. It is 'from nothing' insofar as God creates not by forming an already existing and therefore co-eternal matter, but by bringing about the fundamental conditions for everything to exist. The formula of *creatio continua* asserts - with specific emphasis over against deistic notions of creation in early modern times - that God's creative action is not just an initial act at the beginning, but that his creative agency is the continued condition for the possibility of the existence and the functioning of the created order. It is an important element of the Christian notion of creation that God sustains the created order in its regularities and in its interaction of rule-governed structures and advance into novelty, so that his interaction with his creation happens within the structure of his creation and not by contradicting it in arbitrary bursts of new creativity. This is the foundation of the trust of Israel and of the Christian community in the faithfulness of God in sustaining his created order which can be disturbed and perverted but cannot be abolished.

These important insights still present, however, a restricted picture of God's creative action which can lead to a serious impoverishment of the doctrine of creation, since it seems to be limited to bringing about and maintaining created being. It seems especially important for our theme to take up the insistence of a broad stream in the Christian tradition that creation has to be understood as a triune act where God creates through the Word and by the life-giving Spirit. On this view, God is not only the ground of being, but also of intelligibility and truth. As the result of God's free personal trinitarian action the being of the world is contingent being and its intelligibility is contingent intelligibility. It is not the expression of necessary logical laws, but the intelligible ordering of creation through the divine Word. Creation has therefore an inherent but derived rationality not as an emanation from the divine being and not by participation in the divine substance, but in virtue of the free creativity of God's Word, his Reason and Self-expression in the otherness of created being. Reference to the Spirit as life-giver indicates that created being has the specific characteristic of the self-

148

transcendence of life which makes it capable of responding to God's creative will.[16]

The special status of human beings in creation is in Christian belief expressed by understanding human being as created in the image of God. There is a long tradition which has interpreted this almost exclusively in terms of human reason which images divine Reason. This has in my view more impeded than helped an adequate understanding of human rationality, because it has led to an isolation and absolutization of reason which separates it from the relational being of humanity and can lead to a dualistic anthropology which may result in a problematical denigration of matter. I therefore follow recent proposals to interpret the doctrine of the *imago Dei* within the framework of a trinitarian theology as the distinction of human beings to be as persons-in-relation and as their finite freedom to relate in free personal action to the relational order in which they exist as part of God's creation.[17] This does not exclude human rationality as being part of the image of God, but it integrates it as an important aspect into the relational being of humanity.

The story of the Fall combines these two elements, relationality and rationality, in a very significant way. It interprets the rebellion against God as the denial of the relational character of the orientation of human life as grounded in God. The tempting suggestion of the serpent in the narrative 'Eritis sicut Deus' is to take the place of God as the ground and focus of the basic orientation of human life in possessing knowledge of good and evil which is neither enabled nor limited by God as the ground of being and meaning. The cause and the effect of the Fall as the abuse of finite freedom and the denial that the relationality of human existence is rooted in the relationality of God's being is a fundamental self-deception in which human beings deny the basis for the orientation of their lives. The loss incurred in the Fall is therefore not a loss of rationality as an important aspect of being in the image of God, but a fundamental disorientation of human rationality, be it epistemic, moral or aesthetic, which leads to the application of the formal capacities of rationality for the wrong ends. This disorientation includes deception about the possibilities, the norms and the goals of action; it leads to a distortion of the view of reality that informs (or rather, disinforms) the use of human rationality. Because of this disorientation, human rationality is not only fallible, but fallen.

The Christian understanding of redemption through Christ in the Spirit contains many elements that are relevant for assessing the way in which the basic beliefs of Christian faith shape the understanding of the foundation and exercise of human rationality. First of all, the Christ event is interpreted as the revelation of God, the disclosure of the creator in the reconciler, and as the revelation of the

---

[16] I have developed this interpretation of the doctrine of creation in more detail in my contribution to the *Festschrift* for Eberhard Wölfel 'Theologie der Schöpfung im Dialog zwischen Naturwissenschaft und Dogmatik', in: W.Härle, M.Marquardt, W.Nethöfel (eds.), *Unsere Welt - Gottes Schöpfung*, Marburg 1992

[17] Cf. comprehensive proposal for a reshaping of the doctrine in Colin Gunton's 'The Human Creation: Towards a Renewal of the Imago Dei', C.E.Gunton, *The Promise of Trinitarian Theology*, Edinburgh 1991, 104-121.

true destiny of humanity to be in the image of God by being conformed to the image of Christ. Secondly, this revelation is interpreted as the Incarnation of the eternal Word of God in Jesus Christ as the Son. Thirdly, it is seen as enabling human beings in the power of the Spirit to relate adequately to God as the ground of all being meaning and truth in faith, love and hope. The main thrust of the Christian understanding of redemption in all three points is that the relationship between God and his fallen creatures is restored and transformed in such a way that human beings are now enabled to relate adequately to God. The implications of these beliefs for a theological understanding of rationality are, that in overcoming the contradiction of sin, God discloses the fundamental orientation for human life and enables human beings in faith to follow this orientation in all dimensions of their life, including their rationality. The revelation of God in Christ is therefore the restoration of the universe of meaning on which a view of reality rests, insofar as the ground of all intelligibility, the Word, becomes incarnate in a human life which discloses God as the ground of all being and meaning through the story of a human life which is lived in accordance with the will of God the creator. Christians claim that where this is accepted as the fundamental orientation for human life in the Spirit, the disorientation of sin is overcome in a fundamental reorientation of life in all its dimensions, so that the effects of fallen rationality are overcome in redeemed rationality.

For Christians this is not the whole story, although it is believed to be the ultimate disclosure of truth, in the sense that the orientation of life which it offers is not subject to a further reorientation. What is still hoped for is that what is disclosed in the particularity of the Christ event will be disclosed universally when God brings about his Kingdom and when his Lordship is universally recognized by the whole of his creation. Again it is worth noting that the main metaphors in which the hope of Christian faith is expressed, such as the Kingdom of God, have a relational character which emphasize the reciprocity of God's eschatological action and the response of creation. If we accept the view that the essential attribute of God which summarizes and qualifies all other attributes is love, then the main model for the final eschatological state will be that of an agapeistic community of God and his creation where God's love is universally disclosed so that it can find a universal response from creation. Among the images in which hope is expressed in Christian faith is that of the beatific vision which expresses the ultimate transparency of all reality for God as its ground of being, meaning and truth. This image is used to express the belief that in the eschaton the orientation that is *in via* only given in faith will be universally evident *in patria*. For the understanding of rationality this eschatological dimension of Christian faith has a twofold dimension. With the image of the *visio beatifica* it provides an important limiting concept. On the one hand, this image implies that there is a final state in which everything will be evident and where truth, goodness and beauty will be jointly actualized. There is therefore an ultimate horizon for human rationality where what can here be only fragmentarily known and expressed in fallible beliefs will be made evident. This belief in the transparency of everything from the perspective of the *eschaton* supports the claims for the universality of rationality. But, on the other hand, it is also clear that this universal transparency is only achieved in the *eschaton*, and cannot be achieved or demonstrated *in via*. Although the ultimate rationality of everything will be clear *in patria*, we can now only anticipate this state in faith, in the basic trust in God who is the ground of all rationality and of its disclosure. This is an important qualification of the claims of human rationality. Though its unity and universality is presupposed, it is here and now only fragmentarily present in specific particular forms. To claim anything more is to presume upon God's freedom to bring about his Kingdom.

4 FUNDAMENTAL BELIEFS AND THE MARKS OF RATIONALITY

On the basis of this sketch of the fundamental beliefs of Christian faith we can now relate this view of reality to the marks of rationality which we have described in the previous section.

1. Because the world is seen as an ordered cosmos of inherent contingent rationality in which intentional human action is possible, it provides the context in which the *consequence criterion* can be applied to the interpretation of reality as well as to the rational organization of the world. This correlation of contingency and intelligibility which excludes both a deterministic world-view and the interpretation of reality in terms of pure indeterminacy is perhaps the most important contribution Christian theology has made to the rise of modern empirical science.[18] Furthermore, it is the contingent rational order of creation which makes it possible that human action can have effects according to regularities of the world as the field of human action. This is both the foundation for moral responsibility as well as for aesthetic achievement.

2. Because the world is created through the Word in the Spirit and bears the imprint of its triune maker, it is intelligible, precisely with regard to the contingent regularities which form the necessary presuppositions of intentional action. Because of this 'knowability' of the world as creation, human agents can develop beliefs which can entail valid *inferences* about the possibilities, norms and ends of their actions.

3. The intelligibility of the world is according to Christian belief not grounded in properties which it possesses apart from its creator, but is rooted in its character as the self-expression of God's Word. It is therefore a *semiotic* universe, a universe of signs. The semiotic activity of human rationality is in this way correlated to the semiotic character of the world itself. This semiotic character of the world can be obscured through the alienation of sin so that it is no longer understood as the address of the creator in his Word to his human creatures. The self-disclosure of God in Christ through the Spirit is therefore interpreted as the restoration of the ability to understand the worldly reality in its relation to God as its creator, redeemer and saviour. Therefore it can be claimed that the biblical witness to this divine self-disclosure provides the interpretative framework, Calvin's 'spectacles', in which the semiotic structure of the world can be adequately related to its ground in God.

4. Because the world is a semiotic universe and because human beings have the capacity for semiotic communicative action, therefore human rationality presupposes the fundamental *communicability* of the reasons for human action, the

---

[18] Cf. T.F.Torrance, *Divine and Contingent Order*, Oxford 1981.

norms and goals of action and the circumstances of human activity in the world. Because of this communicability human rationality always has a social character and a historical dimension in which the reasons, norms and ends of rational action, be it interpretative or productive, can be communicated synchronically (so as to enable joint action or social justification) and diachronically (so as to make traditions of interpretation and action possible).

5. The criterion of *consistency* for human rationality reflects the unity of the world as a an ordered and intelligible universe which is rooted in belief in God as the creator of all being, meaning and truth. Since this criterion of consistency is grounded in God, it is therefore neither necessary nor, indeed, appropriate to postulate a ideal of consistency that is based on any finite criteria. The criterion of consistency is one of 'open' consistency that can accept penultimate inconsistencies as long as they can in principle be reconciled within the framework expressed in the fundamental beliefs of Christian faith.

6. One aspect that follows from the fact that the fundamental beliefs of Christian faith include the notions of the Fall and of the redemption of humanity, is that human rationality is seen as, in principle, *fallible* and also as *capable of being corrected*. The claim that is based on these fundamental beliefs is, in fact, even stronger in that it asserts that human reason is in a fallen state and in need of correction, unless it is illumined by the divine Spirit. As we have attempted to show, this concerns not so much the formal capacities of ratiocination as the fundamental orientation of human rationality. If, however, rationality is understood as the intelligent pursuit of appropriate objectives the disclosure of truth with regard to the possibilities, norms and ends of action is indeed central for the quest of rationality itself.

7. The orientational character of the fundamental beliefs of Christian faith does not impose a uniform character on all pursuits of rationality. Rationality will take *different forms* in *different contexts of application*. However, the Christian view of reality implies that none of these contexts of application is totally autonomous or independent nor that the forms of rationality which are appropriate in one particular context of application should be enforced as the normative rational ideal for all other contexts. The understanding of rationality that is developed within the framework of the fundamental beliefs of Christian faith requires that all forms of rationality are to be seen as ultimately grounded in the rationality with which God the creator invests his creation. It therefore functions as a fundamental critique of all forms of reductionism that have dominated the discussion and exercise of rationality throughout history and especially in the modern era.

8. This anti-reductionist thrust of an understanding of rationality that is formulated on the foundation of the fundamental beliefs of Christian faith is rooted in the *integrative character* of the view of reality of Christian faith. This integrative character is not associated with a particular theory of rationality, but grounded in the understanding of God as the ground of all truth, goodness and beauty. The integration of our rational ideals with our moral and aesthetic ideals is eccentric in character in that God and not a particular concept of rationality (or morality or beauty) is the principle of integration of the Christian view of reality. If God is therefore seen as the ultimate reference-point of rational ideals, moral norms and aesthetic values, this implies for a view of rationality based on

the view of reality of Christian faith that there exists, on the one hand, a necessity for integration in which rationality is related to God as the ground of all being, meaning and truth and thereby rationality is related to all other dimensions of existence as they are grounded in God. On the other hand, however, this leads also to a restriction on limited forms of integration based on finite integrating principles. If God is seen as the principle, or more correctly as the agent of integration, then this leads to forms of open integration which counteract restricted, 'closed', forms of integration. This is the twofold implication of the eschatological hope which forms part of the fundamental framework of Christian beliefs.

9. The framework in which rationality should be rooted and in which the exercise of rationality should be conducted is therefore an ontological or metaphysical framework in which the ground and ultimate criterion of all rationality is God as the ground of all being, meaning and truth.

The view of rationality at which we have arrived in this way is one which could be dubbed *relative* or *relational* rationality. In contrast to views which develop an absolute ideal of rationality which then functions as the criterion for what we can believe in and what we can theologically assert, we have developed a view which explains rationality by relating it to God as the ground of all being, meaning and truth on the basis of the fundamental beliefs that are asserted, implied or presupposed in Christian faith. In being interpreted as relative rationality on the basis of its relationship to God as the ground of being and meaning, rationality is also related to the values of goodness and beauty, since God is not only the ground of rationality, but also the source of all goodness and the perfection of beauty. An understanding of rationality is in this way suggested which is part of a view of reality which is based on the fundamental beliefs of Christian faith and which provides a framework of orientation for the exercise of rationality in which human rationality itself can be seen as enabled and limited by its relation to God. The question now is: What follows for theology as a rational pursuit from such an understanding of rationality?

5 RATIONAL THEOLOGY AND THEOLOGICAL RATIONALITY

The theological interpretation of rationality that we have sketched shows clearly that theology does not have to chose between a rationalist understanding of rationality where theology has to justify its claims before the judgement-seat of autonomous reason and a fideist understanding of theology where the pursuit of theological insight is seen as fundamentally divorced from the pursuit of rationality. The first can be seen as resting on a deficient understanding of rationality where rationality is restricted to autonomous reason and the question of the conditions of the possibility of human rationality is arbitrarily brushed aside. The second, the fideist option, would seem to be based on a deficient understanding of God which implicitly denies that God is not only the creator of all being, but also of all meaning and truth. The theological notion of rationality which we have attempted to delineate introduces a strong commitment to rationality into the understanding of theological practice, since it sees rationality in all its forms as enabled by God's relationship to the world and to human beings, and this applies to theological activity just as much as to any other form of intentional action. Theology, however, has the additional task of reflecting on the conditions of the possibility of human rationality and in this way of relating the pursuit of rationality to God as the condition of its possibility. This commitment to rationality also includes a strong critical element, since the understanding of rationality as relative rationality acts as a powerful critical principle against the absolutization of any rational principle that cannot be properly related to the understanding of God as the source of all being, meaning and truth. It is one of the implications of this conception of relative rationality that it applies, first and foremost, self-critically to theology itself which in its own attempts at rational theological practice is called to exemplify the understanding of rationality as relative rationality.

The self-critical application of rationality in theology has far-ranging implications for the current practice of theology in all its disciplines. It challenges the deeply-rooted practice of modern theology of defining the standards of rationality apart from any reference to the view of reality that is asserted, implied and presupposed in Christian faith. If rationality can be adequately understood within the framework of fundamental beliefs of Christian faith both with regard to its foundation and with regard to the criteria of its practice, then it seems questionable whether it is rationally advisable to suspend these fundamental beliefs in doing theology. The history of modern historical criticism in theology is a very interesting example of the implications of this suspension of the fundamental beliefs of Christian faith, which has led to an inherently problematical separation of historical factuality and theological meaning. The reason of this split which has troubled biblical exegesis since the times of Reimarus is not that scholarly methods of investigation and interpretation *eo ipso* necessitate a sceptical attitude towards the factual basis of Christian beliefs. Rather, it is rooted in fundamental beliefs which include an understanding of history which is thoroughly anthropocentric in that only human agents can be seen as agents in history and which is based on an understanding of the regularities of nature as a closed system of natural laws which excludes the possibility of divine action.[19] Furthermore, it presupposes an understanding of theological truths as necessary eternal truths which remain in an irreconcileable contrast to the contingent structure of history. There is no immediate rational justification for theology to accept a set of fundamental beliefs that presents, in effect, a less comprehensive notion of rationality than that of the relative contingent rationality which is rooted in the basic beliefs of Christian faith. In this sense it could be that Barth's maxim: '*Kritischer* müßten mir die Historisch-Kritischen sein!'[20] is indeed a good principle of a rational theology.

The same point could be made with regard to philosophical criticism and with regard to the moral criticism of Christian theology. Many versions of the philo-

---

[19] Cf. W.Pannenberg's critique of such a view of history in 'Heilsgeschehen und Geschichte', in: *Grundfragen systematischer Theologie*, 3rd ed. Göttingen 1979, 22-78, especially, 45-54.

[20] K.Barth, *Der Römerbrief*, Vorwort zur zweiten Auflage, 11th reissue of the 2nd ed., Zürich 1976, XII. It is one of the ironic aspects of the history of the interpretation of this *dictum* that it is often taken as an appeal to be less critical than the historical critics.

sophical critique of and in Christian theology presuppose an understanding of the Divine based on fundamental beliefs in which God is conceived in *a priori* notions of absoluteness, atemporality and immutability which openly contradict the Christian understanding of God as an essentially relational being who relates freely to the temporal and mutable structure of his creation. Again there seems to be no immediate rational obligation to subscribe uncritically to these fundamental beliefs rather than to those expressed in Christian faith. And the same applies to the moral criticism of theology which is grounded in a notion of goodness which sees it as an autonomous property that cannot be related to being or beauty.

This does not mean that the fundamental beliefs of Christian faith function as the critical test of all other methods of rational investigation based on different sets of fundamental beliefs, but are themselves exempt from all criticism. As I have argued, the criterion of the fundamental status of beliefs rests on faith as the unconditional trust determining all dimensions of life in God as the source of all being, meaning and truth. Beliefs are fundamental insofar as they are necessarily implied and presupposed in this act of faith which provides the fundamental orientation for human life.

Faith itself is, however, not an absolute criterion for this fundamental status, since it is understood as being constituted in the self-disclosure of God. The constant self-critical task of theology is to explore whether what are regarded as fundamental beliefs are in fact implications and presuppositions of faith, and whether specific forms of faith are the appropriate and adequate response to God's self-disclosure. Before the *eschaton* Christian theology has to be constantly engaged in the critical assessment of the relations of beliefs to fundamental beliefs, of fundamental beliefs to faith and of faith to the self-disclosure of God.

The main criticism that might be put to this theological conception of rationality is that it is either an imperialist notion of rationality which attempts to impose the fundamental beliefs of Christian faith on all notions of rationality or an isolationist notion of rationality which takes its theological conception out of the public debate about the possibilities, norms and ends of rational human action. In my view, it does not have to be either. Many modern discussions of rationality presuppose that there must be a set of foundational criteria of rationality to which all participants in any rational endeavour subscribe, that there is a universal common ground which defines what can be called rational and what are the criteria of its application. This overlooks the fact that notions of rationality are always part of belief-systems or views of reality which determine which ends should be pursued in rational action and what could count as appropriate means to achieve them. Our notions of rationality are irreducibly perspectival, they are person-relative and, at least, partially socially and historically determined. However, this does not mean that there is no other option left than a relativism of different conceptions of rationality. Rather, what is required is a notion of *dialogical rationality* in which different notions of rationality can engage in dialogue that might support forms of exchange and cooperation, and clarify the agreement and disagreement between the partners in dialogue.

For a dialogue based on the mutual exchange of different partners, it is necessary that two fundamental criteria are observed. The first is the *independence* of the partners in dialogue. Their positions must be recognized as, at least, relatively autonomous in order to make mutual reciprocity in exchange possible. The second is, that there, is some notion of the *interdependence* of different positions, of a common ground where the different positions can meet in the recognition of some truth or value that they may reach from different perspectives. This notion of the interdependence of the different partners in dialogue will be construed differently from different perspectives. It is, however, not a condition for the success of the dialogue that the partners agree on how they construe the interdependence of their positions and in this way the possible success of their exchange, but only that within their different frameworks they are able to recognise disagreement or agreement when it is reached.

The theological understanding of rationality as relative rationality which I have outlined can, I think, satisfy both these conditions for dialogue. Insofar as it is grounded in Christian faith as the basic orientation of human life, it is independent and relatively autonomous, since the particular self-disclosure of God is seen as the foundation for all properly fundamental beliefs. However, since in Christian faith God is seen as the ground of the possibility of all being, meaning and truth, and not just of the being of the believer, the meaning of faith and the truth of Christian beliefs, Christians can be confident that all truth they encounter, and all rationality they find is also grounded in God, even where this is not acknowledged and recognized. The conviction of God as the ground of all being, meaning and truth defines from the Christian perspective the common ground on which dialogue about rationality and rational dialogue can be conducted and which is the foundation of the confidence that rationality and truth will be ultimately effective. Nicholas Rescher ends his book *Rationality* with the statement: 'It is a fact of profound irony that assured confidence in the efficacy of reason requires an act of faith.'[21] From the perspective of a theological understanding of rationality this is no doubt profound, but it is neither ironic, nor does it come as a surprise.

---

[21] N. Rescher, *Rationality* (note 8), 230.